THE NEW POLITICS OF THE OLD SOUTH

THE NEW POLITICS OF THE OLD SOUTH

An Introduction to Southern Politics

Edited by

Charles S. Bullock III and Mark J. Rozell

ROWMAN & LITTLEFIELD PUBLISHERS, INC.
Lanham • Boulder • New York • Oxford

ROWMAN & LITTLEFIELD PUBLISHERS, INC.

Published in the United States of America
by Rowman & Littlefield Publishers, Inc.
4720 Boston Way, Lanham, Maryland 20706

12 Hid's Copse Road
Cumnor Hill, Oxford OX2 9JJ, England

British Library Cataloguing in Publication Information Available

Library of Congress Cataloging-in-Publication Data

The new politics of the old South : an introduction to Southern
   politics / edited by Charles S. Bullock III and Mark J. Rozell
      p. cm.
   Includes bibliographical references and index.
   ISBN 0–8476–8612–4 (alk. paper). — ISBN 0–8476–8613–2 (alk.
paper)
    1. Southern States—Politics and government—1951–. I. Bullock,
Charles S., III 1942– II. Rozell, Mark J. III. Title
F216.2.885 1998
320.975'09'045—dc21   97–36019
                                                              CIP

ISBN 0–8476–8612–4 (cloth : alk. paper)
ISBN 0–8476–8613–2 (pbk. : alk. paper)

Printed in the United States of America

TM
⊖∞ The paper used in this publication meets the minimum requirements of
American National Standard for Information Sciences—Permanence of Paper
for Printed Library Materials, ANSI Z39.48–1984.

Contents

Part IV: The Soul of the South

Acknowledgments

This project benefited from the assistance of the following individuals: Wesley Joe, a graduate student at Georgetown University, produced the index. Cheryl Hoffman and Lawrence Paulson of Hoffman-Paulson Associates provided copyediting assistance. Jakub Krawczyk assisted with proofreading the manuscript. Steve Wrinn, acquisitions editor at Rowman & Littlefield, played a major role in developing the idea for this volume and assisting us through various stages of publishing. Finally, we thank Dean David C. Brown of American University for the generous support that he provided for the project.

Part I

Introduction

_____

I

Southern Politics at Century's End

Charles S. Bullock III and Mark J. Rozell

In the five decades since V. O. Key published *Southern Politics,* the region has been transformed. At midcentury, Key found a still solidly Democratic South—a region in which no Republican had been elected to the U.S. Senate or the governor's mansion in decades and where more than a generation had passed since a Republican collected a single electoral college vote. In some communities Republicans in the electorate were as rare as in elective office.

Key's South had an electorate in which black voters were even scarcer than Republicans. While he observed that "In its grand outlines the politics of the South revolves around the position of the Negro" (1949, 5), much of the political capital was expended in keeping African Americans away from the levers of power. Since implementation of the 1965 Voting Rights Act, black votes have become the mainstay of the Democratic Party—the vote without which few Democrats can win statewide. The votes cast by African Americans have elected a black governor (Virginia's Douglas Wilder), seventeen members of Congress, and hundreds of legislators and local officials. Currently in the five Deep South states' (Alabama, Georgia, Louisiana, Mississippi, and South Carolina) congressional delegation, black Democrats outnumber white Democrats by a margin of seven to four.

For approximately a century after Reconstruction, the South provided the foundation on which the national Democratic Party rested. When the party was in eclipse in the rest of the country, little more than the southern foundation could be seen. During the few periods of Democratic control of the presidency and Congress, as in the New Deal era, the South made a major contribution. To an extent, this partisan unity was part of a more extensive bulwark supporting white supremacy.

Partisan change and black mobilization have not been continuous but

3

have come at different paces in various locales and for different offices. Nonetheless, viewed from today's vantage point, the changes have been massive and, according to the most recent measurements taken in 1996, continue. In the chapters that follow, the nature of the change will be delineated for each of a dozen southern states. This introductory chapter sketches broadly the patterns of the South's politics for which the state chapters will provide greater detail.

The Presidency

Republican gains in the South have followed a trickle-down pattern (Bullock 1988; Aistrup 1996). The initial GOP wins came in presidential elections, and it is for the presidency that the post-Key South has most enthusiastically supported Republicans.

From 1876 through 1948, in only two elections did a Republican presidential nominee carry even one southern state. In 1920, Tennessee, with a large GOP mountain enclave, and Oklahoma supported Warren Harding's call for a return to normalcy. Eight years later, Tennessee, Oklahoma, and four other Rim South states (Florida, North Carolina, Texas, and Virginia) rejected New York, anti-Prohibition nominee Al Smith. The 1920 and 1928 exceptions had no lasting impact on partisan loyalty, and the South returned to the Democratic fold throughout the Roosevelt era. In 1948, Alabama, Louisiana, Mississippi, and South Carolina broke with the Democratic Party over the racial planks adopted by the national convention and supported the Dixiecrat candidacy of South Carolina governor Strom Thurmond (at that time a Democrat).

Some have seen the Dixiecrat rift as foreshadowing a two-party South. More accurately, the Thurmond support marks the end of the solidly Democratic region, but the GOP breakthrough occurred not in the Deep South where Thurmond flourished but in the Rim South. In 1952, the Deep South united behind Adlai Stevenson even as all Rim South states except Arkansas rallied to Dwight Eisenhower. Four years later, the pattern reappeared, and Louisiana became the first Deep South state to vote for a Republican. The Eisenhower years also saw the first Republicans elected to the U.S. House in decades from Florida, North Carolina, Texas, and Virginia.

The crucial election for the Deep South came in 1964, in the immediate aftermath of the Civil Rights Act that extended federal protections to public accommodations, school desegregation, and equal employment opportunities. Barry Goldwater, one of a few Republicans to break with his party's traditional support for civil rights, rejected the legislation as an unconstitutional invasion of states' rights. His stand, coupled with President Lyndon Johnson's outspoken support for the bill, prompted the five Deep South states to vote Republican for the first time in generations— except for Louisiana, which had been in the Eisenhower column in 1956 (Carmines and Stimson 1989). Goldwater's popularity also elected the first Deep South Republicans to the U.S. House, with Georgia and Mississippi each sending one member of the GOP while Alabama elected five.

In 1968, much of the South broke away from the two major parties to support the independent presidential candidacy of Alabama governor George Wallace, then a champion of segregationist policies. The presidential campaign of former vice president Richard M. Nixon devised what became known as the Republican "southern strategy"—the use of racial wedge issues such as affirmative action and crime to drive white traditional Democratic voters in the region to the GOP. Nixon fared well enough in the South to win the presidency in a close contest and profoundly influenced the strategies adopted by future GOP presidential campaigns.

Since 1972, the South has voted primarily for Republican presidential candidates, with the exception of the 1976 election. In that, the initial post-Watergate election and the first with a Deep South candidate in more than a century, the South almost resumed its solid Democratic voting pattern as all of the states of the Confederacy except for Virginia voted for Jimmy Carter. The reconciliation was short-lived, and during the three elections of the 1980s, the only Democratic success came in Georgia in 1980, when that state remained loyal to its former governor.

While the South has continued to be the most Republican region in the 1990s, Democrats made a comeback as their ticket boasted not one but two southerners. In both presidential elections of this decade, the home states of the presidential and vice presidential nominees (Arkansas and Tennessee, respectively) voted Democratic. Louisiana, the first Deep South state to vote Republican, was the only state in the subregion to support the Clinton-Gore ticket in both elections. Democrats narrowly carried Georgia in 1992 and in 1996 took Florida for only the second time in more than a quarter century.

In 1996, the twelve-state South provided Bob Dole with 65 percent of his 159 electoral votes as he secured two-thirds of the region's electoral college ballots. By holding Dole to "only" two-thirds of the South's electoral votes, Clinton traveled the path marked by Earl and Merle Black (1992). The Blacks noted that to win the presidency, Democrats did not have to win the South, they only needed to deny Republicans a sweep, for if Republicans carry the entire South, they win the presidency with only a third of the remaining electoral votes (Black and Black 1992, 56). In 1992, Bill Clinton became the first Democratic president elected without carrying the bulk of the South.

Congress

The key position of the South in GOP presidential success is now being paralleled in Congress. In the mid-1990s, the South's congressional delegation is more Republican than that of the rest of the county. Overcoming the Civil War–induced antipathy toward the GOP took longer in congressional than presidential elections. Since 1972, the South has been at least as Republican as the rest of the nation in presidential elections, with the sole exception of 1976 (Bullock 1988, 225). In Congress, however, southern Republicans continued to lag their northern cousins, although, since 1978, interelection changes in party fortunes in the South paralleled those in the non-South.

As shown in figure 1.1, not until 1992 did the GOP's share of southern Senate seats (46 percent) outpace its proportion in the remainder of the nation (42 percent). In the next two elections, the southern advantage increased, so that in the 105th Congress, Republicans have 71 percent of the seats from the twelve southern states, while half the remaining seats are held by Republicans.

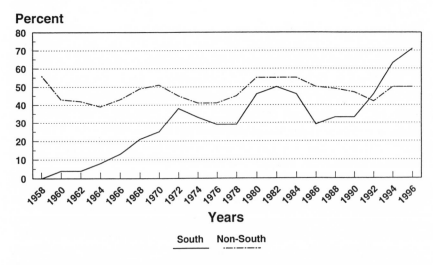

Fig.1.1. South and Non-South, Republicans in the U.S. Senate, 1958–1996 (in percent)

GOP Senate gains in 1996 came in the South. There Republicans picked up two of four open seats, winning their second Alabama seat and scoring their first win in Arkansas since the introduction of popular election of senators. Woody Jenkins came within six thousand votes in Louisiana of giving Republicans a third southern seat. In the rest of the nation, the parties swapped seats, as Larry Pressler (R) was unseated in South Dakota while Republican Chuck Hagel picked up the open Nebraska seat.

The broadening of the base of GOP House success in the South coincides with Republican breakthroughs in presidential voting. The onset of continued Republican victories in the Rim South states of Florida, North Carolina, Tennessee, Texas, and Virginia sowed the seeds for taking congressional seats. Success came slowly as Republicans won urban seats in Charlotte, St. Petersburg, and Dallas in the 1950s and 1960s. After 1964, as figure 1.2 shows, the GOP share of southern House seats trended upward but with setbacks in midterm elections when Republicans held the White House, as in 1974, 1982, and 1986.

Even in taking control of the House, Newt Gingrich's fellow southerners trailed the northern wing of the GOP. Only after several disaffected Democrats followed Georgian Nathan Deal's lead and shifted partisan allegiance did Republicans have a slightly larger share of the southern House seats (56 percent) than the non-Southern (53 percent). In the 105th Congress, Republican House control rests entirely on the GOP's advantage

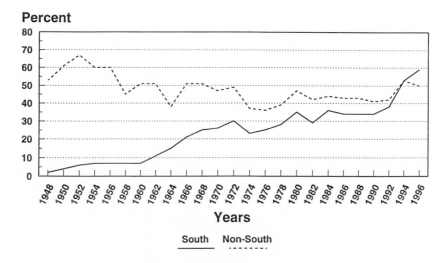

Fig. 1.2. South and Non-South, Republicans in the U.S. House, 1948–1996 (in percent)

in the South, where 59 percent of the seats are filled by Republicans; in the remainder of the nation, Democrats hold a one-seat majority.

Perhaps there is no more compelling evidence of the increased influence of the South in the 105th Congress than what an examination of the leadership of both chambers reveals. As of the first session (1997), southern members hold the following positions in the House: speaker (Newt Gingrich [Ga.]), majority leader (Richard Armey [Tex.]), and majority whip (Tom DeLay [Tex.]). Southerners chair such leading House committees as Ways and Means, Appropriations, Commerce, National Security, and Intelligence. On the Senate side southerners hold these positions: president of the senate (Vice President Al Gore [Tenn.]), president pro tempore (Strom Thurmond [S.C.]), majority leader (Trent Lott [Miss.]), assistant majority leader (Don Nickles [Okla.]), and GOP conference chair (Connie Mack [Fla.]). Lead committees chaired by southerners include Appropriations, Foreign Relations, Rules, Government Affairs, Armed Services, Intelligence, and Energy and Natural Resources.

In the twelve-state South, Republicans registered a net gain of three seats in 1996, building on the nine seats in 1992 and nineteen in 1994 that they added. The 1996 pickup of six open seats (two in Alabama, one in Mississippi, one in Oklahoma and two in Texas) was reduced by the defeats of two GOP freshmen in North Carolina and one in Texas. Further gains in 1998 and 2000 may be modest, since conditions associated with GOP success—that is, Democrats representing small concentrations of African Americans and Democratic legislators with voting records too liberal for their districts—are less common now (Brady, Cogan, and Rivers 1997).

Governorships

As early as 1972, Republicans' percentage of southern governorships approximated the share outside the region, with about a third of all chief executives being Republicans. After the 1994 election, Republicans led six southern states. This number increased by one in 1995 when Mike Foster won the Louisiana governorship and grew by another one in 1996 when Jim Guy Tucker resigned as Arkansas's chief executive after being convicted of a Whitewater-related felony and was succeeded by GOP lieutenant governor Mike Huckabee.

Since their first gubernatorial victories in 1966 (Arkansas and Florida), Republicans have had difficulty retaining governorships following the retirement of a member of their party. The most extended series of successes came in Virginia, where three Republicans held the state's top spot from 1969 through 1981. With seven states holding gubernatorial elections in 1998, partisan competition may be keen, as Republicans will have five states at risk. While Democrats will have only two seats at risk, they may be less favorably positioned than the Republicans, since both Lawton Chiles in Florida and Zell Miller in Georgia have reached the two-term maximums set by their states, so that both seats are open. All of the five Republicans may seek reelection. As of 1997, Georgia remained the last southern state not to have elected a Republican chief executive in the twentieth century.

State Legislatures

In keeping with the trickle-down theory of partisan realignment, success in state legislatures has proven more elusive to the GOP than in higher offices (Bullock 1988, 235). Not until 1984 did Republicans fill more than 20 percent of the seats in lower chambers of the South, a figure only about half as large as their share of U.S. Senate seats. Growth in state senates has come even more slowly than in state lower chambers.

The 1994 elections initiated the period of Republican majorities in some southern state legislatures. The GOP won majorities in the Florida and Tennessee Senates and the lower chambers of North and South Carolina. The next year, the two parties split the forty-member Virginia Senate. The 1996 elections saw Republican majorities emerge in the Florida House and Texas Senate. The success in Florida marked the first time since Reconstruction that Republicans have had majorities in both chambers of a state legislature. Across the region, Republicans had a net gain of ten house seats, as they added eight in South Carolina and seven each in Florida and Georgia while losing seven in North Carolina. Southern senates experienced modest changes in 1996, as Democrats registered a net gain of one seat, although they took two seats to regain a majority in the Tennessee upper chamber.

Shifts in seats may slow in elections held during the next four years, as incumbents produced by the redistricting early in the decade become entrenched. Republicans may make modest gains, but the next major change may come early in the next century when districts are adjusted to reflect population shifts. Suburban growth, coupled with the tendency of suburbia to be strongly Republican, leads to the projection that with a new round of seat reallocation, the GOP will make further gains.

Partisanship in the Electorate

Partisan shifts in the ranks of southern officeholders result from changes in party loyalty among voters. Most states in the region do not require voters to formally identify with a party when registering to vote, a carryover from the era of one-party politics. Instead, states that lack party registration allow voters to choose either party's ballot in the primary, and voters may ask for the ballot of the other party at the next primary. In states with partisan registration, like Florida, Michael Scicchitano and Richard K. Scher show that the GOP has gone far toward eliminating the Democratic advantage.

Where party registration figures are unavailable, surveys help fill the gap. Table 1.1 presents figures from exit polls conducted during the 1996 general election. Eight of the twelve states included in this volume showed more Democrats than Republicans, while Florida had equal numbers of Democrats and Republicans. Louisiana is the last state in which Democrats continued to command the loyalty of most voters. Only in Arkansas and Louisiana did the differences in support for the two parties exceed 10 percentage points; in most states, regardless of which party enjoyed a small edge, the differences were within the margin of error. Statistically, Republicans have drawn even with Democrats, except in Bill Clinton's home state and its neighbor to the south.

Party loyalties have weakened substantially in the last forty years, and the numbers of independents have grown. Even many southerners who identify as Democrats or Republicans nonetheless split their tickets. Old habits die slowly, so Republican candidates have frequently run ahead of their party identification numbers. Republican nominees for major offices such as president, governor, and U.S. senator usually secure larger shares of the vote than would be expected on the basis of party identification data. These gaps have been greatest and were first observed in presiden-

Table 1.1
Party Identification at the Time of the 1996 General Election (in percent)

State	Dem.	Rep.	Ind.	State	Dem.	Rep.	Ind.
Alabama	41	36	23	N. Carolina	42	39	18
Arkansas	45	25	30	Oklahoma	45	38	17
Florida	39	39	23	S. Carolina	35	39	25
Georgia	38	34	28	Tennessee	39	37	24
Louisiana	53	29	18	Texas	37	41	22
Mississippi	45	37	18	Virginia	35	36	29

Source: Exit polls reported on All Politics (http://www.allpolitics.com).

tial elections. When Richard Nixon swept the South in 1972, fewer than one southerner in five was strongly or weakly identified with the GOP (Stanley and Castle 1988, 239). In 1984, when Ronald Reagan repeated the feat, Republican Party identifiers stayed well below 25 percent.

Focusing on the party identification or voting preferences of the southern electorate obscures a growing chasm running along the racial fault line. African Americans support Democratic nominees up and down the ticket at rates of 80 percent and higher. White support for Republicans, while not nearly as uniform as black voting for Democrats, is increasing.

Figure 1.3 shows that across the five most recent presidential elections, Democrats have polled about a third of the white vote in the South. The varied appeal of Democratic nominees in the rest of the nation has not been reflected among southern whites, who found Bill Clinton no more attractive than Jimmy Carter in 1980 or even Michael Dukakis. The data in figure 1.3 also suggest that having a southerner (or even two southerners) at the top of the Democratic ticket does little to enhance the appeal to the region's white voters.

For years, southern Democratic candidates for Congress did relatively well, even as their party's presidential nominees struggled in the region. In the mid-1990s, the success rates for southern congressional Democrats sagged to the level of their party's presidential candidates. The collapse came as white support for congressional nominees converged with the levels of support for Democratic presidential candidates. Figure 1.3 shows

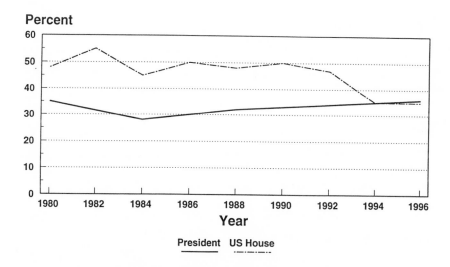

Fig. 1.3. Southern White Democratic Votes for President and U.S. House, 1980–1996 (in percent)

that in 1994 and 1996, Democratic House nominees performed no better among white voters in the region than the party's presidential candidates. The up-and-down, off-year-to-presidential-year oscillation that had marked white congressional voting since 1980 ceased in 1994. After seven elections in which between 45 and 55 percent of the whites voted Democratic, support fell to barely a third.

In 1996, similar levels of white support appear for southern Democratic senatorial candidates. No Democrat running for the Senate managed a majority of the white vote in a southern state. Exit polls reported in table 1.2 show that eight of eleven Democratic nominees polled between 31 and

Table 1.2
Racial Voting Patterns in 1996 Southern Senate Elections (in percent)

State	Candidate	Party	Voter Race	
			Black	White
Alabama	Bedford	D	84	34
	Sessions	R	12	65
Arkansas	Bryant	D	—	43
	Hutchinson	R	—	56
Georgia	Cleland	D	83	37
	Millner	R	12	59
Louisiana	Landrieu	D	91	32
	Jenkins	R	9	68
Mississippi	Hunt	D	67	13
	Cochran	R	31	86
North Carolina	Gantt	D	89	36
	Helms	R	10	63
Oklahoma	Boren	D	—	37
	Inhofe	R	—	60
South Carolina	Close	D	78	32
	Thurmond	R	20	65
Tennessee	Gordon	D	77	31
	Thompson	R	21	68
Texas	Morales	D	79	31
	Gramm	R	19	68
Virginia	Warner, M.	D	77	42
	Warner, J.	R	19	58

Sources: Exit polls reported on All Politics (http://www.allpolitics.com).
— Not reported.

37 percent of the white vote. Even the two Democrats who managed more than 40 percent of the white vote lost. All but three Republicans got at least 60 percent of the white vote, and one of those who failed to break that threshold, Georgia's Guy Millner, suffered from the presence of a Libertarian candidate.

Race and Republicanism

For more than thirty years, Democrats have dominated the African American vote. During much of that period, down-ticket Democrats also turned in respectable showings among whites. The data presented above demonstrate that Democrats, at least as far down as U.S. House candidates, are struggling to retain enough of the white vote to win. Several factors have promoted GOP growth (see Beck 1977; Campbell 1977; Stanley and Castle 1988), which, like the spread of kudzu, has continued largely unchecked, seeping further down the ballot and affecting larger numbers of voters. The region continues to attract upscale whites; older southerners, who maintain a degree of loyalty to the party of their ancestors, die; younger voters are more likely to support Republicans; and newly affluent native southerners are more predisposed toward the GOP. White gravitation toward the GOP has not equaled African American support for Democrats, although GOP pollster Whit Ayres (1997) reports that in South Carolina, fewer than 10 percent of white males identify with the Democratic Party.

GOP success among white voters has enabled Republicans to increasingly dominate office-holding in white constituencies. As reported in table 1.3, Republicans hold more than three-fourths of the congressional seats in districts less than 10 percent black. At the other end of the scale, only Democrats get elected in majority-black districts. As recently as 1991, Democrats still had most of the seats even in the districts that were less than ten percent black. Since the beginning of the decade, Republicans have made the greatest gains in districts with 30 to 39.9 percent black populations; Republicans held 36 percent of the seats in these districts in 1991 but now control 64 percent. For Republicans to win in districts with this kind of concentration of African Americans, the GOP candidates must be doing much better with one of the racial groups, or black voters must be turning out in much smaller numbers.

The GOP is running out of room for further gains in the kinds of districts in which the party has done best. Of the eleven districts with the smallest concentrations of blacks, many of the voters are Hispanic. Texas

Table 1.3
District Racial Composition and Percentage of GOP House
Seats, Controlling for Racial Composition of the District,
102d and 105th Congresses

% Black	105th	N	102nd	N
0–9.9	78.4	51	44.4	36
10–19.9	56.7	30	36.7	30
20–29.9	50.0	24	21.4	28
30–39.9	63.6	11	36.4	22
40–49.9	25.0	4	0	2
≥50	0	11	0	4

Hispanics in particular have shown little inclination to elect Republicans.

In much of the South, the current division of whites between the parties makes for close contests. Of eleven states that elected senators in 1996, in only Mississippi, Oklahoma, and Tennessee did the winner break 55 percent. The Louisiana contest ended in almost a dead heat, and Democrat Max Cleland won the Georgia seat with a plurality.

The Role of Religion

As Green et al. point out in this volume, the role of religion in southern politics continues to receive insufficient attention, excepting perhaps increased awareness of, and interest in, the Christian Right movement. To understand fully the transformation of modern southern politics requires an examination of the religion factor.

As with race and party, the religion factor is characterized by elements of change and continuity. Whether from the left or the right, religious-based organizations and churches have had a profound impact on the region's culture and politics. Much of the civil rights movement of the 1950s and 1960s grew out of the black churches in the South and the religious groups committed to furthering social justice issues. Beginning in the late 1970s, the seeds of the contemporary Christian Right movement were planted by pastors of evangelical churches in the South.

For years white southern Protestants comprised the core of the solid Democratic South. By the 1960s, Green et al. show, the key "high-commitment" evangelical Protestants began to leave the Democratic Party at the presidential level. By the 1990s this bloc shifted to the GOP side in congressional elections as well. Other white Protestant groups followed this pattern, while the coalition of minorities—mostly blacks, Catholics, and seculars—increased in numbers and voted heavily Democratic. Consequently, changes in partisan patterns and demographics help explain the rising fortunes of the GOP in the South (and ultimately in national politics) and the increased representation of blacks in state legislatures, local offices, and congressional delegations. These changes have provided important incentives for the parties—and key interests on both sides—to organize in the South and to mobilize these competing groups in elections.

National Implications of GOP Expansion in the South

Prolonged GOP attacks have pulverized the bedrock on which Democratic congressional majorities rested for decades. Today, the South leads the nation in supporting Republican congressional and presidential efforts. Indeed, GOP successes in winning southern Senate seats set an exceptionally high threshold for Democrats in the rest of the country if their party is to reacquire majority status in the upper chamber.

To assess the consequences of Republican gains in the South for partisan control of Congress, we begin by reviewing the partisan makeup of the Senate over time. The third column of table 1.4 shows the number of Democrats in each Congress beginning with the 86th, the last Congress before John Tower (Texas), the first popularly elected Republican, arrived from the Old Confederacy.[1] In the fourth column are the number of southern Democrats (i.e., those from the twelve states examined in this volume), and the fifth column reports the numbers of northern Democrats. In column six is the number of Democrats who would have served if the southern contingent had been at the level for the 105th Congress (seven). Figures in this column show that had the realignment at the senatorial level occurred earlier, say, by the time that Jimmy Carter lost the presidency, then only once since 1980 would the Senate have had a Democratic majority. Republicans would have had fifty-nine senators during the first six years of the Reagan presidency, which would have been the largest majority enjoyed by either party since the Eisenhower era, if each election had produced seven southern Democrats and everything else had remained constant. The Republican Senate majority would have persisted through the last Reagan biennium and the Bush presidency. The one Democratic majority would have come in President Clinton's first congress.

The important point to take from table 1.4 is the infrequency in the last

Table 1.4
Numbers of Senate Democrats If Southern Democrats Were at 1996 Levels

Year	Congress	Democrats	Southern Seats	Northern Seats	ND + SD 1996
1958	86	64	24	40	47
1960	87	64	23	41	48
1962	88	67	23	44	51
1964	89	68	22	46	53
1966	90	64	21	43	50
1968	91	58	19	39	46
1970	92	55	18	37	44
1972	93	57	15	42	49
1974	94	61	16	45	52
1976	95	62	17	45	52
1978	96	59	17	42	49
1980	97	47	13	34	41
1982	98	46	12	34	41
1984	99	47	13	34	41
1986	100	55	17	38	45
1988	101	55	16	39	46
1990	102	56	16	40	47
1992	103	57	13	44	51
1994	104	47	9	38	45
1996	105	45	7	38	45

two decades of Democratic majorities if Republican strength had been at the levels attained in the South in 1996. If Republicans can maintain the successes that they have achieved in the South in the mid-1990s, Democrats will have to do better in the rest of the nation than they have done in most elections since 1968. If the southern wing provides Democrats with only seven senators, Democrats in the remainder of the country must win at levels they have attained only five times in the last forty years in order to eke out fifty-one seats. Even in their best performance in table 1.4, the 1964 sweep, the North could supply only forty-six Democrats.

Table 1.5 presents data for the House similar to that in table 1.4, but it begins with 1948, when Democrats regained control of the House. The picture of what might have been in the House is much less frightening for Democrats than the hypothetical Senate figures in table 1.4. Even if southern Democrats had held the same share of seats in the past as they do today (41.2 percent), the Democratic Party would have chosen the speak-

Table 1.5
Numbers of House Democrats If Southern Democrats Were at 1996 Levels

Year	Congress	Democrats	Southern Seats	Northern Seats	ND + SD 1996
1948	81	263	111	152	197
1950	82	234	109	125	170
1952	83	213	105	108	154
1954	84	232	104	128	174
1956	85	234	104	130	176
1958	86	283	104	179	225
1960	87	263	104	159	205
1962	88	258	100	158	204
1964	89	295	95	200	246
1966	90	248	89	159	205
1968	91	243	84	159	205
1970	92	255	83	172	218
1972	93	243	80	163	210
1974	94	291	88	203	250
1976	95	292	86	206	253
1978	96	277	82	195	242
1980	97	243	74	169	216
1982	98	269	87	182	232
1984	99	253	78	175	225
1986	100	258	81	177	227
1988	101	260	81	179	229
1990	102	267	81	186	236
1992	103	258	81	177	231
1994	104	204	62	142	196
1996	105	207	54	153	207

er in all but one Congress from the 94th through the 103rd if the party's nonsouthern strength remained at the size that actually existed. Had the GOP capitalized on southern conservatism earlier, additional Republican congressional control would have come during the first half of the period shown in table 1.5, which shows hypothetical Republican majorities from 1948 through 1972 with three exceptions (1958, 1964, and 1970). A strong GOP contingent in the South would have resulted in more variation in partisan control of Congress than the unprecedented forty years of Democratic dominance from 1955 through 1994.

If Democrats regain the strength they had outside the South during the 1980s and suffer few additional losses in the South, then the GOP will be relegated to minority status once again. Under the post-1980 apportionment, Democrats averaged 180 of the 313 northern seats. The 1990 census shifted a net of 9 seats to the South, and with Democrats averaging 57.5 percent of the northern seats, that would be approximately 5 Democratic and 4 Republican seats reassigned to the South. Subtracting 5 from 180 would leave an average Democratic strength in the seats assigned to the North for the 1990s of 175. If Democrats can attain that number of northern seats, then they need hold on to only 43 southern seats. If Republicans keep the 77 southern seats that they hold now, northern Democrats will need a minimum of 164 seats, a threshold they have fallen below in the analysis in table 1.5 only five times between 1958 and 1992. In the elections during this period when northern Democrats failed to achieve 164 seats, they were never more than 6 seats below what they would need to fashion a majority with 54 southern seats. Another way to look at it is that Democrats will need 54 percent of the nonsouthern seats to achieve a majority if Republicans control 77 of the 131 southern seats.

Continuing Shifts in Party Composition

Thus far in this chapter, we have shown that Republicans are competing better in the South for a wider range of offices than ever before. GOP gains ride on increased levels of support among the region's white electorate. Approximately two-thirds of the white vote went to Republican nominees for president, U.S. senator and U.S. representative in 1996. In contrast, while the 1996 exit polls show some Republicans attracting more than 10 percent of the black vote, African Americans remain distinctly loyal Democrats.

As a result of these patterns, African Americans constitute a growing share of Democratic supporters. Indeed, the bulk of the votes for Bill Clinton in Georgia, Louisiana, Mississippi, and South Carolina came from blacks. In Louisiana's U.S. Senate contests, 52 percent of the votes cast for Mary Landrieu came from blacks. As African Americans cast larger shares of the total votes for Democrats, it is likely that the nominees of the South's traditional party will become more responsive to blacks.

Growing participation in GOP primaries, such as has occurred in Florida, Georgia, South Carolina, and Texas, means that the Democratic primary electorate has a higher black percentage than the general election turnout. Since African Americans are, on balance, more liberal on socioeconomic issues than whites, Democratic primary voters may rally to the side of liberal candidates. For example, in 1988, Jesse Jackson led the presidential primaries in the Deep South by capturing almost all of the black votes, while many whites voted in the GOP primary (Bullock 1991). Even if a black candidate is not nominated, the likelihood increases of nominating more liberal candidates or of pulling candidates to the left in search of votes. In 1990 in Alabama and Georgia, for example, the Democrats who advanced to the gubernatorial runoffs were the two most liberal candidates in the field. If Democratic nominees stake out positions further to the left in order to secure support from blacks—the most reliable component of the Democratic Party—these liberal policy stands will drive additional whites to the GOP, rendering the Democratic primary electorate even more liberal. If these cycles continue, the result will be a Democratic Party with such a narrow base that it has poor prospects for winning statewide contests.

A similar cycle in which the Democratic Party becomes smaller, blacker, and more liberal is also under way at the elite level. Georgia's congressional delegation since 1995 has consisted of three black Democrats and eight white Republicans. The other four Deep South states each have a majority Republican congressional delegation augmented by one white Democrat and one black Democrat.

In each state legislative body with a GOP majority, most white legislators are Republicans. In other chambers with Democratic majorities, the black caucus has the potential to be a swing vote. For Democrats to continue organizing these chambers and reaping the benefits of legislative leadership and committee chairs, they must be attentive to at least portions of the policy agenda of the black caucus. Being too responsive to black concerns runs the risk of creating issues that can be exploited by Republicans in the next election.

The implication of the southern wing of the Democratic Party drifting leftward is that in Congress an important counterweight is lost. The success of the Democratic Party in Congress stemmed, in no small part, from its ability to appear liberal in the North but moderate to conservative in the South. To achieve this Janus-like image required that northerners allow southerners to march to the beat of a different drum, and vice versa. In the words of Speaker Sam Rayburn, "You have to go along to get along." This orientation often produced moderately progressive legislation that both northern liberals and southern conservatives could tolerate, even as neither group saw it as ideal. The Democratic downfall of the mid-1990s results at least in part from the demands that southerners be "good" (i.e., liberal) Democrats if they hoped to achieve influence and status within the party. To secure promotion to exclusive committees like Appropriations or Ways and Means, Democrats had to demonstrate loyalty to the national party's goals. Southerners who placed responsiveness to their constituents above adherence to the party line foreclosed the prospects of achieving a seat on a power committee and risked eligibility to lead even subcommittees of lesser committees.

Recent defeats and retirements have decimated the ranks of conservative southern Democrats. No southerner—not even a liberal one—has served in the top positions of the Democratic leadership team since the resignation of Speaker Jim Wright (Tex.) in 1989. With only a handful of southern moderates and conservatives left in Congress, the counterweight that could force the Democratic Party to chart a more moderate course is absent. If congressional Democrats continue to appear to be well to the left of the GOP, Republican efforts to recruit good candidates and win more offices in the South will be helped. Increasingly, white southerners equate the Democratic Party with failed liberal reforms. The last thing that Democrats in the South need is actions and pronouncements from the congressional wing of the party that underscore such perceptions.

The chapters dealing with individual states will more fully explore some of the themes set out in this chapter. Each state, of course, has it own unique features, so that no two have taken the same path toward greater participation of minority groups and the emergence of two-party competition.

Note

1.   Upon his election, Tower became the first Republican from the twelve-state region since Edward Moore represented Oklahoma from 1943 through 1949. Two other one-term Republicans had been elected from Oklahoma in the 1920s.

References

Aistrup, Joseph A. 1996. *The Southern Strategy Revisited.* Lexington: University of Kentucky Press.

Ayres, Whit. 1997. Telephone interview by author. 17 February.

Beck, Paul Allen. 1977. "Partisan Dealignment in the Postwar South." *American Political Science Review* 71: 477–96.

Black, Earl, and Merle Black. 1992. *The Vital South: How Presidents Are Elected.* Cambridge: Harvard University Press.

Brady, David, John F. Cogan, and Douglas Rivers. 1997. *The 1996 House Elections: Reaffirming the Conservative Trend.* Stanford: Hoover Institution.

Bullock, Charles S., III. 1988. "Creeping Realignment in the South." Pp. 220–37 in *The South's New Politics: Realignment and Dealignment*, edited by Robert H. Swansbrough and David M. Brodsky. Columbia: University of South Carolina Press.

Bullock, Charles S., III. 1991. "The Nomination Process and Super Tuesday." Pp. 3–19 in *The 1988 Presidential Election in the South*, edited by Laurence W. Moreland, Robert P. Steed, and Tod A. Baker. New York: Praeger.

Campbell, Bruce A. 1977. "Change in the Southern Electorate." *American Journal of Political Science* 21: 37–64.

Carmines, Edward G,. and James A. Stimson. 1989. *Issue Evolution: Race and the Transformation of American Politics*. Princeton, N.J.: Princeton University Press.

Key, V. O., Jr. 1949. *Southern Politics in State and Nation*. New York: Knopf.

Stanley, Harold W., and David S. Castle. 1988. "Partisan Changes in the South: Making Sense of Scholarly Dissonance." Pp. 238–52 in *The South's New Politics: Realignment and Dealignment*, edited by Robert H. Swansbrough and David M. Brodsky. Columbia: University of South Carolina Press.

Part II

The Deep South States

―――――

2

South Carolina: The Heart of GOP Realignment in the South

John C. Kuzenski

South Carolina, according to Barone and Ujifusa's (1993, 1140) apt description, "stands as one of America's great success stories" in the mid-to-late 1990s. Having emerged after the Civil War as one of "the poorest states in the union, with income levels less than half the national average and with high levels of illiteracy and disease," the state, these authors noted, "is part of the booming Atlantic seaboard and Piedmont ... filling up with new retirement condominiums, factories and office buildings, giant airports and shopping centers, and leading the nation's economic growth." This growth was traditionally buoyed by such plums as the massive military complexes that stretched from Charleston Harbor up through Shaw Air Force Base to Fort Jackson in Columbia. Then, in the early 1990s, foreign companies came bearing healthy doses of foreign investment, which developed the state's economy even further.

Against this backdrop, and given what is already known and well documented about the South's growing Republicanism, the growth of the South Carolina GOP is one of those phenomena that should surprise no student of party politics. What remains to be explored is why South Carolina politics "has been moving, more than any other state in the South, toward the Republicanism exemplified by its native son ... Lee Atwater" (Barone and Ujifusa 1993, 1141–42). The overwhelming successes that the party has enjoyed in the Palmetto State have enabled it to construct an electoral strategy that perhaps no other southern Republican organization has heretofore thought possible: instead of reacting defensively to a black-white Democratic coalition by attempting to drive whites into the GOP, South Carolina's Republican leaders "are coming closer to doing it the other way around, uniting almost all whites with enough blacks to make a huge majority" (Barone and Ujifusa 1993, 1142).

There can be no doubt that contemporary GOP maneuvers in this regard mark a clear shift of strategy; the state's modern Republican Party was born out of racial division in the 1940s and made its greatest development along these lines in the 1950s and 1960s in terms of winning the hearts and minds of South Carolina voters. Somewhere along the way, that success with voters turned into a winning of legislative and executive political positions without the endemic race-baiting found in the successful GOP campaigns of other southern states—even to the point of including a large share of the black vote in the winning candidacies of Republicans such as Governor Carroll Campbell. What comes around goes around, however. As the century comes to a close, the state party appears to be undergoing yet another change that will alter at least the base of its power, if not its control of state politics. This chapter is devoted to exploring and explaining the dramatic shifts that have defined the South Carolina Republican Party, in an attempt to make better sense out of what was, for all intents and purposes, the Deep South's first viable challenger to Bourbon Democratic power.

The Setting for Growth

Virtually nonexistent until the early 1960s, as in most southern states, the modern Republican Party in South Carolina is best understood as an organization that effectively had "two birthdays" representing the large-scale movement of its two factions into GOP ranks. The slightly older, mainstream faction, according to Topping, Lazarek, and Linder (1966, 92–93), was the first to come to the party; they were "attracted to the party . . . by the traditionally more conservative stand regarding business and fiscal matters," as well as "by the Eisenhower/Nixon ticket. . . . They are mostly younger, prospering businessmen, typified by [former state GOP chair] Drake Edens and [Charleston businessman and U.S. Representative] Arthur Ravenel." In South Carolina, where voter turnout has traditionally been among the lowest in the nation, such a small band of dedicated voters can prove its effectiveness; in the 1952 presidential election, Adlai Stevenson carried the state with only 45 percent of the vote compared to Eisenhower's 40 percent. Had it not been for Virginia senator Harry Byrd's independent bid, the results could have been even more promising.

The great migration of the second faction of Palmetto Republicans occurred in 1964, with the defection of Senator Strom Thurmond from Democratic into GOP ranks. In 1948, Thurmond had led many southern Democrats into the ranks of the States' Rights, or "Dixiecrat," movement as a result of the Truman administration's early civil rights policies. He carried the state with 72 percent of its 1948 presidential vote and won a solid belt of other southern states as well. These "mad Democrats," as Topping, Lazarek, and Linder (1966) describe them, had little or no political refuge between 1948 and 1964. Faced with a purely regional movement, they could do nothing but continue voting largely as they had for years before—for white segregationist Democrats at the local level and usually for Democrats who would make only cosmetic moves on the civil rights front for president. Thurmond finally decided in 1964, in the face of Lyndon Johnson's civil rights agenda, that the Democratic Party no longer stood for the values he had joined it to uphold and promptly switched to the Republicans. Thousands of "mad Democrats" across South Carolina quickly followed suit, watching as the Dixiecrat movement aligned with a national party that offered an alternative to what Thurmond called the "socialistic" policies of the Democratic Party.

The second wing of the state party was thus born, and its members' "dissatisfaction . . . with the National Democratic Party can be traced mostly to the civil rights issue. Rural and small town voters constitute the bulk of this faction" (Topping, Lazarek, and Linder 1966, 93). The South Carolina Republican Party throughout the rest of the 1960s and into the 1970s was, therefore, a symbiotic but eclectic alliance of white-collar pro-business traditionalists and blue-collar or rural racists. In the early stages of its existence, there was little doubt about which faction controlled the agenda within the state GOP. The party was Thurmond, and vice versa. He convinced controversial but popular Second District congressman Albert Watson to support Barry Goldwater's bid for the presidency in 1964; when congressional Democrats stripped Watson of his two years' seniority in retribution, Watson also jumped ship to the Republicans. He continued his segregationist bids for reelection, but now against national Democrats—using flyer headlines such as "The South Under Attack!" and "Democrat Bosses Plan to Rule with Negro Vote." The early support given to legitimize the GOP by these two pivotal figures in Carolina politics put the state ahead of the pack in the South's discovery of the post-Reconstructionist Republican Party.

Two important points should be made about this period of Republican development. First, the party was, by this time, substantially better organized and coming closer to major victories than any other Republican organization in the Deep South (and many in the rim South, as well); it kept the Democrats to popular vote victories of 51 percent or less in the presidential elections of 1952, 1956, and 1960, and Goldwater won the state with 59 percent of the vote in 1964 (Bass and DeVries 1976, 254). Thus, it magnified the general pattern found in other states across the

region. Republican fortunes were skewed even more favorably by the
defection of Thurmond in 1964 and Watson shortly thereafter. This
addresses the second point: Republican growth in South Carolina is due
in large part to the political skill and pragmatism of its early leaders. The
early defections of Thurmond and others provided the state GOP with a
strong base of legitimacy much sooner than most other southern states.
As a result, South Carolina got a head start on the Republican Revolution.
Subsequently, this brand of southern Republicanism was strongly influenced by key personnel of the 1970s and 1980s. Alexander Lamis (1990,
63–64) remarks:

> As the South Carolina experience unfolds, it is instructive to remember
> what took place in Mississippi during the same period. The radically differ-
> ent approaches of the leaders in these sister states of the Solid South empha-
> size the importance that the actions of elites have in altering patterns of
> behavior that are too often viewed as dependent on all-powerful sociologi-
> cal forces. Here, political leadership made the difference, and two states
> with similar backgrounds diverged significantly.

The Actions of Elites: Reactions of Party Leadership

Democratic leaders in South Carolina have often found themselves in a
precarious position since the mid-1960s. Long accustomed to the fruits of
a monopoly on political power, as Key (1949) characterized such organizations, they were not accustomed to having to fight for control of the
organs of government or for voters' loyalties. This need for struggle, in
turn, was engendered by their national party's adoption of Great Society
principles, which left little to nothing for the state party to offer the state's
majority-white, conservative electoral base. As in other states throughout
the South, party leaders in South Carolina thought they had found a
workable plan in moving toward incorporation of African American concerns after passage of the Civil Rights Act (CRA) and the Voting Rights
Act (VRA). Unfortunately for state Democrats, historically low voter-
turnout figures in South Carolina, particularly among blacks, have not
gotten substantially better, and the party has been characterized as being
in strategic and organizational disarray (Bass and DeVries 1976; Sampson
1984; Graham and Moore 1994). Key (1949, 670) attempted to hold out
hope for southern Democratic parties by noting that "within southern
politics there is a powerful strain of agrarian liberalism." It can safely be
said that, fifty years after Key's seminal work, that strain has not emerged
as a utilizable power. South Carolina Democrats have pinned their hopes

on forging a coalition between blacks and liberal-to-moderate whites, which has not been a consistently winning strategy. This may be because, in the words of a colleague in a recent telephone conversation with the author, "it could be a step up if the Democrats [in South Carolina] get the moderate white vote—all two or three of 'em."

This is not to say that the South Carolina Democratic Party is slowly inching toward its grave. Narrow beams of light have shined brightly from time to time in the political savvy of some of its veterans, such as Senator Ernest "Fritz" Hollings; popular up-and-comers such as Charleston mayor Joseph Riley provide it with a steady stream of viable candidates for higher office. In those rare instances where the black electorate has been able to exhibit a modicum of trust in what is widely perceived to be an old-boy network of white Democrats, the payoff has been a temporary bulwark against creeping Republicanism. Nevertheless, recent developments in redistricting have also made it worthwhile for many prominent black leaders to ally with Republicans at times. This adds to the dilemma for Democratic leaders, as they lose the support of what is increasingly their most important bloc vote. The critical truth is that it takes some degree of coordination to make narrow beams of light shine with some brilliance. A preoccupation with learning the rules of a new era's political game while trying to hold on to a perpetually slippery electorate has often left South Carolina Democrats fumbling in the dark for meaningful direction.

White Carolinians continue to leave Democratic Party ranks precisely because it is increasingly viewed as the party of the liberals or the party of the blacks—and often, as both. Black Carolinians remain generally loyal to the Democratic cause, but they have forsaken that alliance for temporary peace with the Republicans when specifically black political interests have dictated that course—a pattern about which black Sixth District representative James Clyburn (1997) recently noted, "I never supported that—there's something sinister about that."[1] The end result in all but some county and local elections in the 1990s has been a "white Democratic Party" and a "black Democratic Party" in the state, competing from different positions for electoral victories that would realize a broader set of common political interests.

The Republican reaction has been considerably more focused and pragmatic. This tone was set by Senator Thurmond shortly after African Americans began registering to vote in substantial numbers, and proved to be an invaluable lesson to future generations of South Carolina Republicans. In 1957, he set the legendary twenty-four-hour-plus single-member filibuster record in the U.S. Senate in objections to mild civil rights extensions proposed by the Democratic leadership.[2] In 1964, Thurmond wrestled a Democratic colleague to the ground outside a committee room to prevent a quorum on pending civil rights legislation; he won the match, but his colleague "was able to complete the quorum after the [committee] chairman rescued him" (Duncan 1991, 1341). After blacks enjoyed full franchise protections under law, however, Thurmond toned down these types of flamboyant actions and took a more pragmatic course. In 1971, he became the first southern senator to appoint a black staff aide, and he was the first to sponsor an African American for a federal judgeship. He furthered this change of course in the 1980s by voting in favor of extensions of the VRA and creation of the Martin Luther King Jr. federal holiday. Thurmond has, in effect, left the "Thurmond Republicans" behind in the name of reelectoral pragmatism. If African Americans in the state are not as a group overwhelmingly supportive of him, it is also true that as a result of the conciliations he has made in the last twenty years, they have not found reason to come to the polls en masse to ensure his defeat.

Barone and Ujifusa (1993, 1142) point out that limited Republican gains were made in the state "in the 1960s and 1970s by opposition to busing and appeals to traditional values; most white southerners didn't want to rally to a past they were proud to have overcome." The Thurmond metamorphosis proved that conservative Republicans who blunt the potential for overt racial division—and thus blunt increased black voter turnout in response to that division—can comfortably win reelection on the strength of the white Republican wave.[3] It also paved the way for the ascendancy of the other wing of the party to dominate South Carolina Republican concerns in the 1980s and 1990s, as racism and segregation increasingly began to take a back seat to economic growth as a Republican priority.

Graham and Moore (1994, 94–95) argue that the gubernatorial campaign of 1970, between ardent GOP segregationist Watson and Democratic racial moderate John West, "marked the end of an era of racial politics in South Carolina," particularly since it was clear after Watson's poor showing in affluent white areas of the state that the "racial issue reduced . . . support from more moderate Republicans." Watson lost the election with his antiblack rhetoric. While doing well in parts of the rural upstate, he lost crucial Republican strongholds such as metropolitan Charleston, with its old-moneyed and powerful elite. A new cadre of well-educated and progressive elites, represented most notably by Lee Atwater and Carroll Campbell, learned their lessons from this era well and carried that new pragmatism into their own political battles. Atwater rose to the position of senior party adviser before becoming one of President George Bush's key strategists, while Campbell topped an eight-year career in the general assembly and four terms as a U.S. representative with his election as governor in 1986.

New Breed of Masters: The Campbell Years

Governor Campbell (1986–1994) began his service as South Carolina's chief executive after he eked out a win in the general election over Democrat Mike Daniel; he did so largely as a result of being able to hold the Republican vote together after convincing chief primary rival Thomas Hartnett to run for lieutenant governor instead. Hartnett lost his bid for the number-two slot, but Campbell was elected with a vote that marked the first "Republican governor . . . in an election where both parties were united" (Graham and Moore 1994, 96). Since then, he has become "an exemplar of governing conservatism," and in "1991, [Bill] Clinton told the *Wall Street Journal* that Campbell was the conservative he admired most" (Barone and Ujifusa 1993, 1142–43). Campbell proceeded to build on the reforms of his predecessor, Democrat Richard Riley, on many fronts— business development, education, tax, health, and the like. He also vetoed or refused to sign several redistricting plans the state senate had created for itself, claiming that they would not gain Department of Justice (DOJ) approval under the VRA. When DOJ rejected the plan as the governor had predicted, it reinforced the governor's image as an enlightened progressive and the Democratic senate as anachronistic buffoons. The redistricting debacle was brilliant positioning, as Campbell won the sympathies of many black voters, increased his prestige as a governor in control, and diminished the position of the state senate, South Carolina's locus of political power. In 1990, Campbell won reelection with 69 percent of the vote; among African Americans, the Republican incumbent won 25 percent of the vote.

This feat was even more extraordinary given that his opponent was a black state senator who lambasted pro-Campbell black leaders as "Uncle Toms" (Barone and Ujifusa 1993, 1143). The Campbell experience indicates that Republicans who can avoid the race-baiting endemic in other states can create a superior electoral coalition. If and when their Democratic opponents resort to the race card in an attempt to drive a wedge into that group, as Campbell's opponent did in 1990, it is the Democrats who become the extremists, and they suffer from the split-coalition dilemma. The predominantly rural "racist Republican" white vote present in other states (Kuzenski and Corbello 1995) appears also to be alive in South Carolina (Sinclair 1984), but it is a vote with nowhere else to go on election day than into the pocket of the Republican nominee. Moderate-to-liberal whites, who have become a swing vote in many state elections, and some African Americans as well, are polarized against Democratic candidates who invoke racial appeals for victory—thus exacerbating the Democrats' defeat. Charlotte mayor Harvey Gantt made a particularly apropos comment about this twisted dynamic of race and politics in South Carolina shortly after becoming the first African American student at Clemson University in 1963; he commented, "If you can't appeal to the morals of a South Carolinian, you can appeal to his manners" (Bass and DeVries 1976, 258).

Growth in the South Carolina GOP is thus divided into two distinct phases since its effective inception in 1964: between 1964 and the early 1970s, growth was spurred by the antiblack leadership the party attracted, which in turn attracted vocal and active antiblack rank-and-file supporters. The later 1970s were a period of transition, in which key leaders such as Thurmond began to back away from their earlier creation. This paved the way for the second era in GOP development, marked by the rise of economic concerns and the suppression of racial hostility in the party's campaigning. While growth was sustained by the in-migration of job- and money-seeking Republicans who were attracted to the state by its economic upswing (Black and Black 1987), it is nevertheless the case that native Carolinians also provided the backbone of this movement and dominated it through the mid-1990s. The traditionalistic society of South Carolina, as Graham and Moore (1994) characterize it, thus moved— albeit slowly—back to an even more traditional notion that predates the Bourbon use of race as a political weapon: the desire to find prosperity.

Changing Tides in the Republican Wave?

The great dilemma South Carolina Republicans faced as their party developed the means to dominate the state's political agenda was essentially the same problem Democrats faced after passage of the VRA: lesser elements of the coalition will remain loyal as long as they believe they can wrest control of something worth controlling. By the mid-1990s, the South Carolina Republican Party was clearly something worth controlling, and two elements of their coalition that have mass appeal in the Palmetto State—the "Thurmond-Watson Republicans" of pre-VRA days and the Christian Right—found themselves in a strong position to register protests with the progressivist party leadership that had seemingly forsaken moral and traditionalist cultural issues to concentrate on South Carolina's economic potential. Current governor David Beasley, who converted to the Republican Party after a thirteen-year stint in the house of representatives,[4] is now the state's leading Republican figure at a pivotal time in the party's development. Beasley is a born-again Christian conservative, which, Democratic humorists noted, gave him two essential skills in politics—handling snakes and speaking in tongues (Guth 1995; Barone and Ujifusa 1995). He has also attempted, however, to hold on to the party's pro-business "Atwater Republican" support as the successor to the Campbell legacy. It is difficult to place Beasley as clearly representative of one faction of the party or another. James Guth (1995, 137–38) noted that in his 1994 campaign for governor, Beasley

> ran a quiet "two-tiered" campaign for governor. First, he traveled to hundreds of conservative churches to recount his religious conversion, a stump speech which was distributed via audiotape all over the state.... At the same time, he did not neglect traditional Republican constituencies, cultivating business groups, fellow GOP state legislators, and, most important, Governor Campbell's formidable electoral machine.

In a 1988 interview, Democrat Beasley said that his fellow party leaders were taking for granted that South Carolina was a Democratic state and that they "were the party that has been running the state while the Republicans have been promoting themselves" (Reed 1988). "If black Democrats and white Democrats will begin vocalizing what we've been doing, providing good government with good, conservative fiscal policies and a balanced budget," Beasley continued, "that will take care of the black-white issue." As a result of his 1985 religious conversion, Beasley soon found that his Democratic identity was at odds with his moral and social beliefs, which precipitated his 1991 conversion to the Republican Party. His attempt to restrict racial appeals in favor of economic ones was difficult to complete in 1994, however, given the nature of the electorate he had to win over in his new Republican primary.

In 1994, with help from the anti-Democratic sentiment that swept the country that year and on the backs of the Republican right, Beasley was elected governor with a meager 50 percent of the statewide vote. The previous year, "the Christian Coalition flooded ... GOP precinct meetings, narrowly controlled the state Republican convention, and elected Henry McMaster as state GOP chairman"; rather than turning the state party completely over to the religious right, however, McMaster initially "proved rather independent, staving off Coalition efforts to gain operational control and working to keep disgruntled regulars from setting up alternative organizations" (Guth 1995). The religious right and the Thurmond-Watson conservatives had always been a noteworthy part of the state's Republican base, but they were subjected to the domination of white-collar, business-oriented progressives during the Campbell years. In order to defeat Democratic challenger Nick Theodore, Beasley had to turn out as much of these elements of the party as he could. He succeeded, with the assistance of Campbell and McMaster, but at the clear cost of alienating important segments of Campbell's winning coalition: a *Greenville News* poll taken immediately before the 1994 general election, for example, showed Beasley as the choice of only 6 percent of the state's black voters (compared to Campbell's 25 percent in 1990), leading significantly among white males, and doing particularly well in the rural counties of the state (American Political Network 1994)—just as Albert Watson had done in 1970.

Part of the reason for this change in voter composition was the different call to action from Campbell's that Beasley had to issue in order to mobilize sufficient numbers of the disaffected Republican coalition. He was outspokenly against abortion and a state lottery; he also made an issue of the Confederate battle flag that had been flying over the South Carolina statehouse since 1962. He pledged to keep it flying as a source of remembrance and pride in the state's accomplishment and sacrifice in the Civil War. In 1995, however, the governor reversed his opinion, claiming that he had beseeched God for an answer to the issue after a rash of hate crimes in the state directed against African Americans. Just prior to his epiphany, Beasley's special race relations committee had issued a call for the flag to come down. In 1994, the NAACP had threatened a boycott if the flag were not removed; prominent state business leaders, worried that such an issue would overshadow efforts to attract further business and industry to South Carolina, helped sponsor flag-removal legislation that cleared the state senate but subsequently failed in the house (see Harrison 1996). The governor was attempting compromise on an issue on which he had boxed himself into a corner during his 1994 campaign in an attempt to hold together the winning Republican coalition. Then the entire affair blew up in his face.

Beasley recommended that the flag be brought down from atop the capitol's rotunda and placed at a Confederate memorial on the statehouse grounds instead; this brought immediate condemnation from prominent African Americans such as state senator Darrell Jackson, who claimed that the only proper place for the battle flag was in a museum. Jackson noted that the Beasley plan removed one flag from the rotunda but placed two others at the statehouse grounds' two Confederate war memorials (Burritt 1997). While whites had mixed reactions to the plan and the numbers supporting the rotunda flag appeared to be dropping slightly, the contingent still fighting the War of Northern Aggression was vociferous; the most popular bumper sticker at sportsmen's exhibitions and gun shows as 1996 faded into 1997 read "Dump the Governor—Keep the Flag." Sixth District congressman James Clyburn (1997), who indicated strongly that he believes the governor's flag proposal has hurt him considerably more with whites than helped him with blacks, noted that Beasley "was trying to have his cake and eat it, too" on the issue. He was trapped between antiflag African American and business concerns on one hand and his 1994 "welcome to the party" social conservative voter coalition on the other.

The flag controversy and other racially loaded issues, neatly suppressed by preceding Republican and Democratic elites in the name of economic progress, may represent an end to the uneasy but effective partisan truce that brought such massive reforms and development to South Carolina over the last decade. One other substantial factor in the equation has been the state's reapportionment and redistricting plans, which have for the last thirty years been effected primarily by the courts. Although this pattern may be abhorrent to civil rights proponents and states'-righters alike, it is nevertheless probably the case that having the matter taken largely out of their hands by a politically sheltered entity such as the U.S. district court has enabled these interests to work in greater harmony on the economy-building that characterized the Riley and Campbell years. The days of court-ordered redistricting may or may not be over with the production of the 2000 census, but the current, heretofore unseen alliance between black Democrats and Republicans will have a marked effect on party election success at both the state and the congressional level.

Reapportionment in the Palmetto State

South Carolina's history of legislative reapportionment since the time of the VRA has been one of constant judicial actions, perhaps more so than in any other state covered under the act. Legal advocacy has often been the only effective means available to black voting rights groups in the state, since the post-VRA federal courts in particular have changed from courthouse rings of local machine appointees into judicial activists prepared to tackle the sticky business of gerrymandering. This, among other things, however, reinforces a white attitude that stemmed from a comment once made about Supreme Court Justice Hugo Black. Alluding to

Black's brief flirtation with the Ku Klux Klan, *Washington Post* writer David Yoder jokingly noted that Black "used to put on a white robe and run around scaring black people; now he puts on a black robe and runs around scaring white people" (1996).[5] Judicial redistricting is a process that Republicans have learned to manipulate recently to their favor in working with African Americans. Judicial frustration with the endless stream of such litigation may signal the end of this alliance, to the joy of the state Democratic Party and general assembly alike.

Prior to the landmark "one person, one vote" principle handed down in the Supreme Court case of *Reynolds v. Sims* (377 U.S. 533, 84 S.Ct. 1362, 12 L.Ed.2d 506 [1964]), the state senate had been composed of forty-six seats, one for each county. As a result of the *Reynolds* decision, a suit, *O'Shields v. McNair* (254 F.Supp. 708, 711 [D.S.C. 1966]), was quickly filed against the state of South Carolina to change its method of apportioning seats in the general assembly, and the assembly responded to what became its judicial mandate in 1966 by creating a fifty-member state senate that represented twenty-seven districts. The fifty-member senate plan survived for just one year, however, before the South Carolina Supreme Court ruled it unconstitutional (*State ex rel. McLeod v. West*, 249 S.C. 243, 153 S.E.2d 892 [1967]). The Democrat-controlled senate redrew its district boundaries still again, reverting to a forty-six-member body elected from a combination of single- and multimember districts. This plan, for the 1970 elections, was rejected two years later by a three-judge federal panel in *McCollum v. West* (Civil Action 71-1211 [D.S.C.7 April 1972]). The most noteworthy objection, according to critics of the plan, was the senate's insistence on maintaining the integrity of county lines while drawing senate districts.

Initially, the federal courts did not balk completely at the notion of county-based districts, and in as late a case as *Burton v. Sheheen* (793 F.Supp. 1329 [1992]), a three-judge panel called the general assembly's "preeminence of county lines" policy "highly rational." The problem for state legislators was the population shift. The 1970s exhibited an impressive amount of growth along the coast, from Charleston's Battery northward to the Grand Strand of Myrtle Beach, as well as the suburbanization of the Greenville-Spartanburg metropolitan area. During this time, it was becoming progressively more difficult for the senate to maintain neat divisions of county boundaries within the broader context of legislative districts. Those districts, in turn, were increasingly scrutinized by the courts for compliance with section 5 of the VRA.

Following the decision in *McCollum*, the general assembly came up with several redistricting plans in 1972; one was finally approved by the court.

In *Simkins v. Gressette* (495 F.Supp. 1075 [1980]), however, a number of black plaintiffs filed suit against both Democratic and Republican state party leaders in an attempt to stop the 1980 state senatorial elections. The plaintiffs' request for another three-judge panel was denied in the Charleston Division of the U.S. District Court for South Carolina, because, in the words of the court, the fact that:

> the State of South Carolina had complied in every respect with the guide-lines determined by the court in a previous case for the apportionment of the South Carolina Senate operated to prevent the court from reaching an uncontradicted finding of discriminatory intent necessary to overcome the factors compelling denial of equitable relief in form of an order directing reapportionment prior to the 1980 primary and general elections.

Although the senate won the case, *Simkins* was a warning shot across the senate's bow, and following the 1980 census it attempted once again to contrive an acceptable redistricting plan. Democratic *and* Republican leaders, both respondents or targets in the case, struggled to find a compromise that would satisfy the perceived interests of the *Simkins* plaintiffs as well as their own desire to maintain county-boundary integrity. The final plan, passed in 1983, eliminated the old multimember districts that had caused so much controversy among black plaintiffs in the past. Act 257 of the 1983 legislative calendar created forty-six single-member districts in the state senate and even went so far as to divide some counties to comply with the one-person, one-vote principle now firmly established under VRA-based judicial review. While the state began to accept candidate petitions to file for office under the new plan, it simultaneously filed a declaratory judgment action in the U.S. District Court for the District of Columbia seeking a declaration of the plan's compliance with section 5 of the Voting Rights Act (*South Carolina v. United States*, 585 F.Supp. 418 [D.D.C.], appeal dismissed, 469 U.S. 875, 105 S.Ct. 285, 83 L.Ed.2d 164 [1984]). The court refused to approve the plan until it had received pre-clearance from the Department of Justice, however, and subsequently declared all candidate filings to that date null and void. In a subsequent case, *Graham v. South Carolina* (Civil Action 3:84-1430-15 [D.S.C. 13 June 1984]), a federal judicially imposed redistricting scheme went into effect for the state senate. The *Graham* plan contained forty-six single-member districts that split a total of twenty-six of the state's counties; nine of these districts were majority black.

Later in the year, the senate approved and had precleared a replacement for the interim *Graham* plan; it created ten majority-black districts in terms of total population, but only seven measured by voting-age population. The results, nevertheless, were dramatic: in 1983 the first black state senator since Reconstruction was elected (the result of a special election that year in a redrawn District 7); four African Americans found their way into the chamber in the 1984 elections. By 1990, six black senators had taken the oath of office. At the same time, however, Republicans in the general assembly found their numbers on the rise (see table 2.1). The trend was a signal to South Carolina Republicans that there was an advantage to be gained in assisting African American redistricting interests; bolstered by increasing numbers of voters, the party thus focused on one of the last hurdles to controlling state politics: the ability to win and hold legislative districts. As a result, legal advocacy became as popular a lobbying tactic in the offices of the state Republican Party as it was in the strategy sessions of the Statewide Reapportionment Advisory Committee (SRAC).

In 1991, the South Carolina Republican Party first attempted to ally itself with black redistricting advocates in the state by filing suit unilaterally

Table 2.1
Republican and African American Representation in the South Carolina General Assembly, 1965–1995

	Republicans		African Americans	
	Senate	House	Senate	House
1965	0	1	0	0
1967	6	17	0	0
1969	3	5	0	0
1971	3	11	0	3
1973	3	21	0	4
1975[a]	3	17	0	12
1979	2	16	0	13
1981	5	17	0	14
1984	6	20	1[b]	19
1988	12	33	4	15
1991	11	42	6	14
1993	16	50	7	18
1995	18	63[c]	6	24

Source: Compiled by author from data in the *South Carolina Legislative Manual.*
N (senate) = 46; N (house) = 124
[a]From this point forward, two-year intervals expand owing to missing data.
[b]Filled by 1983 special election, won by black candidate.
[c]Majority control of chamber.

against the continuation of a court-ordered reapportionment plan; the plan had been hammered out by a federal district court after a 1990–1991 impasse between Governor Campbell and the general assembly could not be broken. In *Burton v. Sheheen*, state GOP chairman Michael G. Burton claimed that plans for redistricting both chambers of the general assembly and South Carolina's congressional districts were unconstitutional under the VRA because of changes in population. Three weeks later, the SRAC filed its own lawsuit, *Statewide Reapportionment Advisory Committee v. Campbell*, and by court order upon motion, the two actions were combined under the *Burton* name (*Burton v. Sheheen*, 793 F.Supp. 1329 [1991]). The U.S. District Court for the District of South Carolina, Columbia Division, ruled against the plaintiffs, noting that it did "not tread unreservedly into this 'political thicket'" but that nevertheless the legislature's goal of attempting to minimize the splitting of county lines was a rational one. As such,

> Our plans meet the de minimis standard of *Chapman*, the deviation standard of *Karcher* and the retrogression standard of *Beer* as applicable to each plan. In addition the plans protect the traditional and legitimate policies of South Carolina. . . . It is ordered, therefore, that the [court's attacked redistricting plan] shall be the lawful election districts for each of those bodies . . . until [plans are passed by the assembly, signed by the governor] and approved by the United States Department of Justice pursuant to 42 U.S.C. sec. 1973c.

Any relief Democrats in the general assembly may have felt over the *Burton* decision was to be short-lived. In June 1993, the U.S. Supreme Court vacated the plan established by the case and accepted an amicus curiae brief from the federal solicitor general's office in support of the original *Burton* plaintiffs. The solicitor general's argument was varied, with the main points being that (1) the lower court erred by considering the case in light of only section 5 of the VRA, and not section 2; (2) it refused to resolve the issue of racially polarized voting in South Carolina; (3) there was no basis for its finding that districts with 50 percent or more black voting-age population could be considered "black opportunity districts"; and (4) it gave undue deference to state policy in taking care to maintain existing county or precinct boundaries where possible.[6]

The *Burton* court, on remand, pressured the general assembly for its own redistricting plan, which finally emerged in February 1994. The legislation became law without Governor Campbell's signature, as he advised the assembly that he believed the plan did not go far enough in creating black-majority districts and that it would subsequently be rejected by the Justice Department. In May 1994, that is precisely what happened. Scrambling to find a new plan that would meet preclearance requirements, the general assembly found itself in the midst of a flurry of negotiation letters between its officers, the Department of Justice, the SRAC, the governor's office, the South Carolina Republican Party, and other interested parties. Having finally hammered out what, pending DOJ approval, was perceived as a workable plan in time for the 1996 elections, the assembly met further resistance with the filing of yet another Republican-SRAC cooperative challenge in federal court. This time, however, the Republicans and the SRAC worked in concert from the outset of the case.

In *Smith v. Beasley* (946 F.Supp. 1174 [1996]), plaintiffs argued for an annulment of a number of 1996 state legislative elections and a declaration of unconstitutionality for the plan under which they had taken place. The court gave the plaintiffs half a wish: six state house districts and three senate districts were ruled unconstitutional, and the general assembly was ordered to fix the problem before 1 April 1997. The court refused, however, to invalidate any of the recently held elections, to the chagrin of Smith et al. What is particularly notable about the *Smith* decision is the bench's increasing frustration over the redistricting fracas in the Palmetto State. It is tangible in a number of points throughout the decision, and it is increasingly directed at both the Republican Party and the Department of Justice as parties to the flurry of litigation in which black plaintiffs presumably have the most significant standing. Point 56 of the *Smith* decision, for example, cites the notes of an expert witness taken during a phone call with attorney Nancy Sardeson of the DOJ Voting Rights Section; the notes were finally produced at trial over vehement objection, and in part read "Broke [former Democratic house speaker] Sheheen's back—came out of Judiciary Committee," "9 new black districts," "Blacker than usual," and perhaps the most inflammatory comment, which eventually made local news headlines, "Screw white boy Democrats."[7] Point 57 continues:

> The Department of Justice's advocacy position is evidenced in many memoranda, letters and notes of telephone conversations, but most particularly by the apparent epidemic of amnesia that has dimmed the memory of many DOJ attorneys who were involved with South Carolina's efforts to produce a reapportionment plan that would pass preclearance. Attorney Sardeson identified a DOJ map of South Carolina House districts that was produced under court order. On this map she had written the letter "B" on certain districts and the letter "W" on others. In her testimony, she would not concede that "B" indicated a black district or that "W" indicated a white district. She stated: "I am not going to speculate . . . as to why I wrote that on the map." As to another map of South Carolina House districts identified as "SRAC," which is synonymous with the Black Caucus, she had written notes connected by arrows to various districts. Most of these notes are racial in con-

notation: "Black Caucus Amendment"; "SRAC adds an additional district"; "Will it elect?" [Footnote 6]—It was fitting that Department of Justice moved to intervene as a party defendant in the House case, because it had been a most important participant in the process leading to the creation of the challenged districts.

Smith is, at this time, the most recent federal case involving redistricting in South Carolina. The controversy in South Carolina was made markedly more heated by the Supreme Court decision in Shaw v. Reno; in Shaw, the U.S. Supreme Court rejected the notion that race should be a predominant legitimate factor in drawing legislative boundaries. This decision paved the way for lower courts, as the District Court for South Carolina did in Smith, to lambaste the DOJ for its "aggressive" handling of such cases and to take jabs at Republican organizations, as the same court did in Burton, for playing "friend" when it has its own obvious interests at heart in the decisions.

Given the aftermath of Shaw, and awaiting the outcome of a likely appeal to Smith, the legal advocacy strategy of South Carolina Republicans may be coming to an end. The Shaw decision is an unanticipated setback for GOP redistricting experts across the region who have been eager to assist African Americans in packing black-majority districts so as to keep those voters out of the resulting heavily white—and heavily Republican—remainder. In South Carolina, however, the timing of this setback is almost ideal for the Republican Party; it now controls the state house of representatives and four of the state's six U.S. congressional districts. The Sixth Congressional District, a black-majority area that reaches from northern Charleston to carefully selected neighborhoods in Columbia, is sacrificed to black Democrats in exchange for substantial white majorities in the five others (see table 2.2). Republicans have yet to capture South Carolina's traditional base of power, the state senate, but they are only nine seats away from that feat.

James Clyburn (1997), who has represented the Sixth District since it was redrawn in 1992, argues that the district will survive scrutiny under Shaw, since in his view the district is not substantially existent by virtue of race—"it brings together common economic interests, communities of common interest, the military reservations . . . and the like." He is also one of the few African American leaders on record as being skeptical of the alliance forged between black and Republican leaders over the redistricting battle, forcefully noting:

I never supported that—there's something sinister about that. Republicans, of course, are using it to their advantage, and it's in their interest to do so,

Table 2.2
Demographics of South Carolina Congressional Districts

	Incumbent	Race		% Rural	1992 Presidential Vote			Income[a]
		White	Black		Clinton	Bush	Perot	
1st	R	77	20	25	53	33	14	13,112
2d	R	72	25	40	52	36	11	13,807
3d	R	78	21	58	51	35	13	11,813
4th	R	79	20	36	54	33	12	13,011
5th	D	68	31	63	45	42	12	11,009
6th	D	37	62	51	62	31	6	8,628

Source: Michael Barone and Grant Ujifusa, *Almanac of American Politics, 1996 Online* (http://www.politicsnow.com).
[a]Per capita income.

but it has nothing to do with an interest in the political situation of blacks . . . [which is why] I have been advocating some other methods of election [than single-member districts]. We brought up a bill before to move to another method . . . and it was ignored; I'll bring it up again this term, and it will be ignored again.

The method Clyburn advocates is proportional representation, first brought into the contemporary spotlight by Professor Lani Guinier during her tumultuous efforts to become a DOJ civil rights appointee in the Clinton administration. The alliance forged between black Democrats and Republicans in redistricting battles, however, has, in Clyburn's opinion, transferred to the front of maintaining single-member districts. African Americans from safe VRA-engendered districts have the same interest in protecting their turf as do Republicans whose districts are now more lily-white and conservative than ever. With proportional representation, united Democrats win; without it, the racial wedge continues to create three distinct parties in South Carolina's (and the region's) partisan battles: the overwhelmingly white Republicans, African American Democrats, and the increasingly marginalized white Democrats who have become swing voters in both parties' attempts to establish or maintain power.

Conclusion: Fire from Within?

If Republican electoral victories in South Carolina are somehow slowed by the current state of changing party loyalties and the "racialization" of party identification, it will likely be as a result of tumult within the party itself and not as the result of scheming by the state's dwindling base of old-time white Democrats who cling disorganizedly to the perquisites of legislative control. It is not an unknown phenomenon; Bullock (1988, 571) points out that GOP growth in the South was once delayed by a combination of southern Democratic incorporation of black political strength and the "one-two punch of Watergate and the Carter candidacy." There is no more Carter factor—Clinton lost substantially in South Carolina in both 1992 and 1996—and Watergate is a remnant of the past. South Carolina Democrats' attempts to incorporate black voting strength have largely backfired; while blacks are still usually a loyal bloc in statewide elections, such as the marginal reelection of Senator Ernest Hollings in 1992, groups like SRAC have made it policy to press judicially (if not legislatively) for as many black-majority districts as possible. When race has become a prominent factor in South Carolina elections, the marginalized, traditionally Democratic white electorate has increasingly sided with the Republicans—a trend that appears to be gaining in strength and significance.

Republican growth in current-day South Carolina appears to be threatened only by the loss of control of the party that the socially moderate Atwater faction suffered in 1994. Even then, the debate should be framed not in terms of *whether* the party will continue to grow but rather in terms of *what type* of growth it will be, backed by *which* groups in the intricate mosaic of South Carolina Republicanism. This Pandora's box was opened almost by necessity in 1994 to ensure continued GOP control of the governor's mansion; Beasley played the public opinion surveys well in expanding the party's reach to alienated evangelicals and secular rightwingers alike to bring them enthusiastically to the polls. Once elected, however, he found himself caught in a crossfire between business elites on one side and these newly invigorated populist Republicans on the other. On the flag issue in particular, he angered the part of that new Republican base that can appreciate revelations from God only up to the point where those revelations begin interfering with their rebel legacy.

Using terms like "liar" against the governor in connection with the flag incident, letters pouring into the state GOP offices after Beasley announced his plan were also devoid of money during the party's 1997 fund-raising efforts; by one estimate, the party came up at least $300,000 shorter in its postflag drive than the previous year (Burritt 1997). Members of the wealthy Republican old guard along the Atlantic coast seem hesitant to help make up for the shortfall, given their continuing questions about the new focus of their state organization. McMaster, reelected in 1996 as state Republican Party chair, announces on the party's World Wide Web page that the South Carolina Republican Party "is big enough for all," and by most accounts he has done a reasonable job of trying to hold diverging factional interests at bay. Still a product of the 1994 surge by the Christian Coalition, however, he appears to have no reservations about pushing that group's social agenda. For example, in May 1996, he received a report before the state convention from a panel he had appointed to rewrite the party's five-year-old platform and declared that the South Carolina GOP was "pro-life" on the abortion issue, and "that's the way it's going to stay." The emphasis in rewriting the state platform was to downplay specific legislative goals and stress general political principles; most of the biggest changes in the document came in the area of social and moral principles. These actions led one old-guard party activist, who was also a member of the Republican National Committee, to remark that "traditional Republicans have just ceased to get involved. They sit on the sidelines and complain, but they don't get involved. So we're probably getting what we deserve" (Karr 1996).

While pragmatic statesman Thurmond attempts quietly to live out his final declared term as U.S. senator and the coastal old guard such as Ravenel struggle to find their place in this new party coalition, others have reveled in the sensationalism that drives the new breed of white Republican into action. State attorney general Charles Condon, who appears to enjoy playing Boris Yeltsin to Beasley's conciliatory but fumbling Mikhail Gorbachev, has already positioned himself to capture the populist segment of the GOP vote by vehemently espousing pro-flag views such as "if we give them this one, what will they want next?"—a racially loaded message to white Republicans that is marginally reminiscent of the Watson years. Condon's first headline-grabbing action of 1997 was to write Governor George Pataki of New York objecting to the removal of the Georgia state flag from the Albany state house after Pataki and Georgia governor Zell Miller had discussed the political intricacies of such a maneuver. The question of why South Carolina's attorney general had any reason to become a party to this negotiation was lost on his growing number of white supporters in the Palmetto State, where the Georgia flag is generally as likely a candidate for display as the state's own blue palmetto-and-crescent design at outdoor expositions, barbecues, fairs, and other festivals for the masses.

Republican strategy in voter recruitment, coalition building, and legislative redistricting throughout the late 1980s and early 1990s was both impressive and effective in South Carolina. The party learned from the likes of Thurmond very shortly after passage of the VRA, when Democrats quickly embraced black concerns as a means for their own survival (Lamis 1990), that neutralizing the African American concern over white Republicans was a good way of winning elections. Simultaneously, by helping some black interests "screw the white-boy Democrats" in court over the perpetual redistricting fracas, Republicans were able to obtain a number of changes in the legislative boundaries that favored their candidates during a period when Democrats controlled the general assembly. By the mid-1990s, as the Republican steamroller gained power, however, the idea of driving it became more attractive to coalitional hangers-on. The Beasley campaign's active solicitation of their participation in his gubernatorial bid, combined with the anti-incumbent frustration that marked the 1994 elections, became all but a written invitation to storm the state party convention, install new leaders who were sympathetic to the agitated right, and begin effecting changes to the Campbell coalition that will mark the organization through the opening years of the next century.

Ravenel may have been correct when he said in his unsuccessful runoff bid for governor in 1994 that the election marked a battle "for the soul" of the South Carolina Republican Party (Barone and Ujifusa 1995). Two points, however, need to be clarified. First, although the election clearly represented a battle, it was not the war; coming years will tell how successful the pro-business, "old money" faction will be in reassuming control of the party they largely constructed in the 1980s. The second point to be made is that in a battle for souls, there are winners and losers—and to the victors belong the spoils. As long as conservative born-again Christians and conservative secular voters are so concerned about political affairs that they are able to maintain their control over party organs, the democratic mechanism has worked. There are ramifications to the emphasis on social conservatism that the party has taken with its new statewide platform, not the least of which is the increasing dilemma of racial polarization along lines of party identification. But since a twist of fate, the Thurmond-Watson defections, propelled the South Carolina GOP light-years ahead of its southern neighbors back in the 1960s, it may be only fitting that the Palmetto State is now the first in the region to experience the newest phenomenon of large-scale Republican success, bitter factional disputes for party control of the winning machine, the likes of which have not been seen since Bourbon Democrats dominated the landscape. We know the results of that era of southern politics already, which is why South Carolina is positioned to be such an interesting experiment in the ability of history to repeat itself. The lab rats are already scuttling for position in the elections of 1998 and beyond.

Notes

1. The author would like to thank Representative Clyburn for agreeing to this interview, and his staff, as well as Professor Gardel Feurtado of the Citadel, for arranging it, during an otherwise hectic series of events for Black History Month on the campus of the Citadel.

2. Duncan (1991, 1341) describes this as a "weak civil rights measure," led by segregationist senator Richard B. Russell of Georgia "largely to boost the national standing of their Southern colleague and presidential aspirant, Majority Leader Lyndon B. Johnson of Texas. Thurmond alone insisted on protesting."

3. This is not to argue that Thurmond and others of his ilk have been totally uninterested in the black vote; to the contrary, the pattern in South Carolina is that they have sought—and received—it in greater percentages than in many other southern states. The black Republican vote in South Carolina is still usually minuscule compared to black Democratic strength, however. The "tightrope act" for the GOP therefore consists of maintaining fundamentally conservative policy positions but carefully presenting them in a manner that is devoid of racial overtones.

4. Beasley ultimately worked his way up to Democratic majority leader in the state house of representatives before his resignation and conversion to the GOP.

5. The column was reprinted in a number of major newspapers that day, including the *Denver Post, St. Louis Post-Dispatch,* and *Charlotte News and Observer.*

6. Summary of the solicitor general's amicus brief, found in decision of *Smith v. Beasley,* 946 F.Supp. 1174 (1996).

7. The comment was in a story by the Associated Press Political Service, 19 June 1996; it was subsequently run in newspapers across the state and wound up in an editorial that appeared in the *Rock Hill (S.C.) Herald,* 1 September 1996.

References

American Political Network. 1994. "Governors '94—South Carolina: Latest Poll Shows Statistical Dead Heat." *Hotline* 8, no. 34, 2 November.

Barone, Michael, and Grant Ujifusa. 1995. *The Almanac of American Politics 1996.* Washington: National Journal.

_____. 1993. *The Almanac of American Politics, 1994.* Washington: National Journal.

Bass, Jack, and Walter DeVries. 1976. *The Transformation of Southern Politics: Social Change and Political Consequence since 1945.* New York: Basic Books.

Black, Earl, and Merle Black. 1987. *Politics and Society in the South.* Cambridge: Harvard University Press.

Bullock, Charles S., III. 1988. "Regional Realignment from an Officeholding Perspective." *Journal of Politics* 50: 553–74.

Burritt, Chris. 1997. "Focus on a Disputed Banner." *Atlanta Journal-Constitution,* 24 January. Retrieved via Westlaw Information Service, doc. 1997 WL 3951226.

Clyburn, James. 1997. Interview with author at the Citadel, Charleston, S.C. 18 February.

Duncan, Phil, ed. 1991. *Politics in America.* Washington: Congressional Quarterly Press.

Graham, Cole Blease, Jr., and William V. Moore. 1994. *South Carolina Politics and Government.* Lincoln: University of Nebraska Press.

Guth, James E. 1995. "South Carolina: The Christian Right Wins One." Pp. 133–46 in *God at the Grass Roots: The Christian Right in the 1994 Elections,* edited by Mark J. Rozell and Clyde Wilcox. Lanham, Md.: Rowman & Littlefield.

Harrison, Eric. 1996. "South Carolina Governor Wants to Lower Rebel Flag." *Los Angeles Times,* 27 November.

Karr, Gary. 1996. "Run to the Pragmatic Right to Win South Carolina." Associated Press Political Service (newswire), 22 February.

Key, V. O., Jr. 1949. *Southern Politics in State and Nation.* New York: Knopf.

Kuzenski, John C., and Michael K. Corbello. 1995. "Racial and Economic Explanations for Republican Growth in the South: A Case Study of Attitudinal Voting in Louisiana." *American Review of Politics* 17: 129–43.

Lamis, Alexander P. 1990. *The Two-Party South.* 2d ed. New York: Oxford University Press.

Reed, David. 1988. "State Democratic Party: In Search of Its Soul." Associated Press Political Service (newswire), 26 March.

Sampson, Gregory B. 1984. *The Rise of the "New" Republican Party in South Carolina, 1948–1974: A Case Study of Political Change in a Deep South State.* Ph.D. diss., Department of Sociology, University of North Carolina at Chapel Hill. Ann Arbor, Mich.: University Microfilms International, no. AAC 8508619.

Sinclair, Dean T. 1984. "The Growth and Development of the Republican Party in South Carolina from 1970 to 1980: A Study in Electoral Geography." M.A. thesis, Department of Geography, University of South Carolina.

Topping, John C., John R. Lazarek, and William H. Linder. 1966. *Southern Republicanism and the New South.* Report issued to the National Republican Party and New Haven Ripon Society. Cambridge, Mass.

Yoder, Edwin. 1996. *Washington Post,* 18 June.

3

Georgia: Election Rules and Partisan Conflict

Charles S. Bullock III

Election laws matter. Key passages in the last half century of Georgia's political history have been shaped by the state's unique electoral laws. At times the laws have maintained the status quo, but at other times Republicans trying to displace the century of Democratic dominance have benefited from application of the rules.

In 1947 the state became the laughingstock of the nation with its much-publicized three-governors controversy, produced when governor-elect Eugene Talmadge died before inauguration. The outgoing governor, the lieutenant governor, and the son of the deceased governor-elect all claimed the state's highest office, and only a split decision by the state supreme court settled the matter in favor of the lieutenant governor. Twenty years later, the GOP suffered a defeat that set it back a generation when Georgia's unique majority-vote requirement allowed the legislature to prevent the electorate's plurality choice, a Republican son of a textile mill owner, from ascending to the governorship. The floodgate holding back Republican ambition was breached in 1992 when the minority party turned the tables and exploited the majority-vote requirement to win a Senate seat in a rare general election runoff.

Background

V. O. Key (1949) characterized Georgia politics as "Rule of the Rustics." While farmers and small-town residents had disproportionate influence in every state prior to the one-person, one-vote revolution of the 1960s, rural counties had greater influence in Georgia politics than elsewhere. Not only did rural voters have more than their fair share of the legislative seats, but also their influence in elections was magnified at city dwellers' expense.

The Georgia apportionment system allocated at least one seat in the state house of representatives to each county, and since the state's 159 counties are outnumbered only by Texas, the lower chamber had a large membership. As a slight genuflection to population differences, the eight most populous counties received two additional seats, while the next thirty largest counties got a second seat, for a total of 205 representatives. In the key Democratic primaries for statewide offices and often for congressional contests, victory hinged on winning county unit votes rather than popular votes. The analogy here is the presidential electoral college. Each county's unit vote total equaled twice its number of seats in the state house, so that Fulton County, which includes most of Atlanta, had six votes. Three tiny counties with only a few hundred voters each could easily offset the Atlanta vote, and in the days of boss-controlled counties, manipulating the rural vote was far easier than campaigning successfully in large urban counties. A state official from that era observed, "Give me five good men in 100 rural counties and I could run the state under the county unit system" (Campbell 1983). The urban-rural tradeoffs led the foremost practitioner of rustic politics, three-time governor Eugene Talmadge, to assert that he never wanted to carry a county with a streetcar line.

The county unit system was ruled unconstitutional just before the 1962 election, and while its demise did not affect the outcome, its passing coincided with the victory of the first modern business-oriented governor. Carl Sanders defeated Herman Talmadge's former lieutenant governor and in so doing dismantled the Talmadge machine that had promoted three decades of bifactionalism.

Close behind the demise of the county unit system came nationally applicable court decisions mandating equipopulous legislative districts. These orders had a more immediate racial impact in Georgia than elsewhere in the South. Atlanta's black population ensured some African American seats in the legislature once districts had equal populations. In 1962, Leroy Johnson won a senate seat, thereby becoming the first member of his race to serve in a southern state legislature in modern times. When the house was redrawn to eliminate counties as the basis for representation, African Americans entered that chamber, as shown in table 3.1.

Redistricting also opened the door for more Republicans. Two north Georgia counties, like the mountain areas of Tennessee and North Carolina, had sent Republicans to the legislature, but the minority party could have caucused in a phone booth. Once urban counties got more than the three-seat maximum awarded by the county unit system and apportioned these seats into single-member districts, upscale neighborhoods began electing Republicans. A GOP growth spurt came in 1964 as

Table 3.1
Partisan and Racial Makeup of the Georgia General Assembly and Congressional
Delegation, 1963–1997 (in percent)

	Georgia House		Georgia Senate		U.S. House	
	Rep.	Black	Rep.	Black	Rep.	Black
1963	1.0	0	5.6	1.9	0	0
1965	11.2	3.4	16.7	3.7	10.0	0
1967	10.2	4.4	14.8	3.7	20.0	0
1969	13.8	5.9	12.5	3.7	20.0	0
1971	11.3	6.3	10.7	3.7	20.0	0
1973	16.1	7.8	14.3	3.6	10.0	10.0
1975	13.3	10.6	8.9	3.6	0	10.0
1977	13.3	11.7	7.1	3.6	0	0
1979	11.7	11.7	8.9	3.6	10.0	0
1981	13.3	11.7	8.9	3.6	10.0	0
1983	13.3	11.7	12.5	7.1	10.0	0
1985	13.3	11.7	16.1	10.7	20.0	0
1987	15.6	13.3	17.9	10.7	20.0	10.0
1989	20.0	13.9	19.6	12.5	10.0	10.0
1991	19.4	15.0	19.6	14.3	10.0	10.0
1993	28.9	17.2	26.9	16.1	36.4	27.3
1995	36.7	17.8	37.5	17.9	72.7	27.3
1997	41.1	18.3	39.3	19.6	72.7	27.3

Barry Goldwater, the first Republican to carry the state's electoral votes,
also contributed to the election of the first GOP member of Congress from
Georgia in this century.

The GOP seed, watered by Goldwater, seemed destined to produce a
bountiful harvest in 1966, when Democrats nominated for governor
Lester Maddox, a restaurateur known for his racist rantings in the *Atlanta
Journal-Constitution* and for chasing off prospective black customers with
an axe handle. Republicans countered with Bo Callaway, scion of a textile fortune, who epitomized country-club Republicanism. Maddox's
underfunded campaign was largely ignored by the Democratic hierarchy
at the state capital, but his attacks on blacks and communists and the tradition of voting Democratic stirred the same rural passions that had
elected the Talmadges a generation earlier (Bartley 1970, 69–72). Some
urban, better-educated whites who deplored Maddox but could not
bring themselves to support the conservative Republican mounted a

speaking abilities. Nor did the incumbent replenish his campaign trea-
sury, depleted by the runoff. By the time that Congress adjourned and Talmadge returned to Georgia, momentum was running against him. On the
morning after the election, Talmadge was swept from office as Atlanta
suburbs delivered majorities of better than two to one to the GOP upstart.
Even majority-black Fulton County gave the Democrat no help, casting 57
percent of its votes for Republican Mack Mattingly. The dynasty founded
by the man who never wanted to carry a county with a streetcar ended in
the urban counties he had ignored, with the coup de grace administered
by African Americans in repayment for father Gene Talmadge's race bait-
ing. Herman Talmadge's 27,000-vote defeat came in spite of President
Carter's 236,000-vote majority. Despite little prior practice, many Georgians had learned to split their ballots.

The Mattingly victory provided one of the few bright spots for the
GOP. In the state legislature, even landslide victories by Reagan in 1984
and Bush in 1988 provided little coattail pull, and the GOP did not exceed
its pre-Watergate highs until the late 1980s. Sandwiched between Reagan's 362,000-vote majority and Bush's slightly larger margin was Mattingly's 1986 defeat by 22,000 votes. Underscoring the GOP's inability to
make down-ticket headway, Aistrup (1989) showed Georgia to have the
weakest Republican Party in the region. During the 1980s, Republicans
never managed more than 20 percent of the congressional delegation, a
poorer performance than in any other southern state.

Awakening from Dormancy

Rip Van Winkle slept in the Hudson Valley for 20 years, a brief nap compared to the 120 years that elapsed between the time Republican Rufus
Bullock (Duncan 1995) was driven from Georgia's governor's mansion in
1871 and when the GOP again won a statewide office. The breakthrough
came via the same majority-vote requirement that had saved the Democrats in 1966. The presence of Libertarian candidates who captured slivers
of the vote denied majorities to a renegade Democrat running for the public service commission (PSC) and Senator Wyche Fowler, who had
unseated Mattingly. For these offices, failure to poll a majority triggered a
runoff between the top two candidates.

Having lost the state to President Bill Clinton by 13,714 votes, Republicans sought revenge in the runoffs. With no other federal elections to be
decided, an all-star team of national Republicans campaigned for Paul
Coverdell and deluged the state with money. Coverdell, who had come

write-in campaign for former governor Ellis Arnall (1943–47), who had lost the runoff to Maddox.

Unlike in Arkansas and Florida where Republican gubernatorial candidates capitalized on the racial conservativism of their 1966 Democratic opponents, Callaway refused to reach out to African American leaders, explaining that to do that "would be to play politics." The response of the frustrated advisor who had counseled that strategy was, "What the hell do you think you're playing, Bo?" An attack on the outgoing governor, several of whose lieutenants were working covertly for Callaway, dampened their enthusiasm. When the ballots were counted, Callaway had a 3,039-vote lead, but because of the Arnall write-ins, no majority. In the absence of a majority, the choice passed to the general assembly, where the Democratic majority stood by its party.

Despite losing the governorship and the congressional seat that Callaway had held, Republicans won two Atlanta-area congressional seats. GOP prospects were sufficiently promising that in the autumn of 1968 five statewide officials switched parties to support Richard Nixon. This high-profile support proved insufficient as Georgians, still outraged at federal demands that schools be desegregated and barriers to voting eliminated, gave George Wallace a 12-percentage-point plurality.

Richard Nixon's resignation to avoid impeachment sapped GOP vitality, conferring a more pronounced benefit on Democrats in Georgia than elsewhere. Led by her native son, Georgia seemed to be firmly back in the bosom of the Democratic Party as Jimmy Carter rolled up two-thirds of the vote, matching Adlai Stevenson's performances two decades earlier. Democrats had regained all of the state's congressional seats in 1974, and the GOP share of state senate seats in 1977 had fallen by more than half since its high point following the Goldwater election.

As often happens in the South, Georgia Republicans won their first significant subpresidential election in the midst of Democratic disarray. In 1980, Herman Talmadge's ambition for a fifth Senate term foundered in the wake of a highly publicized divorce, bouts of alcoholism, and reprimand by his colleagues for financial misconduct. Like a bleeding swimmer attracting sharks, Talmadge drew three serious primary challengers but took almost 60 percent of the vote in a bitter runoff against Lieutenant Governor Zell Miller. Talmadge returned to Washington believing the general election to be a mere formality now that he had secured the Democratic nomination.

The GOP nominee, an underfunded, little-known typewriter salesman, capitalized on the incumbent's absence. In a series of misjudgments, Talmadge refused to debate his opponent despite the challenger's weak

up 35,000 votes short in the general election, reversed fortunes and retired Fowler, while Republicans captured the PSC seat by an even larger margin (Fenno 1996; Bullock and Furr 1994).

The 1992 election also saw Republicans add three House seats to the one held by Newt Gingrich since 1979, giving the GOP its largest share of the delegation in more than a century. The minority party also took more than a quarter of the state legislative seats.

Redistricting, or How the Democrats Got Mugged by Justice

Republican gains in Congress and the general assembly could not have been achieved without the assistance of the U.S. Department of Justice (DOJ). Georgia, like all southern states except Arkansas, Oklahoma, and Tennessee, must submit districting plans for approval to DOJ or the federal district court sitting in the District of Columbia. This requirement, mandated by section 5 of the Voting Rights Act (VRA), had been designed in 1965 to ensure that obdurate southern governments did not erect new barriers to black political participation as old ones were knocked down. By 1992, the VRA had been amended to bar statutes or practices that had the effect of diluting minority political influence even if that was not their intent. DOJ used this new provision to demand that jurisdictions maximize the number of minority districts.

A long struggle ensued between DOJ and the Georgia General Assembly. DOJ rejected a districting plan adopted in a special session that created a second majority black district. The state's next effort created a third district that almost achieved a black majority. Again DOJ refused to preclear and demanded that a district be distorted so as to link Savannah's black population with African Americans living in Augusta and suburban Atlanta. Adherence to DOJ dictates made possible a third district, with a 57 percent black population, in southwest Georgia.

In putting the finishing touches on the two additional majority black districts, computer technicians went through block by block, placing those with an African American majority in a black district while assigning blocks with white majorities to neighboring white districts. Bleaching districts had both a direct and an indirect benefit for Republicans. The direct impact came from eliminating black voters who were loyal Democrats. Bleached districts became more receptive to GOP candidates, since the bulk of the state's white population now voted Republican in major contests. The indirect effect was that by creating districts more favorable to Republicans, stronger candidates came forward to carry the GOP banner. In 1992, GOP state legislators gave up secure seats to seek nominations in the First and Third Districts, and both triumphed. The First became whiter when 50,000 African Americans in Savannah were excised and put in the Eleventh. The Third lost the black population of Columbus. The other district picked up by Republicans, the Fourth, just east of Atlanta, revealed traces of the direct impact. John Linder, who had lost by 9,000 votes in 1990, eked out a 2,676-vote victory over a liberal, woman state senator. Had DeKalb County not been split along racial lines in order to make the Eleventh District 64 percent black, it would have been easy to increase the black percentage in the Fourth enough to elect a Democrat there while keeping black ambitions alive in the Eleventh.

The effects of racial gerrymandering continued into 1994 in Districts Eight and Ten as Republicans won another three seats, giving them a majority in the state's delegation. The Tenth District had been made more Republican by placing the black population of Augusta and several rural, heavily black counties in the Eleventh. The Eighth had been made whiter by putting Macon African Americans in the Second. The other GOP pickup, the Seventh, shifted parties as a result of growing suburbanization with new, affluent voters not sufficiently attached to the senior Democratic incumbent. The shift toward the GOP continued in April 1995 when Nathan Deal of the Ninth District became the first of five southern House Democrats to change parties during the course of the 104th Congress.

Shutting the Barn Door after the House Is Out

Members of the Georgia House had difficulty swallowing DOJ demands for a third majority-black district. So many members wanted to fight DOJ in court that the final redistricting plan, which received Justice approval, passed only on the strength of the speaker's vote. In North Carolina, a group led by a Duke law professor took the course urged by Georgia dissidents and challenged that state's "Interstate 85" district, which snaked 160 miles along the highway from Durham to Gastonia. In 1993, the Supreme Court held that the challenge constituted a justiciable issue and ordered a hearing on the case. Before the North Carolina challenge could be resolved, a similar suit filed in Georgia became the first racial gerrymander case to be decided on its merits by the Supreme Court. In *Miller v. Johnson* (115 S. Ct. 2475 [1995]), the Supreme Court struck down Georgia's Eleventh District, which stretched 250 miles from suburban Atlanta to Savannah, with a finger curling into Augusta to pick up that city's black citizens. The court concluded that the district violated the Equal Protection

Clause since it had been drawn predominantly on the basis of race. A three-judge federal panel subsequently invalidated the Second District on the same grounds.

When the general assembly failed to devise a remedial plan, it fell to the trial court to correct the wrong identified by the Supreme Court. The new plan adhered to county boundaries except in the Atlanta metropolitan area and did away with land bridges and fingers that reached into urban areas to connect dispersed pockets of African Americans. The plan eliminated black majorities in the Second and Eleventh Districts, while the First, Eighth, and Tenth Districts picked up enough African Americans to become more than 30 percent black.

The 1996 congressional elections were notable for their lack of change. Despite dire warnings that black candidates could not win in districts in which their race constituted less than a majority, Sanford Bishop won the Second District with 54 percent of the vote, while Cynthia McKinney, running in the Fourth, which was more than 40 percent black in registration by election day, took 58 percent against an aggressive challenger. Both black incumbents easily disposed of primary challengers.

Democrats who hoped to take advantage of higher black percentages in the Eighth and Tenth Districts were disappointed as the incumbents secured narrow margins. In these districts with GOP incumbents, as well as in the two with black Democratic incumbents, the voting patterns were quite similar. As shown in table 3.2, Democrats won almost all African American votes while approximately two-thirds of the white vote went to Republicans. The implication of these results, coupled with other data from 1996, such as Harvey Gantt's polling 36 percent of the white vote in

Table 3.2
Support for Democratic Congressional Candidates by Race,
1996 (in percent)

	Voters		
	Whites	Blacks	Candidate
District 2			
Bishop	36	99	Black
District 4			
McKinney	29	97	Black
District 8			
Wiggins	34	94	White
District 10			
Bell	30	98	White

his North Carolina Senate bid (also see table 3.4), was that when white voters cast ballots against African Americans today, it is not because of the candidate's race but is a response to the candidate's party. Neither white nor black Democrats run well with white voters.

If the share of the white vote going for Democrats does not increase, Republicans will be secure in districts until the black electorate exceeds one-third of the total. White partisan loyalties in districts with racial compositions that Democrats could have probably held in the early 1990s may have eroded too much for Democrats to regain them now, despite infusions of black voters.

Partisan Balance

Georgia's partisan strength divided evenly between Democrats and Republicans in the 1990s. In surveys, voters divided into three groups of roughly equal size, with a large pool of independents able to decide election outcomes. Exit polls conducted at the 1996 general election showed 38 percent of the state's voters to be Democrats, 34 percent Republicans, and 28 percent independents. (Georgia does not maintain party registration.)

The GOP is also making strides in attracting voters to its primaries. The GOP held its first statewide primary in 1970, and until the 1990s, few voters participated in the choice of Republican nominees. As recently as 1990, participants in the Democratic primary outnumbered Republicans nine to one. In 1994 and 1996, Democrats still drew more voters in the summer primary than did Republicans, but the ratio had narrowed to three to two. In 1992 and 1996, Georgia's presidential-preference primary came in early March, a week before Super Tuesday. In this balloting, which included only a smattering of special elections and referenda, the two parties attracted equal numbers in 1992, and in 1996, when President Clinton had no opposition, more than 550,000 voters asked for Republican ballots.

Statewide election results also show partisan competitiveness. During the 1990s, the most frequent result has been a near dead heat. In 1992, the networks called Georgia for Bill Clinton soon after the polls closed but later in the evening shifted the state into the undecided category. The early edition of the *Atlanta Constitution* announced that Bush had carried Georgia. When the last ballot was finally tallied, Clinton had won the state by fewer than 14,000 votes. Four years later, Georgia was among the few states that shifted parties as Bob Dole got a 27,000-vote plurality.

Narrow victories also characterized other 1996 results. Democrat Max

Cleland reversed the president's fortunes to take a 30,000-vote plurality in the race to fill Democrat Sam Nunn's Senate seat. Results in the Cleland contest closely paralleled those in the 1992 Coverdell-Fowler election, but the Democratic legislature had changed the rules so that runoffs were needed only if the general election leader failed to secure 45 percent of the vote. Republicans believe that they could have won a runoff had the old rules still been in effect (Perdue 1997). In two PSC races, incumbents—one Democratic and one Republican—won new terms although neither managed to reach 51 percent. The most impressive win came in the contest for secretary of state, where Lewis Massey, the thirty-four-year-old golden boy of the Democratic Party, took almost 54 percent of the vote in defeating thirty-one-year-old David Shafer, former state executive director of the GOP.

Narrow victories were also the rule in 1994, as reported in table 3.3, when the state's constitutional offices were on the ballot. Three Republicans supplanted Democratic incumbents for down-ticket offices with each victor taking 51 percent of the vote or less. Democrat Zell Miller won reelection with 51 percent of the vote, saved by the popular HOPE scholarships. This innovation funded by revenues from the lottery—whose creation had been the major plank in Miller's 1990 campaign—pays for tuition and books at state-supported colleges and technical schools for all Georgia high school graduates with B averages who maintain those grades in college. This program enabled Miller to cut into GOP majorities in suburbia.

Another two Democratic incumbents secured new terms with about 54 percent of the vote each, and in the one office without an incumbent, the Republican won a PSC seat with 54 percent. In only two of nine 1994 con-

Table 3.3
Winner's Share of Vote in Recent Georgia Statewide Elections

	< 50%	50–51%	51–55%	>55%
1986	0	1	0	3
1988	0	0	2	2
1990	0	0	2	3
1992	3	1	0	0
Runoff	0	1	0	1
1994	0	3	4	2
1996	2	2	1	0

Source: Compiled by author from official state election returns.

tests that featured Democratic-Republican opposition did winners accumulate more than 55 percent of the vote.

As another indicator that Republicans have attained parity with Democrats, for the first time two more Republicans than Democrats filed for the state legislature in 1996. Since, as table 3.1 shows, Democrats retain a three-to-two edge in legislative seats, greater GOP candidate activity is not the result of becoming the majority party. GOP recruiters stir up interest in running for the general assembly by predicting that theirs is the party of the future and that it is only a matter of time before they win control of the institution.

Republicans do best in the growth areas of the state. In the 1996 general election, seventy-five thousand more votes were cast for Republican than Democratic state senate candidates even though the Democrats emerged with a thirty-four to twenty-two edge in the chamber (Baxter 1996). By rolling up massive vote totals in suburbia, Republicans overcame their losses to Democrats in nineteen districts and in another fifteen districts in which the Democrat went unchallenged. These figures suggest that Republicans will fare well after the turn of the century, when additional legislative seats are awarded to suburban counties.

Bases of Partisan Support

If Democrats can retain the overwhelming support of African Americans and get more than 40 percent of the white vote, they can fashion narrow majorities. Republicans can win if they get into the midteens in terms of a share of the black vote or pick up two-thirds of the white vote or if African American participation drops. The recent past provides illustrations of the impact of these variables. The analysis by Democratic campaign consultants Alan Secrest and Mike Sanelli (1995) of Zell Miller's reelection showed that 41 percent of the white vote provided a sufficient bulwark for Democrats. They warned, however, that the Democratic share of white support was slipping. Moreover, they noted that the share of votes coming from African Americans declined from 20 percent in 1990 to 18 percent four years later.

Table 3.4 shows the shares of black and white votes going to Democratic candidates in selected contests over the last decade. Presidential candidates have had the hardest time attracting white support, and in the last three elections the Democrat has failed to exceed a third of the white vote. In a two-person contest this is insufficient to win, but in 1992, when Ross Perot took 13 percent of the state's ballots, Clinton got just enough white

Table 3.4
Support for Democratic Statewide Candidates in Selected Elections by Race,
1986–1996

	White Support (%)	Black Support (%)	Party Margin
1986			
U.S. Senator	42	98	22,470 D
1988			
President	28	97	336,539 R
Public service commissioner	52	97	188,894 D
1990			
Governor	48	98	121,037 D
Insurance commissioner	46	96	36,250 D
1992			
President	32	98	13,714 D
U.S. Senator (general)	41	99	35,134 D
U.S. Senator (general runoff)	39	98	16,237 R
1994			
Governor	42	97	32,555 D
School superintendent	42	96	19,450 R
1996			
President	29	92	26,994 R
U.S. Senator	37	83	30,024 D

Sources: 1996 data from exit polls; other years calculated by author using precinct returns.

votes to squeeze out a plurality. White votes for Democrats below the presidential level have drifted downward. The 1986 Democratic Senate candidate ran relatively poorly for that time among whites, but that may have been because he was challenging an incumbent. In 1988 and 1990, state-level Democrats got about half the white vote and won by what would now be considered comfortable margins. In the next two elections, Democrats who faced stiff competition struggled to get to 40 percent of the white vote and could win only with strong black turnout. While the Democratic nominee, Max Cleland, won the 1996 Senate election, he did so with the least white support given any nonpresidential Democrat. Once white support falls below 40 percent, Democrats are unlikely to win unless there is a third-party candidate like the one who pulled 4 percent of the vote in 1996, thereby enabling Cleland to slip by.

African American support for Democrats was lopsided and constant from 1986 through 1994. The two contests surveyed by exit polls in 1996 show lower levels of black support than at any time in the past, and Cleland failed to get 90 percent of the black vote. If Republicans' share of the black vote reaches the midteens and if they can dissuade Libertarians from running for office, Democrats will be hard-pressed to win statewide.

Race is not the only divide in the Georgia electorate. Republicans dominate top-of-the ticket contests in north Georgia. In 1992, Clinton carried only half a dozen counties north of Atlanta, and two years later Governor Zell Miller won only eight counties in that area, including his home county and one of its neighbors. Miller's inability to win his own corner of the state is in stark contrast to the friends-and-neighbors pattern Key (1949) identified. Republicans have also shown strength in the southeastern corner of the state, winning many of the counties between Savannah and Jacksonville, Florida. Five counties in this area were among seventeen that voted consistently for Republicans in competitive statewide contests in 1994 (Bullock 1995). Democrats do best in the diagonal swath of the Black Belt cutting across the middle of the state. This agrarian area has provided strong support for the dominant faction in the Democratic Party as far back as the Talmadge machine, which controlled the governorship for all but ten years between 1933 and 1963 (Key 1949; Bartley 1970).

Urbanization is another indication of partisan strength. Democrats consistently roll up impressive margins in the state's eight counties that have portions of central cities of metropolitan areas. Of the four 1996 elections reported in table 3.5, the Democratic urban margin exceeded 190,000 in the ticket-leading secretary of state contest and was approximately 150,000 in the presidential and Senate contests. The 34 counties in urban areas that do not contain portions of a central cities and that are labeled "suburban" in table 3.5 are reliably Republican. The 117 nonurban counties were hotly contested, except in the race for secretary of state. In each election, the party that carried the rural vote won statewide.

The consistency of GOP success in suburban counties shows up on a number of dimensions. Seven counties that voted consistently for competitive Republican statewide candidates in 1994 are in metropolitan Atlanta, another contains Augusta suburbs, and two more are suburbs of Chattanooga (Bullock 1995, 87). Rare is the Republican state legislator who does not come from suburbia, and in 1997 at least one suburban district in each of the state's metro areas had a Republican legislator.

Table 3.5 also reveals a phenomenon that proved costly to Democrats in 1994. Republican voters seem to be more constant in their loyalties than Democrats. In both urban and suburban counties, votes for the Republican candidates for president, senator, and public service commissioner showed little variation (a range of 7,132 votes across the three offices in urban counties and a range of 4,108 in suburban counties). In contrast, the

Table 3.5
Partisan Support by Level of Urbanization, 1996

	Urban	Suburban	Rural
President			
Democrat	429,948	328,024	295,717
Republican	267,507	504,778	308,476
Democratic margin	162,441	-176,754	-12,759
U.S. Senate			
Democrat	426,489	357,670	319,834
Republican	269,110	503,044	301,815
Democratic margin	157,379	-145,374	18,019
Secretary of state			
Democrat	425,013	383,566	334,884
Republican	232,374	454,842	232,507
Democratic margin	192,639	-71,276	102,377
Public service commission			
(Ryles v. Durden)			
Democrat	371,324	319,043	272,359
Republican	261,978	500,670	276,007
Democratic margin	109,346	-181,627	-3,648
Number of counties	8	34	117

range for Democrats in these three offices in urban counties is almost 60,000, and in suburban counties it is 39,000 votes.

Democrats set themselves up for disappointment in 1994 when their general assembly majority eliminated the straight-ticket punch. Voters can no longer vote for all of a party's nominees by making a single mark on the ballot. To accomplish that end, the voter must individually designate the party's nominee for each office.

As in 1996, GOP vote totals showed greater consistency across the 1994 set of statewide offices. The vote for the 1994 Republican gubernatorial nominee (756,371) was approximated by the insurance commissioner nominee (754,123), the school superintendent (731,644), and the two PSC candidates (753,950 and 705,317). The vote on the Democratic side dropped from 788,926 for governor to 725,134 for insurance commissioner and 709,568 for school superintendent. An unsuccessful Democratic incumbent for PSC ran almost 100,000 votes behind Governor Miller, while in the race for the open seat on the PSC the Democratic nominee trailed Miller by 200,000 votes. The irony is that the consequences of eliminating the straight-ticket punch were known to Democrats before they enacted the legislation. Democrats got 70 percent of the straight-ticket votes, an option exercised by an estimated quarter of the electorate (Bullock 1995).

The source of the drop in Democratic votes may be disproportionately African Americans. A recent study of roll-off in Atlanta and Fulton County found ballot noncompletion to be more common among black than white voters (Bullock and Dunn 1996). This conformed to patterns observed forty years ago in Florida (Price 1957). The critical nature of heavier black roll-off can be demonstrated by looking at a pair of 1994 elections. Democrat Zell Miller won reelection as governor with 42 percent of the white vote and 97 percent of the black vote. Werner Rogers failed in his reelection bid for state school superintendent, although he also polled 42 percent of the white vote along with 96 percent of the black vote. Rogers, as noted above, ran almost 80,000 votes behind Miller. Rogers lost because only 31percent of the registered African Americans cast ballots in the school superintendent's race compared with almost 38 percent who voted in the gubernatorial contest.

Conclusion

GOP success spread slowly in Georgia. Sixteen years elapsed between the initial Republican presidential success and the first statewide victory. Another twelve years passed before Republicans won a state rather than a federal statewide office. By the mid-1990s, the GOP finally dominated Georgia's congressional delegation and held most statewide offices. As of 1997, Republicans held 40 percent of the state legislative seats and seemed likely to take majorities no later than 2002, when redistricting will reassign more seats to Republican-rich suburban areas. Should a Republican win the governorship in 1998, some observers expect enough conservative white Democrats to change parties, lured by the benefits distributed from the governor's emergency fund, that Republicans might cobble together a legislative majority before the turn of the century.

Today it is only at the county level that officeholders remain overwhelmingly Democratic (Bullock 1993). While Republicans win additional local offices with each election, Georgia's multitude of counties, most of which remain untouched by urban development, provide refuge for the declining numbers of "yellow-dog Democrats." Electors who eagerly vote for Republicans for president on down through member of Congress retain traditional partisan loyalties when choosing sheriffs and county commissioners. In 1995, Democrats held all the commission seats in 109 of Georgia's 159 counties, and in 98 counties no Republican held local office. In part, partisan patterns at the local level reflect the absence of choice. The tradition of Democratic dominance in many communities is so strong that, like a taboo, it goes unchallenged. The ambitious do not seriously consider running as Republicans in many counties. The belief that Republicans cannot win becomes self-fulfilling when Republicans do not run.

Although voters maintain a lingering loyalty to Democrats in rural counties, Democratic claims on white voters have shrunk dramatically. GOP pollster Whit Ayres (1997) reports that about a quarter of Georgia's whites identify with the Democratic Party, with women more likely than men to be loyal to the state's traditional majority party. With the 28 percent of the electorate that professes allegiance to neither party dividing their votes fairly evenly between Democratic and Republican nominees, the white electorate remains very much in play.

As their numbers decline, Democrats have sought to change electoral rules to disadvantage Republicans. The replacement of the majority requirement in general elections with a 45 percent threshold ensured Cleland's Senate victory. Two other efforts were before the 1997 session of the general assembly. One bill changes the election of public service commissioners from statewide to single-member districts. Since the four Republicans on the PSC all come from metropolitan Atlanta, some of them would have to move or leave the board. It might be possible to draw the districts so that Democrats could win an Atlanta district and two south Georgia districts.

The other proposal authorizes vote-by-mail to be tried in all or portions of twenty counties in the 1998 general election. Mail ballots usually heighten turnout, so areas selected for participation in the pilot program would tally more votes than the control areas. If communities that vote Democratic are oversampled in the pilot program, it might be sufficient to secure Democratic victories in hotly contested statewide and legislative contests. Of course, if Republicans determined which areas voted by mail, they could tilt the balance in close contests to their advantage. With Democrats still in control of the electoral mechanism—the secretary of state is a Democrat, as are most county election officials—they may have the inside track if a nonrandom process is used to choose counties to participate in the experiment.

If the 1998 elections are as competitive as table 3.3 shows those earlier in this decade to have been, it would take little to tip the balance toward one party or the other. Democrats, who have suffered a series of reverses, are searching desperately for something that will enable them to reverse the trend. As support of the white electorate evaporates but while it still controls the key power positions in state government, Democrats are turning to the rules regulating elections in an effort to hold on. Sometimes the rules have favored Democrats, as in 1966 and the elimination of the majority requirement in 1996. At other times Republicans have been helped, as in the course of redistricting, in 1992, and with the elimination of the straight-ticket punch. The struggle to use election rules for partisan advantage seems likely to continue.

References

Aistrup, Joseph A. 1989. "Top-Down Republican Party Development in the South: A Test of Schlesinger's Theory." Paper presented at the annual meeting of the Midwest Political Science Association, Chicago.

Ayres, Whit. 1997. Interview by author, 17 February.

Bartley, Numan C. 1970. *From Thurmond to Wallace: Political Tendencies in Georgia, 1948–1968.* Baltimore: Johns Hopkins University Press.

Baxter, Tom. 1996. "Rapid Suburban Growth Undercuts 'One Man, One Vote.'" *Atlanta Journal,* 3 December, C2.

Bullock, Charles S., III. 1993. "Republican Officeholding at the Local Level in Georgia." *Southeastern Political Review* 21 (Winter): 113–31.

———. 1995. *Georgia Political Almanac, 1995–1996.* Atlanta: Cornerstone Publishing.

Bullock, Charles S., III, and Richard Dunn. 1996. "Election Roll-Off: A Test of Three Explanations." *Urban Affairs Review* 32 (September): 71–86.

Bullock, Charles S., III, and Robert P. Furr. 1994. "Race, Turnout, Runoff, and Election Outcomes: The Defeat of Wyche Fowler." Paper presented at the annual meeting of the Southern Political Science Association, Atlanta.

Campbell, J. Phil. 1983. Interview by author, 1 March.

Duncan, Russell. 1995. *Entrepreneur for Equality.* Athens: University of Georgia.

Fenno, Richard F., Jr. 1996. *Senators on the Campaign Trail: The Politics of Representation.* Norman: University of Oklahoma Press.

Key, V. O., Jr. 1949. *Southern Politics in State and Nation.* New York: Knopf.

Perdue, Tom. 1997. Telephone interview by author, 29 January.

Price, H. D. 1957. *The Negro and Southern Politics.* New York: New York University Press.

Secrest, Alan, and Mike Sanelli. 1995. *Precinct-Level Analysis of Racial Voting Patterns in Georgia's 1994 General Election for Governor.* Alexandria, Va.: Cooper & Secrest Associates.

4

Alabama: Republicans Win the Heart of Dixie

Harold W. Stanley

Alabama voters backing a Democratic presidential candidate and electing Republicans to almost every office below the presidential level—such a political prospect, unthinkable only a few years earlier, was more realistic than not during the 1996 elections. Republican voting at the presidential level and Democratic loyalties below the presidency had characterized Alabama politics for thirty years. Alabama Republicans had made inroads but lagged behind GOP successes in the other southern states. Yet when the votes were counted in 1996, Republican candidate Bob Dole beat back incumbent president Bill Clinton for Alabama's electoral votes (see table 4.1). And Republicans swept the important contests below the presidency.

The results of the 1996 elections are all the more striking when placed in the context of Alabama politics since the 1960s. In the South, history lingers. As one Faulkner character reminds us, the past isn't dead, the past isn't even past yet. The following review of nearly four decades of Alabama politics focuses on three principal points. First, the political dominance of George Wallace throughout the 1960s, 1970s, and 1980s retarded the growth of the Republican Party in Alabama. Second, despite Wallace's dominance, Republicans did make inroads over these decades. Third, and again despite Wallace's dominance, Alabama blacks moved from political objects to political participants, from political exclusion to full-fledged political clout.

George Wallace

Although Republicans made inroads nationally by courting the discontented who backed Wallace in 1968 (Phillips 1969), Wallace's political

Table 4.1
Alabama General Election Voting, 1946–1996

	Republican			Democrat		
	Candidate	Vote	Vote (%)	Candidate	Vote	Vote (%)
			President			
1948[a]	Dewey	40,930	19.0	Truman	—	—
1952	Eisenhower	149,231	35.0	Stevenson	275,075	64.6
1956	Eisenhower	195,694	39.4	Stevenson	280,844	56.5
1960	Nixon	237,981	41.7	Kennedy	324,050	56.8
1964[b]	Goldwater	479,085	69.5	Johnson	—	—
1968[c]	Nixon	146,923	14.0	Humphrey	196,579	18.7
1972	Nixon	728,701	72.4	McGovern	256,923	25.5
1976	Ford	504,070	42.6	Carter	659,170	55.7
1980	Reagan	654,192	48.8	Carter	636,730	47.4
1984	Reagan	872,849	60.5	Mondale	551,899	38.3
1988	Bush	815,576	59.2	Dukakis	549,506	39.9
1992[d]	Bush	804,283	47.6	Clinton	690,080	40.9
1996[e]	Dole	769,044	50.1	Clinton	662,165	43.2
			U.S. Senator			
1946	—			Sparkman	163,217	100.0
1948	Parson	35,341	16.0	Sparkman	185,534	84.0
1950	—			Hill	125,534	76.5
1954	Guin	55,110	17.5	Sparkman	259,348	82.5
1956	—			Hill	330,182	100.0
1960	Elgin	164,868	29.8	Sparkman	389,196	70.2
1962	Martin	195,134	49.1	Hill	201,937	50.9
1966	Grenier	313,018	39.0	Sparkman	482,138	60.1
1968	Hooper	201,227	22.0	Allen	638,774	70.0
1972	Blount	347,523	33.1	Sparkman	654,491	62.3
1974	—			Allen	501,541	95.8
1978f	Martin	316,170	43.2	Stewart	401,852	54.9
1978	—			Heflin	547,054	94.0
1980	Denton	650,362	50.2	Folsom	610,175	47.1
1984	Smith	498,508	36.4	Heflin	860,535	62.8
1986	Denton	602,537	49.7	Shelby	609,360	50.3
1990	Cabamiss	467,190	39.4	Heflin	717,814	60.5
1992	Sellers	522,015	33.1	Shelby	1,022,698	64.8
1996	Sessions	786,436	52.5	Bedford	681,651	45.5

Continued on next page

Table 4.1—*Continued*

	Republican			Democrat		
	Candidate	Vote	Vote (%)	Candidate	Vote	Vote (%)
			Governor			
1946	Ward	22,362	11.3	Folsom	174,962	88.7
1950	Crowder	15,217	8.9	Persons	155,414	91.1
1954	Abernethy	88,688	26.6	Folsom	244,401	73.4
1958	Longshore	30,415	11.2	Patterson	239,633	88.4
1962	—	—	—	Wallace	303,987	96.3
1966	Martin	262,943	31.0	Wallace, L.	537,505	63.4
1970[g]	—	—	—	Wallace	637,046	74.5
1974	McCary	88,381	14.8	Wallace	497,574	83.2
1978	Hunt	196,963	25.9	James	551,886	72.6
1982	Folmar	440,815	39.1	Wallace	650,538	57.6
1986	Hunt	696,203	56.3	Baxley	537,163	43.5
1990	Hunt	633,519	52.1	Hubbert	582,106	47.9
1994	James	604,926	50.3	Folsom	594,169	49.4

Sources: Adapted from America Votes and the Alabama Secretary of State home page (http://www.alaline.net/alsecst/1996.htm) as of 6 July 1997.

[a]The Democratic candidate did not appear on the Alabama ballot; States' Rights candidate Strom Thurmond won 171,443 votes, or 79.7% of the total.

[b]The Democratic candidate did not appear on the Alabama ballot; Unpledged Democratic won 210,732 votes, or 30.5% of the total.

[c]George Wallace, running on the American Independent ticket, won 691,425 votes, or 65.9% of the total.

[d]Ross Perot won 183,109 votes (10.8%).

[e]Ross Perot won 92,149 votes (6%).

[f]Special election to fill a vacancy.

[g]The National Democratic Party candidate, John L. Cashin won 125,941 votes (14.7%).

dominance and longevity within Alabama retarded Republican development in the state (Bass and DeVries 1976), causing it to lag behind Republican growth in other southern states.

Wallace's political presence on the state scene lasted from the 1960s through the 1980s. Wallace served as governor from 1963 through 1967, 1971 through 1979, and 1983 through 1987; and his first wife, Lurleen, was governor from 1967 through 1968. Thus, a Wallace was governor of Alabama for seventeen of the twenty-four years after 1962. The only other two individuals to occupy the governor's chair between 1963 and 1986 were Albert Brewer and "Fob" James. Only James was elected to the office in 1978; Brewer succeeded to the office upon Governor Lurleen Wallace's death in May 1968. Wallace, the firebrand segregationist of the 1960s, changed during the 1970s and 1980s, but the strident racial appeals that marked his rise to national political notoriety both secured a base of support and limited his ability to expand that base outside Alabama and the South. Another southerner, Jimmy Carter, elected governor of Georgia in 1970, would turn back Wallace's national bid in 1976, presenting a markedly different stance on race and urging voters to "Send them a president, not just a message." As Wallace himself put it on the night of Carter's presidential nomination in 1976, "I had to do things—say things to get elected in Alabama, that made it impossible for me to ever be President" (Carter 1995, 458).

Wallace rose to political prominence with his election as governor in 1962. His 1958 gubernatorial bid had ended in failure, although he did make it to the runoff against Attorney General John Patterson (a majority of the vote was required for the nomination and Patterson led in the first primary but failed to secure a majority of the vote). Patterson defeated Wallace for governor. Wallace got the votes of black voters in the first primary. Patterson took a harsher line on race and lambasted Wallace as the candidate of black voters. Wallace over the next four years repeated the lesson that he learned from his 1958 loss: "John Patterson out-niggered me and I'm never going to be out-niggered again." Wallace's 1962 campaign and his 1963 inaugural address ("Segregation today. Segregation tomorrow. Segregation forever.") marked him as a political leader who could and would milk the race issue for political advantage.

Racial resistance typified Wallace's political stance and public appeal, but to reduce Wallace's political support to the single issue of race underestimates him. V. O. Key Jr. had noted a strong populist streak of defiance in Alabama politics. Unlike Virginia, where deference to the upper orders prevailed, in Alabama "a wholesome contempt for authority and a spirit of rebellion akin to that of the Populist days resist the efforts of the big farmers and 'big mules'—the local term for Birmingham industrialists and financiers—to control the state" (Key 1949, 36). Wallace epitomized this populist rebellion, spoke up for the little guy against the moneyed interests, and added to the mix resistance to federal authorities over racial matters. Over the 1960s, this mix catapulted Wallace onto the national political stage. In the 1970s and later, Wallace sought to leave his racial baggage behind, but times had changed and his physical debilitation after the assassination attempt in 1972 limited his political prospects.

At the University of Alabama in June 1963, Wallace stood in the schoolhouse door to block the registration of two black students and thus defied federal court orders to integrate the university. President John F. Kennedy federalized Alabama National Guard troops to carry out the court order, and Wallace stepped aside. In 1964 Wallace entered Democratic presidential primaries to carry his message to voters outside Alabama. His campaign resonated among voters in Wisconsin, Indiana, and Maryland (Carter 1995, 201–15). His chance of taking the nomination from Lyndon Johnson, the incumbent president, was nil, but Wallace rallied would-be supporters with cries of "Send them a message"—a catchall for voters looking for someone to express their political discontent.

Unable to succeed himself as governor in 1966 (his attempts to repeal that prohibition having failed), Wallace offered his wife Lurleen Wallace as a proxy candidate. She won handily, bettering her closest challenger by 54 to 19 percent in the primary and trouncing James Martin, the near-victor over Senator Lister Hill in 1962, by 63 to 31 percent. In the general election of 1966, Alabama Democrats turned back the Republican contestants who were seeking to expand on the victories secured in 1964 with Goldwater's popular candidacy (discussed below). Her death from cancer in May 1968 meant Lieutenant Governor Albert Brewer, a former Wallace ally, became governor, setting up a political showdown between Brewer and Wallace in the 1970 governor's race.

In 1970, Brewer led Wallace in the first primary, but the runoff campaign was marked by a viciousness exceptional even for Alabama politics. Race mattered, and Wallace forces pulled out all the stops. Wallace himself warned about the danger of electing a governor beholden to the "bloc vote." Distributed among the barber shops, beauty salons, and similarly apt locations around the state were Wallace campaign literature pieces that hit hard at the race issue. For example, one featured a young white girl surrounded by young black boys and urged readers to vote Wallace to prevent the worst. Targeted mobilization campaigns registered and turned out white voters for Wallace (Stanley 1987). Brewer forces did not counter. Some Brewer gambits backfired. A prominent Brewer campaign aide was embarrassed when an attempt to secure photographs of Wallace's brother's home and grounds came to grief when a helicopter malfunction forced a landing on the grounds. Press coverage was extensive but not helpful to Brewer in the closing days of the campaign. During the Watergate investigations, it became known that Nixon forces had contributed heavily to the Brewer campaign coffers. Nonetheless, Wallace won in a runoff election (51.6 to 48.4 percent).[1]

After his 1958 loss to Patterson, Wallace had vowed never to be outmaneuvered on the race issue again. In 1970, his gubernatorial win proved that he was a master at riding the race issue. Events during his governorship suggested that after the 1970 win, despite having resorted to the race issue, Wallace decided to move away from such racial stridency. His near brush with death in the assassination attempt, particularly the awareness that black ministers were praying for his well-being, continued the softening of his harsh stance on racial issues. In 1974, in a state where football is serious business, the governor crowned the first black homecoming queen at the University of Alabama. In other ways, also, Wallace signaled his transformation on race.

A Wallace administration was energized more by the demands of the next campaign than by the demands of governing. Even as Wallace laid the groundwork for presidential bids in the 1970s, an increasing share of state policy was being challenged successfully in the federal courts. Matters in which federal judicial decisions struck down state policy in the 1970s included prisons, mental health, property tax, highway patrol hiring, and redistricting, among others (Bass 1993).

In his 1974 reelection bid, Wallace was a shoo-in. A serious challenger among Democrats and Republicans failed to emerge. Wallace's 1976 presidential bid proved politically deflating, as fellow southerner Carter secured the Democratic nomination and the general election win. Wallace's political future revolved around whether he would seek a Senate seat in 1978 when he would be ineligible to run for governor again (the prohibition on gubernatorial succession had changed since his first term, but an individual could serve only two consecutive terms). Insiders were certain that Wallace would seek to make his mark on the U.S. Senate. As Wallace delayed an announcement about his intentions, Chief Justice Howell Heflin of the Alabama Supreme Court, a prominent public figure because of his efforts at court reform, boldly announced that he would run for the U.S. Senate seat. (The death of Senator James B. Allen meant two U.S. Senate seats were open in 1978. The shorter-term seat had already attracted several candidates, but the six-year term seat was avoided because of Wallace's looming presence.) Heflin's declaration ensured that Wallace would have a hard campaign if he announced. Whether that prospect deterred him is unclear, but Wallace announced that he would not seek a Senate seat. Heflin won handily, and in a surprise, former state legislator Donald Stewart defeated more prominent politicians for the other U.S. Senate seat.

In questionable health, Wallace did not acquire a taste for political retirement, returning in 1982 to run for governor again. He turned back a strong challenger in the Democratic primary and then won 58 percent of the vote in the general election against well-organized and equally well financed Montgomery mayor Emory Folmar. In 1986 the prospect of another gubernatorial term for Wallace loomed large. But rather than seek reelection, in April 1986 Wallace announced his intention to retire from politics: "I have climbed my last political mountain." In a seven-minute statement, Wallace indicated that he had wanted to seek reelection but that his friends and family had prevailed upon him to retire because of his health. Wallace biographer Dan T. Carter relates that as Wallace rode back to the governor's mansion with his son, he uttered only one sentence: "I hope the rich and powerful don't take over now" (Carter 1995, 463).[2]

Key's masterful work, *Southern Politics in State and Nation*, argues that in the absence of political party competition, dominant political figures such as Huey Long in Louisiana or Gene Talmadge in Georgia can provide useful rallying points in politics, imposing a degree of coherence on what would otherwise be a kaleidoscopic, confusing mishmash of factions. Long and Talmadge left a lasting mark and generated enduring opposition, giving their states a degree of political coherence lacking in most other southern states where one party dominated. Wallace endured and generated opposition, but that opposition seldom enjoyed much sustained political success. Democrats loyal to the national party led by Robert Vance and George Lewis Bailes warred with Wallace and his supporters over control of the state Democratic Party. In 1971 a majority of the state senate united in opposition to Wallace's legislative program and delayed its passage. Eventually Wallace's political leverage and the opportunities some opposition senators saw and seized meant that they dropped their opposition. Challenging Wallace did not prove an effective way of gaining statewide election. Wallace's hold on Alabama voters stifled political competition in the state.

The Republican Rise

Although Republicans made headway in the rest of the nation by courting the discontented voters who were sympathetic to Wallace, within Alabama, Republicans were stymied by Wallace's presence. In the 1960s and later, the Republican presence was beginning to make itself felt, but Republican electoral success materialized only sporadically. Growth was not so much consistent and steady as volatile.

At the presidential level, Alabama's electoral votes were cast for Republicans seven times between 1964 and 1996, with Democrats winning only in 1976 and Wallace in 1968. During this period the state was presidentially Republican. Below the presidential level, Republican development was much slower.

Indeed, as early as 1948 the loyalty of Alabama voters to the Democratic Party proved less than absolute; in that year Strom Thurmond's third-party candidacy in opposition to President Harry S. Truman's civil rights agenda garnered all of Alabama's electoral votes. (Truman and the national Democrats were not even officially on the ballot, as Thurmond's States' Rights Party usurped the Democratic line. If Alabama voters wanted to back Truman, they had to write in the vote. In Alabama, a Democratic vote was a vote for Thurmond and states' rights.) Alabama voters liked Ike, but not enough to give his Republican presidential candidacy the state's electoral votes in 1952 or 1956. In 1960, Governor John Patterson cast his lot with Senator Kennedy's presidential bid, but the state's electoral votes were split with Senator Harry Byrd of Virginia (although Byrd had not been on the ballot in November).

The first strong inkling of Republican electoral appeal in Alabama came with Martin's near-upset of U.S. senator Hill in 1962. Hill edged out Martin by only 50.9 to 49.1 percent. Republicans were a political threat to Democratic hegemony, a threat that became all the more real with Goldwater's 1964 presidential candidacy. Goldwater swept the state and carried into office most candidates the Republicans had bothered to nominate (several positions were without Republican nominees).

Goldwater's carrying the state showed that white Alabama voters were willing to vote Republican and that Democratic loyalties could not be taken for granted at the presidential level. Presidential coattails and political conservatism could aid down-ballot Republicans. Yet Republican gains among southern whites were offset by solidly Democratic trends among southern blacks, who were gaining an effective right to vote in the mid-1960s. In the years ahead, southern Democrats would turn back Republican challenges with newly loyal black voter support (Bass and DeVries 1976).

If Goldwater's victory in 1964 showed the potential for Republicans, the 1966 debacle showed that Republicans had a long way to go before they could consolidate their gains. In 1966 Alabama's gubernatorial election provided an opportunity for Republicans to advance and U.S. senator John Sparkman was up for reelection. Republicans eagerly anticipated continuing their winning ways. In a much questioned move, Republicans nominated party chairman John Grenier to run against Senator Sparkman and Congressman Martin, the near-winner over Senator Hill in 1962, against Lurleen Wallace for governor. Sparkman was considered the more politically vulnerable, but Grenier had little statewide visibility. Wallace and Sparkman easily turned back the Republican challengers. Internal squabbling among Republicans added to the dismay of defeat.[3]

Republicans found it hard to recover. Richard Nixon's election as president in 1968 meant a Republican White House would be the target of discontent over federal initiatives on civil rights and other policies. Nixon was popular within Alabama, but his popularity did not translate into a lift for Republican Party development. Republican growth was hampered by Nixon's political necessity to work with entrenched, senior Democratic members of Congress such as Senator Sparkman. Priority was given to working with senior Democrats, not to electing Republicans. When Alabama Republicans nominated a member of the Nixon cabinet, Winton "Red" Blount, to run against Sparkman, the presumed political backing of the Republican White House was not forthcoming. The White House released a letter praising Sparkman for his strong support of the president. Once when Sparkman was campaigning in Alabama, President Nixon sent a White House plane to carry the senator back to Washington to cast a vote in support of the president. When pressed, White House press secretary Ron Ziegler refused to say the president supported Republican Blount against Sparkman: "Well, he doesn't oppose him" was the best Ziegler could offer (Bass and DeVries 1976).

Nixon's Watergate troubles further eroded Republican development. Carter's presidential bid in 1976 initially revived Democratic fortunes in the South, even in Alabama. Statewide, the path to elective office still required the Democratic nomination. Indeed, in the 1978 elections, the winning candidates for the top offices were both former Republicans who had recently become Democrats—Fob James, governor, had been on the state Republican executive committee, and Charles Graddick, attorney general, had been on the Mobile County Republican executive committee. The Democratic Party was a catchall coalition, containing everyone who had aspirations for higher electoral office. Coalitional strains among this all-encompassing collection of interests were considerable. For politically ambitious Alabamians, the Republican Party had some appeal, but the chance to gain elective office was a strong part of that appeal. Initial Republican electoral advances below the presidential level would be more in the nature of flukes than the result of solid preparation. Republican state house members broke into double digits only in the early 1990s; in the state senate in the 1990s (see table 4.2).

Carter's 1976 presidential campaign initially revitalized southern Democrats, but Carter's performance led many Alabama voters to reconsider the desirability of supporting Republicans. A "friends and neighbors" vote was not sufficient for Georgian Carter in 1980. Reagan edged out Carter in Alabama by 49 to 48 percent. Alabamians gave a slightly greater percentage of the vote (50 percent) to Republican Senate candidate

Table 4.2
Partisan Composition of Alabama State Legislature, 1958–1997

	House		Senate	
	Democrats	Republicans	Democrats	Republicans
1958	106	0	35	0
1962	104	2	35	0
1964	104	2	35	0
1966	106	0	34	1
1968	106	0	34	1
1970	104	2	35	0
1972	104	2	35	0
1974	105	0	35	0
1976	103	2	34	0
1978	101	4	35	0
1980	100	4	35	0
1982	97	8	32	3
1984	87	12	28	4
1986	89	16	30	5
1988	85	17	28	6
1990	82	23	28	7
1992	82	23	28	7
1994	74	31	23	12
1996	72	33	22	12
1997	72	33	23	12

Note: Vacancies account for totals that sum to less than 105 for the house after 1974 and 35 for the senate.

Sources: For 1958–1994: *Statistical Abstract of the United States,* annual editions; for 1996: unpublished data from the National Conference of State Legislatures (as of 18 December 1996); for 1997: house and senate Web pages, http://www.state.al.us/house.html and http://www.state.al.us/senate.html (as of 6 July 1997).

Jeremiah Denton, a certified war hero who had spent over three decades in the U.S. Navy, including seven and a half years as a prisoner of war in North Vietnam. Denton's victory helped the Republicans achieve a Senate majority for the first time time since the 1950s.

As the 1980 election neared, most pollsters reported the Carter-Reagan contest too close to call. Such expectations made the GOP victories all the more dramatic considering the large Reagan lead (51 to 41 percent of the vote, 489 to 49 electoral votes), and the unexpected Republican capture of a Senate majority provided a lift for Reagan and the Republicans.

Denton proved incapable of holding on to his seat, losing his reelection bid in 1986. Self-confident, he declined to do the grassroots politicking Alabama voters had come to expect by virtue of Senator Jim Allen's extensive town meetings and travels across the state. Denton explained his absence from the state by claiming that he had more important things to do than "to come to Alabama and kiss babies' butts" (Ingram 1996b). Alabama Republicans lost the Senate seat but gained the governor's chair when Guy Hunt, former Cullman County probate judge, defeated Democrat Bill Baxley after months of Democratic wrangling over who the Democratic nominee should be. Democrats self-destructed and Hunt was the beneficiary. Once the degree of Democratic destructiveness became apparent, other Republicans, who had passed up the opportunity to run for governor, magnanimously suggested that perhaps Hunt should step aside for stronger, more viable candidates such as themselves. Hunt declined.

The Democratic trouble began when Baxley and Graddick survived the first primary, with neither garnering a majority of the vote. For the runoff, Graddick as attorney general issued a ruling holding that voters who had taken part in the first Republican primary could indeed switch over and take part in the Democratic runoff. Observers expected Graddick to benefit from erstwhile Republican primary voters who participated in the Democratic runoff. After the runoff voting, court challenges proliferated. The Democratic Party decided to declare Baxley the Democratic nominee, and voters were enraged. Such decision by fiat was perhaps less politic than submitting the contest to another public vote. Graddick continued his challenge, dropping out only a few days before the general election.

Hunt governed in ways that would strengthen the Republican Party, leaving vacancies rather than appointing Democrats to local office. Hunt was reelected in 1990 but encountered legal problems when the attorney general pressed investigations of Hunt's finances and activities. Hunt was ultimately convicted of illegally using funds raised for his inauguration and resigned as governor. Lieutenant Governor "Little Jim" Folsom, son of former governor "Big Jim" Folsom, became governor.

In the 1992 elections two moderate southerners headed the national Democratic ticket , but Democrats were still unable to break the Republican hold on Alabama's electoral votes. The 1994 elections saw a Republican tide in Alabama as well as the rest of the nation. Republican electoral prospects were brightening, and the politically ambitious began to switch parties. Senator Richard Shelby, elected as a Democrat in 1994, switched to the Republicans a few days after the election (Shribman 1995). Shelby's move made it easier for conservative Democratic officeholders to go Republican. Over the next few years many elected Democrats in Alabama followed in Shelby's footsteps. The Republican majorities in the House and Senate following the 1994 elections no longer meant a loss of congressional influence if Republicans were elected to Congress.

One-party politics characterized the solidly Democratic South for decades after Reconstruction. Alabama was no exception. Some observers conclude that the state is now one-party again, only this time one-party Republican. In light of recent Republican electoral successes, it's hard to recall exactly how far the Republican Party has come in Alabama. One eighty-year-old Alabamian, when asked in the late 1970s to comment on the major political changes he had witnessed over his lifetime, asserted that he now lived in a two-party area. This was strange since no Republican had been elected in the area since Reconstruction. The interviewer feared the interviewee was senile or at least powerfully disconnected from reality. Not so. When pressed, the elderly gentleman recalled that in 1928 one local businessman had been unable to support Democrat Al Smith for president and had voted for Republican Herbert Hoover. The businessman almost had to shut down his business and leave town for his political heresy. The conclusion? Now we have two-party politics; you can vote Republican if you like.

Black Political Clout

Two of the more momentous moments in the civil rights struggle occurred in Alabama: in Birmingham in the spring of 1963, Bull Conner and his police dogs and fire hoses confronted demonstrators; and in Selma in 1965, Sheriff Jim Clark and law enforcement officials beat up demonstrators once they crossed the Edmund Pettus Bridge, seeking to march to the state capitol in Montgomery to protest the inability of blacks to vote in Selma and Dallas County.

Wallace contributed to making Alabama a battleground for civil rights, gaining political notoriety in the process. The Voting Rights Act of 1965, a response to the events surrounding the Selma march, gave blacks in hardcore, defiant areas of the South an effective right to vote. Voting rights drives and the federal registrars assigned to the most resistant areas, as well as the cooperation of local officials in areas that wanted to avoid the assignment of federal registrars, led to great increases in the number of blacks registered to vote. Black political influence at the ballot box was evident. In Dallas County, more moderate Police Chief Wilson Baker defeated Sheriff Jim Clark with black voter support. Politicians learned to count votes, and black and white votes counted the same once they were in the ballot box.

Within Alabama, registration rates among blacks of voting age rose from 5 percent in 1952 to 14 percent in 1960, then to 51 percent by 1966 and to 64 percent in 1970 (Garrow 1978, 7, 11, 189, 200). Restrictive registration practices were reduced and white voter registration rose as well. While some of the rise in white political participation can be attributed to white voter backlash against black political gains, less offputting registration practices, increased political competition, and other nonracial political and socioeconomic factors also played a role (Stanley 1987, 37, 52, 67, 98).

Black political clout was organized through the Alabama Democratic Conference headed by Joe Reed and the New South Coalition started by Birmingham mayor Richard Arrington. These organizations proved potent. In 1984 Mayor Arrington endorsed Walter Mondale for the Democratic nomination rather than endorsing the Reverend Jesse Jackson. Arrington's support proved vital in capturing a large share of the black vote and helping Mondale carry the state.

Black political gains were evident over the decades. Although the share of elected officials who were black lagged behind the black share of the voting-age population, Alabama led the states in the share of black elected officials. Voting rights challenges led counties and towns to adopt single-member districts in which blacks constituted more than a majority of the voting-age population. Before the 1974 election, there were 3 blacks in the 140-member state house; after, there were 13. By 1984 (and subsequently), 5 black state senators and 19 black house members served in the Alabama legislature (see table 4.3). Below the state house level, by the end of the 1980s, black officeholding in Alabama "approached the level of proportional representation" (McCrary et al. 1994, 54). Redistricting, the move to single-member districts, and the creation of majority-minority districts boosted the numbers of blacks elected. Congressional redistricting in the 1990s led to the creation of a black-majority congressional district. Congressman Earl Hilliard, Democrat, was elected as the first black member of Congress from Alabama since Reconstruction (*Chicago Tribune* 1995).

The 1996 Elections

For the 1996 elections the retirement of U.S. senator Heflin in 1995 considerably brightened Republican prospects. Several statewide judicial contests also provided targets of Republican opportunity, and Republicans seized them. Ironically, what had been securely established for decades,

Table 4.3
Black Elected Officials in Alabama, 1971–1993

		State Legislature		
	Total	Senate	House	Both Chambers
1971	105	0	2	2
1973	149	0	2	2
1974	149	0	3	3
1976	171	—	—	15
1977	201	2	13	15
1979	208	—	—	16
1980	238	—	—	15
1981	247	—	—	16
1982	269	3	13	16
1983	309	—	—	—
1984	314	5	19	24
1985	375	5	19	24
1986	403	5	19	24
1987	448	5	19	24
1988	442	5	19	24
1989	694	5	18	23
1990	705	5	18	23
1991	706	5	19	24
1992	702	5	19	24
1993	699	—	—	23

Note: — indicates data not available

Sources: Joint Center for Political Studies, *Black Elected Officials: A National Roster,* annual editions; and *Statistical Abstract of the United States,* annual editions.

presidential Republicanism, was in doubt in Alabama during the general election campaign (Smith 1996). What some called a "split-level realignment," in which voters backed Republicans at the presidential level and Democrats below that, appeared likely to be reversed. Clinton, avoided by white southern Democratic officeholders in the 1994 campaign, was welcomed with open arms in 1996 (Farrell 1996). Dole's campaign failed to catch on, and his weak support in Alabama reflected that failure. In the days just before the election, the president and Dole campaigned in Alabama on the same day (October 24), competing for votes on what should have been secure Dole turf. Clinton ultimately lost Alabama, 50 to 43 percent. The mere fact that a presidential win appeared possible was small comfort for Democrats, as they lost decisively below the presidential level. Indeed, the state Democratic Party chief admitted that Democrats had lost the seven major statewide races but took some solace in the fact that these races were not lost by many votes. In the aftermath of the election, Republicans, for the first time since Reconstruction, controlled a majority of major state offices. The count was Republicans twenty, Democrats only seventeen (Alcorn 1996a).

Republicans had contested far more elections in 1996 than in previous years, with 320 Republican candidates in 461 county races—double the number of seats contested in the previous election (Hetzner 1996).

Democrats lost a Senate seat, leaving Republicans in control of both Alabama seats in the U.S. Senate for the first time since Reconstruction. Republican Jeff Sessions replaced Heflin. Ironically, Sessions, nominated to a federal judgeship by Reagan, had his nomination fail when Heflin cast the critical vote against him in the Judiciary Committee (Associated Press 1996).

Republicans won five of the seven U.S. House seats up for election, a net gain of two. In addition, Republicans swept the state supreme court, the state court of civil appeals, and the state court of criminal appeals (places 1, 2, and 3) and won the presidency of the public service commission.

Among Alabama voters in the 1996 general election, Democrats still outnumbered Republicans (44 to 41 percent). Twelve percent of the voters were former Democrats who had become Republicans over the previous two years (Alcorn 1996b). Among white voters, 30 percent backed the Democrats; among black voters, 90 percent did so (Ingram 1996a).

Party switching by Democratic elected officials continued into 1997, with Secretary of State Jim Bennett the most prominent conversion to the Republicans. By mid-1997 the number of switchers had risen to twelve. This is in addition to the thirty-five who switched between the 1994 election and January 1997 (*Montgomery Advertiser* 1997).

Carl Grafton may have provided the soundest assessment in the aftermath of the 1996 elections: Alabama "is a two-party state with a Republican tendency." Keeping Alabama competitive between the parties and away from becoming a one-party solid Republican state are the significant number of blacks who vote in state and national races and the strong populist tendency among some whites (Alcorn 1996a).

Even so, Republican prospects have never been brighter. Dimming that brightness is the realization that Republicans, not Democrats, are now the incumbents. Whatever ire voters focus on incumbents will hurt Republicans more than Democrats. Morever, although Republicans have gained voter support, party ties mean less than they once did. Voters have less faith in either party. New-found Republican loyalties may well prove fleeting.

Notes

1. "The principal factor that moved Wallace from a deficit of nearly 12,000 against Brewer on May 5 to a commanding majority [33,881 votes] in the space of four weeks clearly was his hammering away at Brewer's black voter support in the first primary. It had as its purpose a consolidation of a white backlash, and in the hands of a master at this kind of political maneuvering, it worked." (Perason 1970, 1, 12)

2. Wallace's son, George Jr., also entered public office, serving as state treasurer. He ran for Congress in 1992 and lost the general election by fewer than 4,000 votes (out of 225,391) to Republican Terry Everest of Enterprise.

3. Republican internal strife was not limited to the 1960s. Congressman John Buchanan of Birmingham, a Methodist minister, was challenged as too liberal by Albert Lee Smith, a former John Birch Society member. Smith's candidacy fell short in 1978, but he won the 1980 rematch with the aid of the Moral Majority.

References

Alcorn, John D. 1996a. "Most State Offices Now in GOP Hands." *Montgomery Advertiser,* 7 November, 1A.

———. 1996b. "Party Loyalty Split in State, Poll Says." *Montgomery Advertiser,* 11 December, 3B.

Associated Press. 1996. "Rejected Reagan Judge Making Bid in Alabama U.S. Senate Primary." *Boston Globe,* 2 June, 16.

Bass, Jack. 1993. *Taming the Storm: The Life and Times of Judge Frank M. Johnson and the South's Fight over Civil Rights.* New York: Doubleday.

Bass, Jack, and Walter DeVries. 1976. *The Transformation of Southern Politics: Social Change and Political Consequence since 1945.* New York: Basic Books.

Carter, Dan T. 1995. *The Politics of Rage: George Wallace, the Origins of the New Conservatism, and the Transformation of American Politics.* New York: Simon & Schuster.

Chicago Tribune. 1995. "Barkley Shoots for Governor's Job." 14 July, 1.

Farrell, John Aloysius. 1996. "Clinton Pleasing Party in South: Centrist Positions Win Praise from Black and White." *Boston Globe,* 27 October, A23.

Garrow, David J. 1978. *Protest at Selma: Martin Luther King Jr. and the Voting Rights Act of 1965.* New Haven: Yale University Press.

Hetzner, Amy. 1996. "Republican Numbers Up: State Races Offer Choices." *Birmingham Post-Herald,* 9 April.

Ingram, Bob. 1996a. "Gun-shy Democratic Chief Analyzes November Rout." *Montgomery Advertiser,* 26 November, 12A.

———. 1996b. "Was '62 Race Really Tight?" *Montgomery Advertiser*, 13 October, 1F.

Key, V. O., Jr. 1949. *Southern Politics in State and Nation*. New York: Knopf.

Montgomery Advertiser. 1997. "Democrats Get Deadline for Switching to GOP." 13 January.

Perason, Ted. 1970. "Wallace Rides Backlash to Narrow Comeback." *Birmingham News*, 3 June, 1, 12.

Phillips, Kevin P. 1969. *The Emerging Republican Majority*. New Rochelle, N.Y.: Arlington House.

Shribman, David M. 1995. "GOP's Dixie Rise: A Case Study." *Boston Globe*, 20 January, 3.

Smith, Gita M. 1996. "Parties Fight over Alabama." *Atlanta Journal-Constitution*, 25 October, A13.

Stanley, Harold W. 1987. *Voter Mobilization and the Politics of Race: The South and Universal Suffrage, 1952–1984*. New York: Praeger.

5

Mississippi: A Synthesis of Race, Region, and Republicanism

David A. Breaux, Don E. Slabach, and Daye Dearing

On the Road to Federal Republicanism

Once considered to be a traditional one-party Democratic state, Mississippi has undergone a dramatic transformation toward a highly competitive two-party system. This transformation is clearly evident when one examines both national and state elections, as well as attitudinal data.

In 1972, when Republican presidential candidate Richard Nixon won Mississippi in a landslide, Republicans Thad Cochran and Trent Lott were both swept into the U.S. House of Representatives from the Fourth and Fifth Congressional Districts, respectively. Six years later, Cochran defeated a white Democrat and a black independent with a plurality of the vote to gain the Senate seat previously held by James O. Eastland. This made Cochran the first Republican senator from Mississippi since Reconstruction. By 1996, Cochran had gradually climbed to a position as the second most powerful Republican in the U.S. Senate, behind Republican Party leader Bob Dole.

Lott won the state's other Senate seat, that of retiring senator John C. Stennis, in the George Bush landslide of 1988. Lott had previously served as House minority whip and had made a mark for himself as a rising Republican star ideologically allied with the activities of Georgia congressman Newt Gingrich. As the state's junior senator, Lott rapidly rose to the third position in the Senate Republican hierarchy.

The positions of Cochran and Lott gained added importance after the 1994 elections that resulted in the Republican takeover of both House and Senate. With the resignation of newly empowered majority leader Bob Dole to run for president, the stage was set for an intraparty struggle between two Mississippians. Both Cochran and Lott announced plans to seek the majority leader's position. Early in the contest many pundits saw Cochran, the more moderate and "senatorial" candidate, as having an advantage within the aristocratic atmosphere of the U.S. Senate. However, as Cochran later quipped, his votes showed him starting ahead and losing ground from there. Lott's rapid ascendancy to the Senate majority leader position just two years into his second term as senator can be explained as an attempt by the Senate to keep pace with the brasher House and the Democratic White House's move to the center of the political playing field.

After Cochran's move from the Fourth District to the Senate, the seat was first held by a Republican, who was quickly replaced by a Democrat. When that Democrat, Wayne Dowdy, unsuccessfully sought to replace retiring senator Stennis in 1988, the House seat went to another Democrat, Mike Parker.

With Lott's move to the Senate in the 1988 election, his Fifth District seat was filled by Republican Larkin Smith. Smith's death in an airplane crash and the subsequent special election to fill his unexpired term resulted in Gene Taylor's reclaiming the seat for Democrats for the first time in seventeen years.

Elsewhere, in the recently created black-majority Second Congressional District, which is mostly composed of the state's Delta region, electoral politics has followed racial and socioeconomic divisions. In the 1982 congressional race, Webb Franklin, a conservative white Democrat-turned-Republican, was able to attract enough of the white vote to defeat black Mississippi House veteran Robert Clark of Holmes County. Capitalizing on the power of incumbency, Franklin was able to turn back Clark's challenge two years later. In 1986, Democrats in the poverty-stricken and newly redrawn Delta district united to elect Mike Espy, a young black progressive candidate. When Espy resigned to accept a cabinet appointment in the Clinton administration, voters in the Delta district elected black civil rights leader Bennie Thompson (Krane and Shaffer 1992).

Jamie Whitten's decision not to seek reelection after more than forty years of service from the state's First Congressional District ultimately resulted in the election of Republican Roger Wicker. Mike Parker, who was elected in 1988 as only the second Democrat from the Fourth Congressional District since 1972, switched from the Democratic to the Republican Party and was easily reelected in 1996. That same year, voters in the Third Congressional District chose Republican Chip Pickering, former aide to Lott, to replace retiring House veteran Sonny Montgomery. Thus today the Republican Party occupies both of the state's Senate seats and three of its five House seats.

By this time, Mississippi could also boast such Republican leaders as Haley Barbour, chair of the Republican National Committee, and Evelyn McPhail, vice chair of the Republican National Committee. Additionally, Mississippians served as prominent members of the platform committees at the 1992 and 1996 Republican conventions and served throughout Washington in various capacities. Mississippi Republicans had found a home in national politics.

Regional Inroads for State Republicans

Owing in part to a tradition of party loyalty and the fact that Mississippi state elections are insulated from trends in national politics by being held in odd-numbered years, Democrats have typically held an advantage over Republicans in state and local elections. Democratic candidates, most notably those running for the state's highest office, have typically been able to win by constructing broad-based, biracial coalitions.

In *Southern Politics in State and Nation* (1949), V. O. Key summarized Mississippi politics as one-party (and one-race, white) Democratic with a conservative, wealthy Delta and a progressive, "dirt farmer" Hills factionalism. The chief cause of the clash between the Delta and the Hills in electoral politics revolved around the issues of taxation and public expenditures. Delta voters embraced the conservative, "no new taxes" position, while Hills voters assumed a more populist stand and hoped for government intervention through public roads, free textbooks, and other populist ideas. The Delta-Hills split clearly manifested itself in the 1947 gubernatorial primary, which pitted Fielding Wright against Paul B. Johnson Sr. In that election, Wright, a Delta native, received his greatest support in the counties along the Mississippi River and in the few rich farming counties in the state's eastern Black Prairie (see figure 5.1). Vestiges of the factionalism continued into the 1960s but have gradually been replaced by a more contemporary Democratic-Republican split within the electorate. In fact, the current political relationships now appear to be a mirror inversion of Key's Delta-Hills dichotomy.

Three gubernatorial elections preceding the 1995 state election illustrate the gradual growth of the Republican Party. In the 1975 gubernatorial election the historically conservative Delta and progressive Hills faced a true dilemma. Political maverick and Democrat Cliff Finch of the Hills ran a populist "workingman's campaign" and was often seen pumping gas or bagging groceries around the state. Though he was a wealthy trial lawyer, the symbol of his campaign became an old metal lunch box (Bass

greater than 60% Wright

Wright's home

Source: V. O. Key Jr., *Southern Politics in State and Nation* (New York: Knopf, 1949).

Fig. 5.1. 1947 Democratic Primary, Fielding Wright vs. Paul B. Johnson

and DeVries 1976). The Republican candidate, Gil Carmichael, also of the Hills, pushed liberal issues, countering much of Finch's support. Carmichael called for ratification of the Equal Rights Amendment, hand-gun control legislation, and compulsory school attendance laws (Carmichael 1996). These issues found a place in the campaign as Carmichael picked up support in the more urbanized areas of the state, winning seventeen counties and driving a deep wedge into the midsection of the state (see figure 5.2). A postelection survey indicated that two-thirds of Carmichael's support came from those who had never before voted for a Republican candidate, while Finch was able to claim victory by combining traditional Democratic voting habits of whites with nearly 80 percent of the black vote (Bass and DeVries 1976).

In 1987, both the Republican and Democratic candidates were labeled as moderates. It was often commented that Republican Jack Reed and Democrat Ray Mabus, both of the Hills, were "singing out of the same hymnal." Mabus had been one of the primary architects of Democratic governor William Winter's Education Reform Act and as state auditor had investigated many local officials who had made up the "good ol' boy" network of Mississippi politics. Reed, chairman of the state board of education, had strongly supported the Education Reform Act and during the 1960s had been one of the few who called for greater racial tolerance

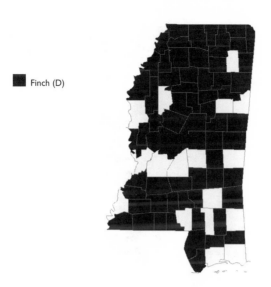

Finch (D)

Fig. 5.2. 1975 Mississippi General Election, Finch (D) vs. Carmichael (R)

and moderation (Krane and Shaffer 1992). Both candidates agreed on the need for progressive reforms in education and government and for diversifying the state's economy.

While the goals of the two candidates reflected a bi- or nonpartisan view, their methods for accomplishing them did not. While Mabus pledged to increase teacher pay in one year while holding the line on taxes, Reed advocated a more incremental process, saying Mabus would indeed be forced to raise taxes (Krane and Shaffer 1992). Because the issue stands of the two candidates were so similar and they were both from the Hills, all that separated them was a choice between Republican and Democratic partisanship and their specific policies for achieving agreed-upon goals.

If Key's description of regional factionalism had held true in the 1987 gubernatorial election, one would have expected Reed to lay claim to the Delta counties as the base of his support. However, the results of the election indicate that the Republican candidate's moderate tax policies played better in the Hill counties, winning twenty-three counties in the eastern half of the state. Clearly, by 1987, the Republican Party had begun to make significant inroads in Mississippi gubernatorial elections. However, Mabus won the governor's seat by sweeping the Delta and River counties and picking up substantial support among the border counties (see figure 5.3).

Fig. 5.3. 1987 Mississippi General Election, Mabus (D) vs. Reed (R)

In 1991, Kirk Fordice of Vicksburg, a river city at the southernmost end of the Delta, brought a new type of Republicanism to Mississippi. By combining the populist workingman rhetoric and opposition to the "establishment" with fiscal conservatism, Fordice cemented the new conservative ideology of the Hills in opposition to the growing progressive tendencies of the Delta.

Democratic incumbent governor Ray Mabus, who had campaigned and been elected as a "reformer" in 1987, faced stiff opposition from reformers and populists in the 1991 party primary. While Mabus outspent Fordice by nearly a three-to-one margin, Fordice became the state's first Republican governor since Reconstruction, winning 50.8 percent of the vote. As in 1987, Mabus gained majorities in the Delta and River counties, while Fordice built upon Reed's vote, extending his support deeper into the Hill counties (see figure 5.4).

In that same year, Eddie Briggs, who had recently switched from the Democratic to the Republican Party, became the state's first Republican lieutenant governor in the modern era. Republicans were also able to make modest gains in the state legislature, where their numbers increased from 7 to 9 in the state senate and from 9 to 22 in the state house. In a special election held the following year as a result of redistricting, Republicans were able to increase their numbers to 13 in the senate and 27 in the house. As a result, just under 23 percent of the 174 legislators were mem-

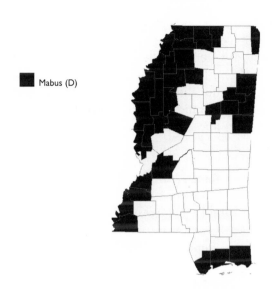

Fig. 5.4. 1991 Mississippi General Election, Mabus (D) vs. Fordice (R)

bers of the state's Republican Party. Also as a result of that same special election, black members (all of whom were affiliated with the state's Democratic Party) increased their numbers from 2 to 10 in the senate and from 17 to 32 in the house, giving them just under 24 percent of the state's legislative seats.

Mississippi's transformation from a one- to a two-party system is also evident when one examines the trend over time in the partisan self-identification of adult Mississippians. In 1982, Democratic self-identifiers held a 36 percent advantage over Republican self-identifiers. Among those adults who indicated that they were likely to vote, the Democratic advantage shrank only slightly to 30 percent. By 1994, self-identified Democrats outnumbered self-identified Republicans by only a 6 percent margin. Among likely voters, Republican self-identifiers actually surpassed Democratic self-identifiers by 7 percent (Shaffer, Jackreece, and Bigelow 1996). Two years later, in the spring of 1996, this nearly equal self-identified partisan split was reaffirmed by polling that showed a statistical dead heat among likely Mississippi voters (Shaffer 1996). Polls have also shown that party and ideological separations among Mississippi voters have come to resemble more closely those found outside the South. College-educated, higher-income, and conservative whites are more likely to identify with the Republican Party, while blacks, lower income, and liberal whites are more likely to identify with the Democratic Party (Krane and Shaffer 1992).

Thus, it appears that the time has come to reconsider V. O. Key's (1949) often-cited characterization of Mississippi politics as fueled by the struggle between the interests of voters who live in the old conservative, aristocratic Delta and those who live in the populist Hill country. It now seems that the Delta-Hills factionalism that existed during the first half of this century within the Democratic Party has been transformed into a struggle between Democrats and Republicans.

Race Remains

With the passage of the Voting Rights Act of 1965, the once conservative Delta and the populist Hills were transformed into a progressive, Democratic Delta and conservative, Republican Hills. Prior to the passage of the Voting Rights Act, only 6.7 percent of the black voting-age population was registered to vote, but by the time of the 1967 gubernatorial election this number had swelled to 59.8 percent, the highest of the seven states originally covered by the act (Bass and DeVries 1976).

Evidence also suggests an overwhelming sense of loyalty among black Mississippi voters to the Democratic Party regardless of their ideological tendencies. In 1994, 86 percent of black Mississippians identified themselves as Democrats, while only 7 percent identified themselves as Republicans. Even among blacks who claimed to have conservative leanings, 79 percent identified themselves as Democrats, while only 14 percent identified themselves as Republicans (Shaffer, Jackreece, and Bigelow 1996). Surveys done in 1996 showed that 84 percent of black Mississippians identified themselves with the Democratic Party, and 55 percent of all Mississippians identifying with the Democratic Party were black (Shaffer 1996).

This is not to say that the political transformation that Mississippi has undergone is based solely on race. While some whites may have once toyed with voting for Republican candidates because of their dissatisfaction with the national Democratic Party's stand on civil rights issues, there is ample evidence of a socioeconomic basis for the growth of the Republican Party within the state. Surveys taken in 1996 show that 69 percent of families making less than $20,000 per year and 68 percent of high school dropouts identified themselves as Democrats, while 63 percent of college graduates and 57 percent of those making more than $40,000 per year identified themselves as Republicans (Shaffer 1996).

The 1995 Elections: Readjusting or Realigning?

On 7 November 1995, Republican governor Kirk Fordice made history by becoming the first Mississippi governor since Reconstruction to be elected to two four-year consecutive terms (he was one of only three allowed this option because of a long-standing constitutional prohibition). During the early weeks of the campaign, polls showed Fordice holding approximately a 10 percent lead over his Democratic challenger, secretary of state Dick Molpus. Attacks not only on public policy issues but also of a personal nature, dominated the campaign. Molpus, who had built a reputation as an education candidate, saw Fordice cut into his support through the use of the PRIME Initiative, which called for a "return to local control of schools." There were also much publicized exchanges in which each candidate suggested the other should be taken "to the woodshed" (Gordon 1995).

As election day neared, Molpus appeared to be cutting into Fordice's lead. Various tracking polls indicated a movement away from Fordice to "undecided" and from "undecided" to Molpus. An article appearing in the *New York Times* just a few days before the election labeled the race as too close to call (Sack 1995).

In the end, the much anticipated campaign proved anticlimactic, with Fordice winning reelection with over 55 percent of the statewide vote. Fordice gained majorities in fifty-three of the state's eighty-two counties. Much of his vote came from those counties with a white majority population (see figure 5.5). Molpus, on the other hand, carried most of the majority-black Delta counties and those in the Black Prairie of east central Mississippi. A geographical representation of the 1995 gubernatorial vote is eerily reminiscent of an inversion of Key's Delta-Hills factionalism.

Fordice's victory, however, did not help any of his fellow Republican candidates seeking statewide office, all seven of whom failed to win. In the lieutenant governor's race, Republican incumbent Eddie Briggs lost in a close contest to Democrat Ronnie Musgrove. As in the governor's race, Delta and Black Prairie counties went heavily for the Democratic candidate, but, unlike in the governor's race, Musgrove was able to expand upon this base of support and capture a majority of the vote in twenty-four counties that Molpus lost.

The open-seat races for secretary of state and commissioner of agriculture presented the Republican Party with an excellent opportunity to build upon its success in the governor's race. However, the general election yielded rather surprisingly lopsided Democratic victories in both

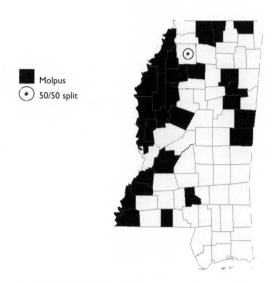

Fig. 5.5. 1995 Mississippi General Election, Molpus (D) vs. Fordice (R, incumbent)

contests. As in times past, the real contest for both offices appears to have been waged within the Democratic Party. Having survived hard-fought primary and runoff primary battles in which they gained visibility, both Democratic candidates coasted to easy victories in the general election.

State legislative elections that year resulted in a senate composed of thirty-four Democrats and eighteen Republicans and a house of representatives made up of eighty-seven Democrats, thirty-two Republicans, and three independents. The Republican Party was able to increase its share from 23 to 28.7 percent of legislative seats. Black members of the state senate remained at ten, and representatives increased to thirty-three in the house, for a total of 27.4 percent of the legislative seats. An interesting note concerning African American legislators—all Democrats—elected in 1995 is that seven out of ten in the senate and twenty out of thirty-three in the house are from Delta, River, or Black Prairie areas of the state.

Table 5.1 illustrates the trend in two-party competition in state legislative races. With the exception of the 1992 special election, the number of contested legislative seats has steadily increased over recent elections. The number of unopposed Republican candidates has also increased over time. These figures attest to the continued growth of two-party competi-

Table 5.1
Legislative Election Competition

	Contested Races	Republican Unopposed	Democrat Unopposed	Independent Unopposed
1987	49	3	122	
1991	61	8	104	1
1992*	80	16	77	1
1995	70	27	76	1

* Special election

tion in the once one-party Democratic state.

Term Limits, A Republican Issue

In 1995, Mississippians were also able to make their voices heard in the term-limit debate. The first citizen-initiated constitutional amendment to be placed on the ballot under the state's new initiative and referendum law, Initiative Measure 4, proposed to limit all elected and appointed officials in state and local government to two consecutive terms, with the exception of certain judicial offices that would be limited to three terms. The proposal also called for term limits on the members of the state's congressional delegation, but a U.S. Supreme Court decision invalidated that section before the election.

The ballot initiative grew to be highly controversial, with proponents and opponents voicing conflicting interpretations of the measure's impact. Proponents, including the incumbent Republican governor, claimed that only a few appointed officials would be affected by the measure, while opponents countered that virtually all appointed officials would face term limits.

When the public finally went to the polls, the proposal was overwhelmingly defeated. Mississippi law requires not only that an initiative receive a majority of the vote to be enacted but also that the majority it receives must represent at least 40 percent of the votes cast in the election (based on the vote for the highest office). The total vote in the governor's race was 819,471, which meant that at least 327,778 votes were required in favor of term limits for the measure to pass. As it turned out, the vote in favor of term limits totaled only 322,277 and, most important, was only 45.7 percent of the total ballots cast on the issue.

By the time the votes were tabulated, only eleven counties provided a majority vote in favor of limiting the terms of elected and appointed officials. Given the continued growth of Republican electoral victories and self-identification, combined with the emphasis on term limits by both the national Republicans and the successful Republican gubernatorial candidate, the term-limits vote could be seen as a contrast. From a county-by-county perspective, the vote did not seem to be tied to other Republican issues. Furthermore, some areas of the state voted against their incumbent officeholder while also voting against the proposal and still others voted for incumbents while voting to limit the terms of those same officials. This indicates that incumbency factors were at best a weak influence on the results.

However, bivariate correlations do indicate some interesting relationships (see table 5.2). Negative correlations are found between the vote for term limits and black voting-age population and region (Delta or non-Delta). This would indicate that the greater a county's African American population (clearly identified with the state's Democratic Party), the less likely that county is to vote for term limits. As for region, previous studies have indicated that apparent regional factors are actually an amalgamation of race, income, and education (Breaux et al. 1996). This would, therefore, imply other demographic factors similar to those influencing party identification.

As further evidence of this, there are positive relationships between the vote for term limits and income, education, and the vote for the Republican gubernatorial candidate. This would, therefore, mean that the higher the income level, education level, and percentage of votes given the Republican candidate within a county, the greater would be the percentage of votes in favor of limiting the terms of elected and appointed officials. Since, as already discussed, income and education are also closely linked to Republican self-identifiers, term limits might well have been a Republican issue, but not the primary issue in 1995.

Table 5.2
Term Limits Bivariate Correlation

	Black Voting-Age Population	Median Income	Region (Delta/ non-Delta)	High School Education or Greater	% Vote for Fordice
% of vote in favor of term limits	-.3643 P = .001	.4466 P = .000	-.3100 P = .005	.4168 P = .000	.3651 P = .001

1996: Race and Region Meet Republicans

The federal elections of 1996 continued the Mississippi trend of voting for Republican federal officials. Since 1964, Mississippians have more often than not cast the majority of their votes for Republican presidential candidates. The only exceptions to this were independent George Wallace of Alabama in 1968 and Democrat Jimmy Carter of Georgia in 1976. Unlike these two fellow southern candidates, Bill Clinton of Arkansas has not fared well in Mississippi. In 1992, the state gave George Bush his highest percentage of votes in the entire country. Bush received 49.7 percent to Clinton's 40.8 percent. Ross Perot's independent candidacy captured 8.7 percent. The 1996 election saw Bill Clinton once again rejected by a majority of Mississippi voters. However, the margin between Clinton and Bob Dole narrowed considerably, from a 9-point difference to 5 points, 44.1 percent for Clinton to 49.2 percent for Dole. Perot once again seems to have been a factor in some counties, and he gained a total of 5.8 percent of the statewide vote.

Not only had Clinton gained a higher 1996 percentage in Mississippi than in his previous campaign, but he also gained more support than other recent Democratic presidential candidates (again, with the exception of Carter in 1976). Michael Dukakis's ill-fated attempt to end eight years of Republican administration in 1988 resulted in a landslide for George Bush in Mississippi. Bush's 20-point victory carried Republican candidates, such as Trent Lott, into previously Democratic positions and solidified the support for other Republican officeholders in Mississippi. Four years earlier, in 1984, Walter Mondale's Democratic bid to replace Ronald Reagan was soundly defeated in Mississippi by an even larger margin, 37.5 percent to 61.8 percent.

As a result, one could theorize that either friends and neighbors voting on the basis of southern proximity or Clinton's attempts to recapture the "vital center" of the electorate could have been factors in this improved Democratic showing. However, county-by-county results of the 1996 presidential election once again show the familiar pattern of state elections (see figure 5.6). In fact, this pattern is bolstered by bivariate correlations between demographics and the voting results of the 1995 gubernatorial election results.

Two strong positive relationships emerge. The first, between the Clinton vote and black voting-age population, comes to .8363, indicating that the larger a Mississippi county's black population, the higher the percentage of votes that county is likely to cast for Clinton. The highest degree of correlation, however, is between the Clinton vote in 1996 and

Fig. 5.6. 1996 Mississippi Presidential Election

the vote for 1995 Democratic gubernatorial candidate Dick Molpus. With a correlation of .9444, these two show an incredible predictive value between gubernatorial-election results and the following year's presidential election.

Other correlations in this matrix (see table 5.3) reaffirm that income and education are factors associated with voting for the Republican candidate. As education and median income levels within a county increase, fewer votes could be expected to be cast for Bill Clinton in 1996.

However, Clinton had little follow-through for other Democratic candidates. Senior senator Thad Cochran coasted to victory over Democrat James W. "Bootie" Hunt. Hunt had few dollars to spend on the campaign and used the situation to dramatize the plight of the less fortunate. By riding a commercial bus to the 1996 Democratic National Convention in Chicago and staying in a homeless shelter, Hunt gained some national attention but saw few results at home. Cochran won eighty of the state's eighty-two counties and received 71 percent of the overall vote. The vote for Hunt could easily be equated with the "yellow-dog" Democrat vote, those likely to vote for a Democratic Party candidate regardless of other factors. In fact, the two counties won by Hunt, Holmes, and Wilkinson, have previously been identified as two of the most Democratic-oriented counties within the state (Slabach and Breaux 1996).

Table 5.3
1996 Bivariate Correlations

	Black Voting-Age Population	Median Income	Region (Delta/ non-Delta)	High School Education or Greater	% Vote for Molpus
% of vote for Clinton	.8363 P = .000	-.7016 P = .000	.4213 P = .000	-.5879 P = .000	.9444 P = .000

In the 1996 races for the U.S. House of Representatives (see figure 5.7), the partisan balance shifted from one Republican and four Democratic members after 1994 to a split of three Republicans and two Democrats. In the Fourth Congressional District, incumbent Mike Parker retained his seat after switching from the Democratic to the Republican Party earlier in the year. Parker had first been elected as a Democrat in 1988, but the party switch provided Republicans with a two-to-three split before the 1996 election. Parker's opponent, Kevin Antoine, a black appointed city official from the state capital, won only one county (Wilkinson).

Second District Democrat Benny Thompson was able to keep the majority-black and solidly Democratic Delta in his pocket, in spite of the fact that Republicans offered the unique scenario of nominating a black candidate, Danny Covington. Thompson won all counties in the district except Yazoo. Yazoo County, the home of Republican National Committee chair Haley Barbour, had been won by Clinton but had not gone for Democratic gubernatorial candidates in the 1991 or 1995 state elections or the 1992 presidential election.

In the First District, one-term Republican incumbent Roger Wicker faced relatively unknown Democratic opposition and won reelection with a greater than two-to-one margin. The surprising aspect of this race is the fact that this district could be described as the epitome of the Hills region. Progressive in political tradition and Democratic in voting behavior, the First District had continually reelected Jamie Whitten by wide margins, even as the rest of the Hills showed tendencies to become more Republican. To have this district face the reelection of a Republican without meaningful opposition speaks volumes on the current state of the Hills' political sensibilities.

Trent Lott's old congressional district on the Mississippi coast has continued to be an anomaly in recent Mississippi politics. The Fifth District had not been held by a Democrat, nor had the region as a whole voted for Democratic candidates, since the 1970s. Democrat Gene Taylor had surprised pundits by winning the seat in a 1989 special election after having

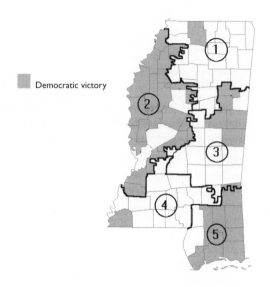

Fig. 5.7. 1996 Mississippi Congressional Elections

lost the regular election only one year before. Given the fact that Clinton never won any of the counties in the district in 1992 or in 1996, Taylor's retaining this seat has been just as surprising to many. However, the combination of a truly conservative bent to his Democratic affiliation and the advantage of incumbency could explain this relatively unusual situation.

Finally, in the Third Congressional District, retiring Democrat G. V. "Sonny" Montgomery left an open seat and a districtwide scramble among Republicans and Democrats alike. The area, part of the Hills region, had been voting for Republican presidential and gubernatorial candidates for a number of years. It was assumed that any Republican nominee would have a natural base of support from Rankin County, bordering the capital of Jackson and one of the state's most Republican counties (Slabach and Breaux 1996), and other pockets of Republican support. The Democrats relied on Democratic voting traditions and the Black Prairie counties. Both the eventual nominees had some name recognition. Republican Chip Pickering had a politically known family and had served as an aide in Washington to Trent Lott. Democrat John Arthur Eaves Jr. laid claim to old supporters from his father's party activism and frequent runs for governor in the 1970s.

The election resulted in another Republican seat and the continued shift within the Hills region. Pickering won fourteen counties with a districtwide total of 61.4 percent. Of the five won by Eaves, one county, Oktibbeha, provided only a five-vote margin of victory.

Where in the Political World Is Mississippi?

Nationally, since the end of World War II, Republicans have been highly successful at capturing the presidency, although they have been less successful in winning congressional seats. However, the year 1994 was a watershed in American electoral politics. Grounded firmly in an ideologically conservative base spearheaded by Representative Newt Gingrich of Georgia, Republicans gained control of both houses of Congress for the first time in almost fifty years and retained control in 1996. Many observers speculate that the cumulative success of the Republican Party at the federal level over the past years has been a primary factor in the development of a two-party system within the state of Mississippi. Certainly, it is easy to agree that the Republican Party in Mississippi has made significant gains in its ability to win elections, capturing a combined five out of seven seats in the U.S. Senate and House, as well as winning reelection for Kirk Fordice, the first Republican governor since Reconstruction. Given these examples, some observers view Mississippi's transformation into a two-party state as the result of a national trend toward more conservative political opinions and voting patterns. Yet this analysis may be incorrect. Mississippi has long been a bulwark of the South's conservative ideals and traditions, and the politics of the state has generally reflected these beliefs. If, as many have suggested, the electoral success of the Republican Party at the federal level embodies a rejection of liberal public policy in favor of more conservative beliefs, it could be argued that Mississippi's conservative political ideology has slowly been adopted by growing numbers of voters in other parts of the nation. In other words, perhaps the electorate in the rest of the country has begun to reflect Mississippi's, and more generally the South's, conservative political nature.

This supposition could be tested in 1999, when Mississippi will have an open-seat gubernatorial election. This election may provide additional insight and information to measure the ideological pulse of Mississippi voters. If Republicans should retain the governor's office, it might strengthen the position of the party within the state. However, if a Democratic candidate should capture the position, it could indicate that the election of Republican governor Kirk Fordice was driven more by candidate personality and less by party ideology. In either case, it may be difficult to analyze the outcome of Mississippi elections in relationship to national trends because statewide elections are not held in conjunction with federal elections and are therefore insulated from the direct influence of national politics.

However, this insulation does not keep Mississippi from influencing national agendas. Mississippi is seeing a resurgence of political power in the federal government. At one time Mississippi could boast of having two of the most senior and powerful members of the House (Jamie Whitten and Sonny Montgomery) and of the Senate (James O. Eastland and John C. Stennis). In fact, at one point the House Appropriations Committee was chaired by Whitten while the Senate Appropriations Committee was chaired by Stennis, who also served as president pro tempore of the Senate. The retirement of these political figures reduced the state's political influence. Now, with the ascension of Trent Lott to Senate majority leader, Mississippi regains some of its old political glory.

Unfortunately, recent studies in anticipation of the 2000 census and reapportionment have shown that Mississippi's influence could once again be jeopardized. The state barely retained five congressional seats following the 1990 census, and from all indications, a seat loss may now be inevitable. Such an occurrence would reduce the state's delegation in Washington, decrease the number of delegates to national nominating conventions, and reduce Mississippi's importance in the electoral college. Beyond that, Mississippi, as do many other states, elects state officials from congressional districts. The loss of one district would require one additional layer of redistricting by the legislature and one more set of submissions to the U.S. Department of Justice for approval under the Voting Rights Act of 1965. Finally, recent Supreme Court decisions regarding majority-black districts will add a new level of scrutiny for any future redistricting efforts, especially when facing the possibility of dividing the state into four rather than five equal portions.

Much of the state's earlier power was based on seniority in Congress, and the same could be said for power within the state legislature. However, the specter of term limits, though defeated, has thrown a new issue into the legislative arena. A second term-limits initiative has already been discussed by supporters of the original effort. The next proposal is likely to be scaled down, applying only to members of the state house and senate. What this means for female, African American, and even Republican legislators only now securing "safe" districts and seniority in the policy process is anyone's guess. Potential ramifications could, however, create both electoral and policy consequences far into the next century.

In 1995, Mississippi elected seven Democrats and one Republican to statewide positions. Democrats continue to control both the state house and senate. Local elected officials are overwhelmingly affiliated with the Democratic Party. These successes appear to be more closely tied to the individual candidates and their issues than to party organizing and party issues.

Of course, this could also be true in the case of the current Republican governor. In short, it might be said that Mississippi voters in the 1990s are more candidate oriented than party oriented. However, party organizations and activities remain important for candidate recruitment and nomination, as well as citizen education. Ensuring a supply of viable candidates rests on organization activities for both parties. This could well be the enduring role for both parties beyond the statutory requirement of administering party primaries. Now that the two parties have ushered in a new era of political competition, it is unlikely that either will easily abdicate its position in Mississippi politics.

The Republican Party has spent decades catching up to the Democrats in Mississippi and eventually surpassing them in organizational acumen. Democrats now find themselves playing catch-up in fund raising and grassroots organizing. The result has been a trend toward more and more successful Republican campaigns at the federal, state, and local levels. However, given the Democratic majority in state and local offices, GOP hopes for the demise of the Democratic Party are unlikely to be realized.

References

Bass, Jack, and Walter DeVries. 1976. *The Transformation of Southern Politics.* New York: Basic Books.

Breaux, David A., Daye Dearing, Don E. Slabach, and W. Martin Wiseman. 1996. "The Three 'Rs' of Mississippi Politics: Unraveling the Impact of Race and Region on Republicanism." Paper presented at the annual meeting of the Southern Political Science Association, 6–9 November, Atlanta, Ga.

Carmichael, Gilbert E. 1996. "Southern Republican Politics, the Mississippi Republican Party: One Candidate's Viewpoint." John C. Stennis Lecture Series. Jackson: Mississippi State University, John C. Stennis Institute of Government.

Gordon, Mac. 1995. "Molpus Chides Fordice for Campaign Tactics." *Jacksonville Clarion-Ledger,* 14 November, 1B.

Key, V. O., Jr. 1949. *Southern Politics in State and Nation.* New York: Knopf.

Krane, Dale, and Stephen Shaffer, eds. 1992 . *Mississippi Government and Politics: Modernizers versus Traditionalists.* Lincoln: University of Nebraska Press.

Sack, Kevin. 1995. "An Underdog Closing In in Mississippi." *New York Times,* 4 November.

Shaffer, Stephen D. 1996. "Public Split between Two Parties." John C. Stennis Institute of Government Political Brief. Jackson: Mississippi State University, John C. Stennis Institute of Government.

Shaffer, Stephen D., Telemate Jackreece, and Nancy Bigelow. 1996. *Stability and Change in Mississippians' Political and Partisan Views: Insights from Fourteen Years of Opinion Polling.* Jackson: Mississippi State University, Social Science Research Center.

Slabach, Don E., and David A. Breaux. 1996. *An Overview of the 1995 Primaries and General Election,* vol. 1 of *Mississippi Votes 1995.* Jackson: Mississippi State University, John C. Stennis Institute of Government.

6

Louisiana: African Americans, Republicans, and Party Competition

Wayne Parent and Huey Perry

On paper, Louisiana looks remarkably similar to its sister states in the Deep South. Louisiana politics in the 1990s, however, remain distinct. The fascinating politics of Huey Long, Earl Long, and Edwin Edwards were only a colorful prelude to the party-switching, racially polarizing, mean and nasty, nationally conspicuous elections involving "Buddy" Roemer, David Duke, Mike Foster, Cleo Fields, Woody Jenkins, Mary Landrieu, and a host of others. Louisiana in the 1990s has been the site of an erratic, often unpredictable, certainly uneven evolution from Democratic dominance to Republican parity and from virtually white-only participation to genuine black political power.

Mississippi, Alabama, and, to a somewhat lesser extent, Georgia and South Carolina mirror Louisiana in politically important demographics like income, education levels, and racial makeup. However, in 1996, when Republican presidential candidate Bob Dole carried all four of those states, Democrat Bill Clinton carried Louisiana in an incredible 12 percent landslide. Louisiana remains the only state in the South with two Democratic senators. Although these Democratic victories involved substantial and usually crucial support from blacks, black candidates still fail to win white support. This chapter will address the unique forces in Louisiana that have tempered, but not stopped, the Republican tidal wave in the Deep South and will also address the emergence of blacks in power and as key players in power politics.

The Emergence of the Republican Party

To be sure, GOP gains in Louisiana have been dramatic. In 1995 Louisianians elected a Republican governor by over a two-to-one margin; in 1996 five of the seven members of the congressional delegation elected were Republicans; in 1996 U.S. Senate candidate Louis "Woody" Jenkins came within six thousand votes of becoming Louisiana's first elected Republican member of that body. Republicans are increasing their numbers in the state legislature (see table 6.1) and winning elections at all levels. Republican voter registration has surged from less than 1 percent in 1960 to over 20 percent (see table 6.2). Republicans have clearly established themselves as equal partners in this two-party state.

The agents of change away from the hundred years of Democratic dominance in Louisiana are similar to those in other states in the South. In 1956 Dwight Eisenhower became the first Republican to carry Louisiana (and, in the Deep South, only Louisiana) with a pro-business "establishment" Republican message that attracted middle-to-upper-income suburbanites. In 1964 Louisiana joined the pattern that established Republican success in the remainder of the Deep South when Republican Barry Goldwater's message of racial and cultural conser-

Table 6.1
Partisan Makeup of Louisiana State Legislature, 1962–1996

	House		Senate	
	Democrats	Republicans	Democrats	Republicans
1962	101	0	39	0
1964	103	2	39	0
1966	103	2	39	0
1968	105	0	39	0
1970	104	1	38	1
1972	101	4	38	1
1974	101	4	38	1
1976	101	4	38	1
1978	96	9	38	1
1980	95	10	39	0
1982	93	11	38	1
1984	91	14	38	1
1986	87	15	34	5
1988	86	17	34	5
1990	89	16	34	5
1992	88	16	34	5
1994	88	16	33	6
1996	77	27	25	14

Table 6.2
Louisiana Voter Registration by Party, 1960–1996 (in percent)

Year	Democratic	Republican	Year	Democratic	Republican
1960	98.6	0.9	1979	89.5	5.3
1961	98.7	0.9	1980	86.5	7.5
1962	98.7	0.9	1981	86.0	8.0
1963	98.5	1.0	1982	85.0	8.4
1964	98.1	1.5	1983	83.5	9.1
1965	97.7	1.6	1984	82.2	10.0
1966	97.9	1.6	1985	79.3	12.8
1967	97.8	1.6	1986	78.1	13.6
1968	97.4	1.9	1987	77.5	14.0
1969	97.4	1.9	1988	75.4	16.4
1970	97.2	2.1	1989	74.8	17.2
1971	96.7	2.2	1990	74.1	17.7
1972	96.0	2.8	1991	73.5	18.1
1973	96.0	2.8	1992	71.5	19.0
1974	95.9	2.8	1993	71.1	19.2
1975	95.2	3.0	1994	70.6	19.4
1976	93.3	3.8	1995	68.4	20.0
1977	92.9	4.0	1996	65.4	21.0
1978	91.8	4.4			

Source: Louisiana Commissioner of Elections

vatism attracted enough middle-to-lower-income whites to carry the state; Republican Ronald Reagan's similar message of strong defense and social conservativism not only carried the state in 1980 and 1984 but also helped George Bush win, although by his smallest margin in the South, in 1988. Republican congressional candidates began winning in the (mostly white) suburban areas surrounding New Orleans, Shreveport, and Baton Rouge and then eventually in (mostly white) rural areas as well.

An examination of the elections leading up the present party system reveals two fairly distinct aspects of Republican appeal. First, as was evident in the Eisenhower victory, is the pro-business, economic appeal to middle-class, white suburbanites. Louisiana's higher proportion of urban centers than Mississippi, Alabama, and South Carolina provides a fertile ground for suburban political messages that obviously resonated in some of Louisiana's consistently strongest Republican parishes; Republicans have been quite successful around Louisiana's largest urban areas of

Jefferson Parish (county) and St. Tammany Parish in suburban New Orleans and the areas in and around Shreveport (Caddo and Bossier Parishes), Baton Rouge (East Baton Rouge and Livingston Parishes), and Lafayette (Lafayette Parish).

The second aspect of Republican appeal was more evident in the Goldwater victory. Republicans carried rural white parishes, especially in Protestant north Louisiana, for the first time. These voters were attracted to Goldwater's opposition to the Civil Rights Act. These conservative policy positions were precursors to the appeal of socially conservative positions on such issues as gun control and prayer in public schools. This second type of Republican voter is now often categorized by using the all-too-limited term "Christian Right." These social/cultural conservatives have formed the second part of the foundation of the Republican coalition in Louisiana.

When Republicans can combine the two appeals of pro-business conservativism and social/cultural conservativism, Republicans are almost impossible to stop. The combination of suburban parishes and rural parishes is a healthy one. Ronald Reagan was probably most adept at combining these messages. Mike Foster, who became only the second Republican elected governor in Louisiana, was also able to win substantial victories in the suburbs and rural areas. If Republicans field candidates that both groups—the pro-business conservatives and the cultural conservatives—find attractive, Republicans will win often in Louisiana.

The Tenacity of the Democratic Party

The continued appeal of the Democrats is quite naturally to other groups. When the 1964 Republican presidential candidate appealed to conservative whites with opposition to the Civil Rights and Voting Rights Acts, black Louisianians of all demographic backgrounds began voting overwhelmingly Democratic. Before the Voting Rights Act, Louisiana's blacks were registered at low rates, mainly because of the restrictions on black voting remedied by that act. Black turnout was higher in south Louisiana than in much of the rest of the Deep South, but still tellingly low. Black votes are concentrated in urban areas (notably Orleans Parish) and many rural parishes along the Mississippi River Delta.

The first significant statewide breakthrough for a black-white Democratic coalition came in the election of Edwin Edwards to the governorship in 1971, after he campaigned hard for black support. He rewarded that support by appointing blacks to visible positions and backing black legislators for leadership positions on reapportionment and important policy positions on education, health, and welfare legislation. Many Democrats like Senators John Breaux and Bennett Johnston followed this successful strategy. However, in 1995, when the first major black candidate for governor made the runoff for governor, friction between black and white Democrats began to show. In that race, which will be covered extensively below, African American congressman Cleo Fields did not receive the endorsement of many of the same white Democratic officeholders that he and many black leaders had supported in previous years.

While black support for the Democratic Party is most noticeable, many whites continued to support the Democrats throughout the Republican realignment that began in the 1960s. The parishes that straddle the Mississippi River between Baton Rouge and New Orleans are the home of a vast chemical industry and of a shrinking group of southern white labor union Democrats. The parishes of Assumption, Ascension, Iberville, St. John the Baptist, and St. Charles are predominantly white and core Democratic parishes. The Catholic, French Acadian parishes concentrated in southwest Louisiana also are part of the Democratic base. This area, which through the past several decades of redistricting roughly makes up the Seventh Congressional District, was the congressional home base of four-term governor Edwin Edwards and current senator John Breaux.

The Uniqueness of the Rules: Louisiana's Open Election System

A brief explanation of Louisiana's unique election system must precede any discussion of Louisiana's contemporary electoral politics. In 1975 the Louisiana legislature, at the urging of Governor Edwin Edwards, adopted an electoral system that was seen as benefiting both the governor and incumbent legislators (Hadley 1985). The system is unique but straightforward. All candidates for office, regardless of party affiliation, run in one election. If any candidate receives a majority of votes cast, that candidate is elected. If no candidate receives a majority, the top two candidates, regardless of party affiliation, compete in a runoff. Unlike the newly adopted California system and similar systems in other states, the Louisiana system allows two Democrats or two Republicans to compete in the final election.

Governor Edwards proposed, and legislators supported, the new system because under it they would often hold an advantage. Incumbents could win outright in the first election, thereby avoiding the cost and unpredictability of running in a general election against an opponent of the other party. However, this unique system can have other consequences as well.

Prelude to 1996: The 1991 and 1995 Races for Governor

As the 1996 elections approached, the two parties in Louisiana were in similar positions. Each had a coalition that was formidable when united but highly vulnerable when divided. To simplify: the Republicans were an uneasy coalition of suburban pro-business conservatives and rural cultural conservatives; the Democrats were a coalition of blacks, some labor union members, and a small number of socially liberal urban whites. Even though the form of the coalitions is similar to those nationally, the proportions and opportunities for disruption are different.

The gubernatorial elections of 1991 and 1995 are particularly instructive. In 1991, in perhaps the most spectacular election in a state with a history of spectacular elections, Louisianians were faced with three major candidates for governor. The first, and early favorite, was incumbent governor "Buddy" Roemer, who was elected in 1987 as a Democrat but had become a Republican while in office, after having alienated the conservative wing by not signing a restrictive abortion bill. The second was two-term former Democratic governor Edwin Edwards. Edwards was initially elected with a black-labor-Cajun coalition that was a winning combination for the Democrats in the 1970s. Edwards had enjoyed high approval ratings until he was tried for racketeering in the middle of his second term; although he was aquitted, the trial tainted his image, and his effectiveness and his approval ratings plummeted. Finally, the ballot included Republican David Duke, who was internationally known as the former grand wizard of the Ku Klux Klan. He had won a seat in the Louisiana House of Representatives and had garnered a striking 40 percent of the vote in his 1990 race for the U.S. Senate against incumbent Bennett Johnston. In the first election Edwards ran first, with solid support of black voters and some labor support. Duke ran second, with a strong showing especially in the rural white areas of north Louisiana. Roemer, who had the support of pro-business Republicans and Democrats who had turned against Edwards after his trial, finished out of the running. Since no one got a majority of the votes, Edwards and Duke were in a runoff.

The Duke-Edwards race offered two choices that were widely disdained by a large proportion of the voters. Democrat Edwards had become unpopular because of perceived unethical and even criminal behavior.

Republican Duke's association with the KKK and use of racist rhetoric caused him to be despised by much of the electorate. Almost all prominent Republican officials refused to support Duke and even endorsed Democrat Edwards. In the end, a bumper sticker summed up the sentiments of much of the electorate: "Vote for the Crook: It's Important." After an election that created an international media circus, Edwards easily won the runoff. The state GOP had not only lost an election but also had to cope with having David Duke as their most visible politician.

The 1995 governor's race illustrated the fact that Republicans were not alone in confronting potentially fatal splits. In that year, several well-known Democrats faced only two Republicans. The Republicans appeared to be in a state of disarray; the candidate endorsed at the state convention, suburban New Orleans state representative Quentin Dastugue, chose not to run, which left former governor Roemer and little-known Democratic state senator Mike Foster, who switched his party affiliation the day he filed to run for office. The same ballot featured four well-known and well-funded Democrats who would have been "firsts" as governors of Louisiana: two women, Lieutenant Governor Melinda Schweggman and state treasurer Mary Landrieu; and African American congressmen Cleo Fields and William Jefferson.

Even though Roemer had lost support from the Christian Right, he was expected to run well because of name recognition. Among the Democrats, Landrieu, who had announced her candidacy a year earlier in a move that angered incumbent governor Edwards (who had not yet announced his own intentions), was seen as the most likely to make a runoff. A Roemer-Landrieu runoff, however, was not to be.

Foster emerged as the choice of the Christian Right. In a brilliant campaign move, he ran as a "Christian and a gun owner" in ads that had this millionaire businessman wearing a welder's cap. In the last few weeks of the campaign, Foster surged to the top of the opinion polls. Fields, who benefited from the exit from the other black congressman's exit from the race, moved into second place, edging out Landrieu and leaving Roemer behind in fourth place.

The Foster-Fields runoff proved to be a nightmare for Democratic cohesion. The feud between Fields and Landrieu erupted as a result of a very heated contest to make the runoff. Fields became upset because Landrieu and others in her campaign allegedly warned African American voters that Fields could not win in the runoff election and that Landrieu could. In effect, the allegation was that African Americans should not waste their vote to achieve symbolic satisfaction when they could help elect someone who would be just as mindful of their interests as Fields.

Fields attacked Landrieu for that allegation, and Landrieu had to deny publicly that her campaign had made such statements. Fields's public criticism of Landrieu probably mobilized enough African American support for him to place second in the election and thus qualify for the runoff. Landrieu blamed her failure to make the runoff on Fields's attack and vented her frustration by not endorsing him. Fields lost to Mike Foster by a landslide.

The 1996 Elections

As Louisiana entered the 1996 elections, both parties had reason for concern about party unity. Democrats had reason to worry after the Fields-Landrieu conflict because now it was Fields's turn to be upset. Landrieu entered the Senate race less than a year after the gubernatorial election and was immediately annointed as the front-runner. Although she slipped to second place in the first election, Landrieu made it into the runoff against Republican state senator Woody Jenkins. Public opinion polls throughout the runoff period indicated an evenly contested campaign. Initially, Fields refused to endorse Landrieu. Although several prominent African American political leaders endorsed her, the majority of African Americans appeared to be taking their cue from Fields. Until Fields decided to endorse Landrieu, African Americans were faced with a very uncomfortable choice: either vote for Jenkins or abstain.

The Democratic Party leadership was in no position to attempt to negotiate between Fields and Landrieu. Fields was upset with the party's white leaders for refusing to endorse him in the gubernatorial election but enthusiastically endorsing Landrieu in the Senate runoff. Fields believed that this double standard was because of his race. It is difficult to argue that Fields's belief had no merit. Ultimately, the national Democratic Party, in the person of Vice President Al Gore, had to intervene to settle the dispute between Fields and Landrieu. The Louisiana contest had national implications, as President Clinton was attempting to reestablish Democratic control of the Senate. Gore persuaded Fields to endorse Landrieu, but Fields's endorsement was weak.

If the Fields-Landrieu conflict was simply a personality clash, it would be difficult to derive any lasting meaning that would facilitate scholarly understanding of Louisiana politics, since personality clashes often occur in American politics. We believe that there was an underlying basis for the Fields-Landrieu feud that helps to promote scholarly understanding of Louisiana politics.

The Fields-Landrieu feud represents a growing tension between African Americans and moderate and liberal whites, currently the two mainstays of the Democratic Party's coalition. This tension is erupting in southern politics faster than elsewhere because the growing Republicanization of political leadership has siphoned away conservative party leaders from the Democratic Party. This development has made it possible for African Americans and moderate and liberal whites to vie for leadership positions in the Democratic Party in the South for the first time since African Americans became active players in the region in the middle 1960s.

Republicans had problems of their own. Despite the tension in the Democratic Party, Republicans were unable to win the seat. In the first election, two Democrats were leading the pack and appeared likely to squeeze the Republicans out of the runoff. In the final weeks of the first election, key Republican leaders began endorsing Jenkins, who was consistently polling best among the Republican contenders. By the final days of the first election, the Republican strategy had worked and Jenkins roared into first place, with Landrieu second.

Jenkins, who clearly represented the more rural conservative wing of the party, had trouble gaining support that might have gone to a more suburban conservative and barely lost the election to Landrieu. Indeed, in the ABC exit poll, 66 percent of self-described moderates voted for Landrieu. Although Landrieu was widely criticized by the Jenkins campaign for being an extremist, primarily because of her pro-choice stance, it was Jenkins who lost the support of the middle. The Republicans, by fielding a candidate who was perceived as too conservative by moderates, missed a golden opportunity to capture an open Senate seat.

Although the Senate race was the most closely watched in Louisiana in 1996, two of Louisiana's seven congressional races had no incumbent running. Republican newcomer John Cooksey won in the newly redistricted Fifth District in rural north Louisiana, and Democrat Chris John won the seat held by Republican convert Jimmy Hayes in southwest Louisiana (Hayes ran unsuccessfully for the Senate seat). Republicans hold a solid five-to-two advantage in Louisiana's congressional delegation.

At the end of 1996 both parties were in a state of conflict and were also highly competitive. Democrats had brought blacks and whites together for a resounding win for President Clinton but had barely found a way to hold on to the Senate seat, even with strong, albeit reluctant, black support for Mary Landrieu. The Republicans had almost pulled together behind a candidate with visible ties to the conservative wing of the party but found themselves short of a victory. This race illustrates well the splits in both parties and suggests that, in years to come, success may well depend on the failure of the opposite party to heal its divisions.

The Development of Black Politics in Louisiana

GOP attainment of parity with the Democrats is only half of the story of Louisiana politics in the last few decades. Equally dramatic is the emergence of African Americans as a potent political force. Blacks in Louisiana, as in most southern states, began to reemerge politically in the immediate post–World War II years. As a result of the well-known and successful efforts by southern states to formally suppress black political participation between 1890 and 1910 (see Kouser 1974), the substantial black political participation that had begun in the Reconstruction era was eventually reduced to a bare minimum between 1910 and 1945 in most southern states. The nation's participation in World War II unleashed a confluence of political, social, and economic forces that opened opportunities for southern blacks to begin redeveloping a political presence. This political reemergence took the form of increased voter registration by blacks. The success of the efforts to suppress blacks politically between 1890 and 1910 and the reemergence of black political participation in the 1940s and 1950s can be seen in table 6.3.

Black voter registration increased dramatically in 1948 and again in 1952. This increase was principally attributable to the U.S. Supreme Court ruling in *Smith v. Allwright*, which prohibited the use of the white primary on the grounds that it violated the Fourteenth Amendment to the U.S. Constitution. The white primary precluded blacks from voting in the Democratic primary, although the small number of blacks who were registered during this period were allowed to vote in the general election.

The white primary essentially denied blacks effective participation in the political process, since the dominance of the Democratic Party meant that the only viable electoral competition occurred in the Democratic primary. Democrats always won the general election because the Republican Party was not strong enough to mount a serious challenge. Realizing that they were denied effective political participation by the white primary system, most blacks were not inspired to attempt to overcome other formal as well as informal efforts to suppress their political participation during this period. After the elimination of the white primary by *Smith v. Allwright*, black voter registration in Louisiana increased considerably in the 1950s and the first half of the 1960s (see table 6.4).

Table 6.3
Black Voter Registration in Louisiana, 1910–1964

	No. Blacks Registered	Est. Black Adult Population	% Black Adults Registered
1910*	730	174,211	0.4
1920	3,533	359,351	0.9
1928	2,054	359,251	0.5
1932	1,591	415,047	0.3
1936	1,981	415,047	0.4
1940	886	473,562	0.1
1944	1,672	473,562	0.3
1948	28,177	473,562	5
1952	107,844	481,284	22
1954	112,789	481,284	23
1956	152,578	481,284	31
1960	156,765	514,489	30
1962	150,898	514,589	29
1964	164,717	514,589	32

Source: James Bolner, ed., *Louisiana Politics: Festival in a Labyrinth* (Baton Rouge: Louisiana State University Press, 1982), 299.

*The data for 1910 are for black males only. Women were not allowed to vote prior to the ratification of the Nineteenth Amendment to the U.S. Constitution in 1920.

The Voting Rights Act of 1965 accelerated the rate of black political participation in the state. African Americans in 1997 comprised 30 percent of the registered voters in the state. There were two major consequences of the increase in black voter registration following the enactment of the Voting Rights Act. One was an increase in the number of moderate and liberal white Democrats elected to office with the help of black voters. The other has been an increase in the number of black elected officials. These two developments occurred chronologically in the order in which they are presented here. One of us (Perry 1996, 1990a, 1983) has suggested elsewhere that this sequence has occurred with enough regularity in the development of black politics to be considered a pattern of black political participation.

Turning to the first impact, the earliest consequence of significantly increased black political participation is usually the election at first of moderate and later of liberal white candidates (Perry 1996, 1990b, 1983). The election of Moon Landrieu, a white liberal and father of Mary Landrieu, as mayor of New Orleans in 1967 occurred precisely in this manner.

Table 6.4
Black Voter Registration in Louisiana, 1965–1996

	Total Voters Registered	Blacks Registered[a]	Blacks as % of Total[b]
1965	1,190,122	163,414	13.7
1966	1,281,919	238,356	18.6
1967	1,285,933	245,275	19.1
1968	1,411,071	279,468	19.8
1969	1,422,900	291,547	20.5
1970	1,438,727	298,054	20.7
1971	1,633,181	347,098	21.3
1972	1,704,890	397,158	22.3
1973	1,712,850	380,490	22.2
1974	1,726,693	391,666	22.7
1975	1,798,032	408,696	22.7
1976	1,866,117	420,697	22.5
1977	1,787,031	413,178	23.2
1978	1,821,026	429,231	23.6
1979	1,831,507	431,196	23.5
1980	2,015,402	465,005	23.0
1981	1,942,941	454,988	23.4
1982	1,965,422	474,238	24.1
1983	1,968,898	476,618	24.2
1984	2,133,363	533,526	25.0
1985	2,175,264	550,225	25.3
1986	2,141,263	549,916	25.7
1987	2,139,861	551,263	25.8
1988	2,190,634	572,133	26.1
1989	2,113,867	552,781	26.2
1990	2,121,302	561,379	26.5
1991	2,103,334	569,603	27.1
1992	2,241,949	626,678	27.9
1993	2,294,043	636,018	27.7
1994	2,257,080	628,578	27.8
1995	2,400,086	689,046	28.7
1996	2,518,896	724,831	28.8

Sources: Data for 1965 to 1979 were taken from James Bolner, ed., *Louisiana Politics: Festival in a Labyrinth* (Baton Rouge: Louisiana State University Press, 1982), 305. Data for 1980 to 1996 were provided by the Office of the Louisiana Commissioner of Elections, Baton Rouge.

[a]Data from Louisiana Board of Registration.

[b]Data from Louisiana Board of Registration.

Similarly, in 1971, black voters exerted a critical impact on the election of Edwin W. Edwards, a U.S. congressman from southwest Louisiana, to the governorship. Edwards defeated state senator J. Bennett Johnston in the Democratic primary principally because of the overwhelming support he received from black voters.

In the general election, Edwards received 202,055 black votes, compared to only 10,709 for Republican Dave Treen (Prestage and Williams 1982). Since Edwards's margin of victory was about 160,000 votes, black support constituted the critical difference. That black voters were able to cast decisive votes for Edwards was attributable to the fact that Edwards and Treen split the white vote, with Edwards receiving 30,000 fewer white votes than Treen (Prestage and Williams 1982, 307–8).

In 1972, state senator Johnston ran successfully for the U.S. Senate seat, receiving the majority of the black vote. Johnston defeated former governor John J. McKeithen. In the 1967 Landrieu election, the 1971 Edwards-Johnston gubernatorial election, and the 1972 Johnston-McKeithen U.S. Senate election, black voters cast the decisive vote for the more progressive candidates. Edwards's 1971 gubernatorial victory and Johnston's 1972 U.S. Senate victory established these two men as fixtures in Louisiana politics for the next 25 years. Edwards and Johnston won easy reelection in 1976 and 1978, respectively, both receiving substantial support from black voters.

The influence of black Louisianians in the 1980 state election was mixed. In the gubernatorial race that year, Edwards could not run for a third term because the state's constitution prohibits a governor from serving more than two consecutive terms. This election occurred the year that Louisiana's new open elections system went into effect. Republican Treen defeated the Democratic candidate, Louis Lambert, despite strong African American support for Lambert.

African Americans had a more positive influence on the 1986 U.S. Senate race. Russell Long, the senior senator, had earlier announced that he was going to retire at the end of the term. John Breaux, a young Democratic congressman, won this race with substantial support from African Americans.

In 1983, Edwards ran for governor against incumbent Republican governor Treen. This was an evenly contested campaign from start to finish, and in the end Edwards won a narrow victory with overwhelming support from African American voters. This was a disappointing defeat for Treen, because he had appointed three African Americans to major positions in his administration and had openly sought the African American vote in the 1983 campaign.

The 1986 Senate race took place against the national backdrop of the 1984 reelection of a popular Republican president. John Breaux, the popular Democratic incumbent, ran against Henson Moore, a popular Republican congressman. Polls conducted deep into the campaign showed Moore leading Breaux by a considerable margin. At just about the time that it was widely believed Breaux was not going to win reelection to a second term, a news story broke that the state's Republican Party leadership had plans to conduct a statewide effort to remove African Americans from the roll of registered voters. This news energized African American voters to turn out to vote at a very high level in support of Breaux. It also caused a fair number of white voters who probably were going to vote for Moore to vote instead for Breaux. There is no doubt that the overwhelming support that Breaux received from an energized African American electorate was responsible for his election.

In the 1990 Senate election, incumbent Democrat Johnston received a very strong challenge from former Klansman David Duke. Although Duke received 60 percent of the white vote, Johnston won the election with overwhelming support from African Americans.

In the 1987 gubernatorial race, Edwards placed second in the open primary election to Buddy Roemer, a congressman from north Louisiana. Edwards decided to drop out of the race and Roemer became governor. In 1991, Edwards ran for governor for the fifth time. This time he placed first in the open primary and entered a runoff against David Duke. Edwards won the election with strong support from African American voters. In 1995, in a historic gubernatorial election, former congressman Cleo Fields from Baton Rouge made the runoff against Republican state senator Mike Foster. Fields was the first African American to run in a runoff election in Louisiana history. Although Fields received substantial support from African American voters, he lost the election by a landslide.

The increase in black voter registration also resulted in large numbers of black elected officials. In 1968, there were 36 black elected officials in Louisiana. Ten years later, in 1978, the number of black elected officials in Louisiana had increased to 333. As Jewel L. Prestage and Carolyn Sue Williams indicate (1982, 306), practically all of these were local officials, most elected from predominantly black constituencies.

It is an axiom of American politics that the higher-level, more prestigious elected offices are the most difficult for blacks to win. Louisiana is no exception. The first black elected to the state legislature, Ernest "Dutch" Morial, was elected to the Louisiana House of Representatives in 1967. After Morial resigned to accept a judgeship, he was replaced in 1971 by Dorothy Mae Taylor, the first black woman ever to serve in the Louisiana legislature. In 1972, seven other blacks were elected to the state house. In 1974, Sidney Barthelemy became the first black ever elected to the state senate. By 1980, the number of blacks elected to the state legislature had increased to twelve—ten in the house and two in the senate (Prestage and Williams 1982, 306–7). Additionally, in 1977, Morial made history for a second time when he was elected the first black mayor of New Orleans.

The 1970s represented a watershed period for black officeholding in Louisiana. During this decade, blacks were able to win election to both houses of the Louisiana legislature and to the mayoralty of the largest city in the state. In the 1980s, the number of blacks elected to the state legislature more than tripled. The city of New Orleans has had a continuous history of black mayoral leadership since Dutch Morial's historic election in 1977. Morial served two terms as mayor and was prohibited by the city's charter from serving a third consecutive term. Morial unsuccessfully attempted to have the voters amend the city's charter so that he could run again.

Morial was succeeded by Sidney Barthelemy, former president of the New Orleans City Council and Morial's chief nemesis on the council. Barthelemy, New Orleans's second black mayor, also served two mayoral terms. Barthelemy was succeeded by Dutch Morial's son, Marc Morial, who was a Louisiana state senator prior to his election as mayor. All three of these African American mayors, except Barthelemy in his election to his first term, won because of overwhelming support from African American voters. In his election to his first term as mayor, Barthelemy ran a deracialized campaign in which he received a majority of the white but a minority of the African American vote (see Perry 1996, 1990a,b,c). Barthelemy defeated in this election a strong African American candidate, William Jefferson, a congressman representing the Second Congressional District, which includes most of New Orleans. Jefferson was the first African American elected to Congress from Louisiana since Reconstruction.

Conclusions

In the last half-century, Louisiana politics has been revolutionized in two ways. First, the Republican Party, once virtually noncompetitive in Louisiana elections, has emerged to achieve near parity with the Democratic Party. Second, African Americans, who make up almost one-third of the population, have overcome suppression to achieve positions of power. In sum, Republicans have won several statewide offices, including the governorship; they control the state congressional delegation; and they have made dramatic gains in the legislature. The party still must contend with internal conflicts before it can become the dominant party in the state. African Americans have gained tremendous ground in breaking registration barriers, winning local offices and congressional seats, but they have yet to overcome the patterns of the past by winning a statewide office.

References

Bolner, James, ed. 1982. *Louisiana Politics: Festival in a Labyrinth.* Baton Rouge: Louisiana State University Press.

Hadley, Charles. 1985. "Dual Partisan Identification in the South." *Journal of Politics* 47 (February):254–68.

Kousser, Morgan J. 1974. *The Shaping of Southern Politics: Suffrage Restriction and the Establishment of the One-Party South, 1890–1910.* New Haven: Yale University Press.

Perry, Huey L. 1983. "The Impact of Black Political Participation on Public Sector Employment and Representation on Municipal Boards and Commissions." *Black Political Economy* 12 (Winter):203–17.

———. 1990a. "Black Politics and Mayoral Leadership in Birmingham and New Orleans." *National Political Science Review* 2:154–60.

———. 1990b. "The Evolution and Impact of Biracial Coalitions and Black Mayors in Birmingham and New Orleans." In *Racial Politics in American Cities,* edited by Rufus P. Browning, Dale Rogers Marshall, and David H. Tabb. White Plains, N.Y.: Longman.

———. 1990c. "The Reelection of Sidney Barthelmy as Mayor of New Orleans." Quoted in Huey L. Perry, "The Evolution and Impact of Biracial Coalitions and Black Mayors in Birmingham and New Orleans," in *Racial Politics in American Cities,* edited by Rufus P. Browning, Dale Rogers Marshall, and David H. Tabb, 2d ed. New York: Longman.

Perry, Huey L., ed. 1996. *Race, Politics, and Governance in the United States.* Gainesville: University of Florida Press.

Prestage, Jewel L., and Carolyn Sue Williams. 1982. "Blacks in Louisiana Politics." Pp. 285–318 in *Louisiana Politics 1982,* edited by James Bolner. Baton Rouge: Louisiana State University Press.

Part III

The Rim South States

7

Virginia: The New Politics of the Old Dominion

Mark J. Rozell

Virginia offers an ideal environment in which to study the changing politics of the South. Once the home of the capital of the Confederacy, it is the first state in the nation to have elected a black governor. Infamous for its support of massive resistance to public school integration in the 1950s and still subject to Justice Department approval of its legislative redistricting because of a poor history of protecting minority voting rights, the state is undergoing a profound demographic transformation that is changing the nature of racial politics and partisan competition. Once a part of the "solid [Democratic] South," Virginia is close to having its first Republican majority legislative chamber since Reconstruction. For many years a Democratic political machine stymied constructive change and kept the party distant from its national organization and leaders, and by the 1980s Virginia Democratic leaders were pointing the way toward a more centrist philosophy that would better promote the party's chances of winning the presidency in the 1990s.

More than in most states, many residents of Virginia are strongly aware of their political heritage, both good and bad. Citizens and leaders wage heated political fights over proposals to build homes or retail establishments on undeveloped lands that were once sites of Civil War battles. Although demographic changes have altered the electoral landscape, much of the political culture of Virginia is conservative in the old sense: enamored of tradition, resistant to change—oftentimes even obviously needed change.

At times the cultural resistance to change has opened the state to ridicule. When Congress approved a national holiday to honor Martin Luther King Jr., the state legislature responded by declaring that date Jackson-Lee-King Day to also honor Confederate heroes Stonewall Jackson and Robert E. Lee. Black members of the state legislature responded on that celebrated date by carrying picture posters of their preferred honorees: Jesse Jackson, Spike Lee, and Martin Luther King.

More recently, the capital city of Richmond was mired for several years in a bitter debate over where to place a statue to a black hometown hero, former tennis star Arthur Ashe, who had died of AIDS. The city council and residents could not agree to place the statue on historic Monument Avenue, which honors Confederate heroes with imposing statues. The city finally agreed to place the statue at a public park.

The historically all-male, state-supported Virginia Military Institute (VMI) attracted national attention when it fought a seven-year-long legal battle with the U.S. Department of Justice to maintain the school's single-sex status. In June 1996 the Supreme Court mandated that VMI admit women. Emotions run deep regarding the Court's decision. In January 1997, GOP state senator Warren Barry addressed the legislative chamber and declared that women had no place at VMI because they are "physiologically different" from men, their presence in the military causes sexual harassment, and "aggressive warrior" men shouldn't be forced "to live in a social slumber party." Most Republican members and some Democrats loudly applauded the speech (Hsu 1997).

For decades the state legislature resisted calls to retire the official state song "Carry Me Back to Old Virginny." Although the lyrics had long been justifiably criticized for being racist, lawmakers defended the song's standing as a bow to tradition. Finally, in 1997 the state legislature struck a compromise in which it approved a measure to grant the song "emeritus" status and to commission the search for a new official state song.

These controversies are illustrative of the modern contradictions of Virginia politics resulting from the reverence to tradition and the need for change. Virginia has progressed enormously in the modern era, yet in many ways it remains a bastion of old-style southern politics.

The Changing Politics of Race and Party Competition

In his seminal work *Southern Politics in State and Nation*, written nearly one-half century ago, V. O. Key Jr. described Virginia as a "political museum piece." He added that "of all the American states, Virginia can lay claim to the most thorough control by an oligarchy" (Key 1949, 19). At that time, the Democratic political machine of Harry F. Byrd dominated state politics. Byrd served as governor of Virginia from 1926 to 1930 and as U.S. senator from 1933 until he retired in 1965. He assembled his machine from the county courthouse organizations of the landed gentry, who preferred stability over economic growth and were fiercely committed to racial segregation.[1]

The machine succeeded in part by restricting participation: in 1945, just 6 percent of the eligible adult population voted in the gubernatorial primary—in a one-party state, the only election that mattered (Sabato 1977, 110). Frank Atkinson described how the state literacy requirement restricted participation by whites as well as blacks. He noted that prospective registrants had to answer extraordinarily difficult questions: for example, How many people signed the Declaration of Independence? or Name the counties in the Twenty-seventh Judicial District. One college graduate who failed the test received a postcard saying, "Yo hav fald to rechister" (Atkinson 1992, 15).

Although the Democratic Party had a minority faction of "antiorganization" members, Key described them as "extraordinarily weak, [having] few leaders of ability, and [being] more of a hope than a reality" (Key 1949, 21). Republicans were few and far between, and their candidates had no hope of winning a general election. In this way, Virginia resembled many other southern states—overwhelmingly conservative, overwhelmingly Democratic. During the 1950s, Virginia's Democratic machine led a massive resistance to school desegregation, choosing to close the public schools rather than obey a federal court order.

Like other southern states, Virginia supported Democratic presidential nominees throughout the early part of the twentieth century. The state's electorate defected to the Republicans only in 1928, when the Democrats nominated a Roman Catholic, Al Smith, who opposed Prohibition. But Byrd himself feuded with Franklin Roosevelt and Harry Truman and dissented from the growing Democratic support of greater civil rights for blacks. Byrd openly expressed his contempt for "Trumanism" and signaled to state Democrats that it was acceptable to vote Republican at the presidential level.

In the 1944 presidential election and thereafter, Virginia supported Republican presidential candidates in every election except the Lyndon Johnson landslide of 1964. In their classic study of southern politics, Earl and Merle Black show that in the period between 1952 and 1964, Virginia was more supportive of Republican presidential candidates than any other southern state (Black and Black 1987, 266). Many of the conservative Democrats of the Byrd machine were more comfortable with Republican presidential candidates than with their more liberal Democratic opponents. In the post-Byrd era, Virginia remained solidly Republican at the presidential level. In 1976, Virginia was the only southern state to back GOP nominee Gerald Ford over Jimmy Carter. When some other southern states were backing Democrat Bill Clinton in 1992 and 1996, Virginia backed George Bush and Bob Dole.

After World War II, the population growth in the southwestern coal-mining counties, the naval activity around Norfolk and Newport News, and the growing number of government workers in the northern Virginia suburbs of Washington, D.C., changed the demographic makeup of the state and weakened the Byrd machine. The influx of black voters and the elimination of the poll tax after passage of the Voting Rights Act further weakened the machine. Byrd machine candidates faced intraparty challenges; most notably, incumbent Democratic senator A. Willis Robertson, father of the Reverend Marion G. "Pat" Robertson, lost a primary election in 1966.

As the national Democratic Party moved to the left, many of the more conservative members of the Byrd machine turned to the Republican Party. Moreover, the influx of relatively affluent professionals in northern Virginia and of promilitary citizens in the Norfolk region provided growing numbers of Republican voters. In 1969, with the Byrd machine in disarray, Virginia elected as its first Republican governor a progressive on race issues who drew attention by enrolling his daughter in the predominantly black Richmond public schools. The Republicans won again in 1973, with a candidate who took a less progressive stance on race issues, and in 1977, with a moderate candidate.

By the late 1970s, Republicans held both the U.S. Senate seats and nine of Virginia's ten seats in the U.S. House of Representatives. Virginia moved toward the Republican ranks more rapidly than did other southern states. Between 1951 and 1980 Virginia elected more Republican governors than any other southern state (Sabato 1983, tables 4–7).

The period of Republican control ended in 1981, when Democrat Lieutenant Governor Charles S. "Chuck" Robb defeated Attorney General J. Marshall Coleman for the governorship. A former Marine married to former president Lyndon Johnson's daughter, and the lone Democrat elected to statewide office in 1977, Robb won the governorship as a fiscal conservative with progressive views on race and social issues. Robb's philosophical positioning proved to be an ideal combination for the evolving Virginia electorate.

Robb's victory and gubernatorial leadership had a profound impact on state politics. He presided over a booming state economy and used revenues from the economic upturn to increase spending for education. Robb could have easily won a second term, but the state constitution prohibits gubernatorial succession.

Nonetheless, Robb had established for the state Democratic Party a winning strategy: to court the Byrd Democrats and some Republicans with strong appeals to fiscal conservatism, and to energize the moderate and liberal wings of the Democratic Party with progressive appeals on race, education, and social issues.

The 1980s, the Reagan-Bush era, were the heyday of the Virginia Democratic Party at the state level. In the 1981, 1985, and 1989 elections Democrats swept all three statewide offices (governor, lieutenant governor, attorney general).

In 1985 the incumbent attorney general, Gerald Baliles, like Robb before him, ran as a fiscal conservative with progressive views on race and social issues. He easily defeated a more conservative opponent. Most significantly, Virginia attracted national attention for electing a black and a woman to the other state offices. State senator L. Douglas Wilder, a grandson of slaves, confounded analysts by handily winning the lieutenant governor race, making him the first black elected to statewide office in Virginia. State delegate Mary Sue Terry won the office of attorney general with 61 percent of the vote, becoming the first woman elected to statewide office in Virginia.

The significance of Wilder's victory in 1985 to racial politics in Virginia should not be understated. At the time, Wilder was substantially more liberal than the leadership of the state Democratic Party. It was no secret that such figures as Governor Robb had serious reservations about Wilder's electability, and some even tried to recruit other leading Democrats to challenge him for the nomination. But when Wilder won the nomination, Robb and other Democrats solidly backed his candidacy, despite predictions that a black candidate would sink the entire statewide ticket. Political scientist Larry Sabato was widely quoted in statewide media when he boldly stated that Wilder's odds of winning were worse than a hundred to one and when he declared the statewide ticket with a black and a woman "too clever by half." The comments exacerbated an already overheated climate of controversial rhetoric regarding the impact of Wilder's race on the elections, and at the candidate's urging, campaign manager Paul Goldman turned up the heat again when he angrily denounced the political scientist as "in danger of becoming the Dr. Schockley of Virginia."[2]

Wilder's victory permanently put to rest the question of whether a black could win statewide office in Virginia. When others went out of their way to draw attention to Wilder's race, he campaigned throughout the state as a traditional southern politician and even ran televised ads in rural communities featuring a rather rotund white sheriff with a thick accent offering his strong support for the Democrat.

What made many Democrats and analysts uncomfortable about Wilder was his unabashed liberalism and preference for playing by his own rules rather than being guided by the leadership of other public figures. Wilder publicly criticized the national Democratic Leadership Council, a group of prominent party moderates then led by Robb, as a pseudo-Republican organization. He was openly critical at times of Governor Baliles's leadership and policy priorities. Wilder and Robb openly feuded with each other with a testy exchange of letters in which Robb characterized the lieutenant governor as not a good team player and Wilder vented his anger at Robb for allegedly taking too much credit for the lieutenant governor's victory.

Although Wilder was at times openly disdainful, Robb left office in January 1986 with enormous popularity—so much so that in 1988, incumbent GOP senator Paul Tribble chose to step aside rather than be challenged by Robb. The Republicans, resigned to their fate, nominated a weak candidate who had never held elected office.

The GOP nonetheless made a bold move by nominating a black minister, the Reverend Maurice Dawkins, to challenge Robb. A fiery speaker with ample experience working with black churches throughout the state, Dawkins claimed that he could put together an electoral majority by appealing to both Republicans and Democratic-leaning blacks with a Jack Kemp–like philosophy of inclusive conservatism. At a post–nominating convention press conference, reporters asked him how he could seriously believe that a conservative Republican would attract the support of blacks. He responded that the black community is not monolithic and quipped, "We're a lot like white folks in that regard."[3]

Dawkins campaigned vigorously in black churches throughout Virginia trying to promote a message of self-reliance and anti–welfare state feeling. Ultimately his conservative message was a difficult sell in the black community. He attracted only 16 percent of the black vote (and just over 30 percent of the white vote) and 29 percent overall against the popular former governor.[4]

In 1989 Wilder led the statewide Democratic ticket as the gubernatorial nominee. Although many party leaders continued to harbor reservations about his electability, they uniformly backed his candidacy. Despite his clear victory in 1985, many critics speculated that his race would prohibit him from winning the governorship of a former Confederate state.

Wilder's candidacy attracted substantial national and international attention because he stood to become the nation's first elected black governor.[5] That a grandson of former slaves stood to accomplish this goal in the state that was the home of the capital of the Confederacy made his possible election all the more intriguing. A content analysis of the press coverage of Wilder's campaign found that elite newspapers helped to boost his campaign with laudatory treatment of what was possibly history in the making (Rozell 1991).

It became clear during the campaign that despite all of the attention paid to Wilder's race and—a year after the odious Bush presidential campaign ads featuring menacing-looking black criminal Willie Horton—the possible temptation for GOP candidate Marshall Coleman to inject subtle racial appeals, neither candidate drew strong attention to the race factor. Indeed, during the campaign and especially during his term as governor, Wilder was more likely to endure criticism from prominent black leaders for downplaying race or for not having been a leader in the civil rights movement than from opponents for exploiting race for political gain.

Wilder won by the slimmest margin for a statewide race in Virginia history. With a record turnout of nearly 1.8 million voters (66.5 percent of registered voters), Wilder's margin of victory was only 6,741 votes.[6] On election night, exit polls projected that Wilder would win by a margin of at least 5 percent, and some news stations early on stated that he had won comfortably, only to backtrack later on as the precincts reported throughout the night that the election was too close to call. Journalists and pollsters later said that many of the voters had lied in exit polls in order to appear racially progressive. That explanation, although credible, angered many citizens who felt that injecting racial motivations into voting patterns had tainted the state's accomplishment in electing a black governor. The state's flagship newspaper, the *Richmond Times-Dispatch*, ran a political cartoon featuring a cigar-chomping white man with a Ku Klux Klan outfit telling the exit pollster that he had just voted for Wilder.

Despite the narrowness of victory and speculation that racially motivated voting nearly cost Wilder the election, the national media celebrated his win as a historic achievement. The three national newsweeklies prominently featured stories on Wilder's victory with the titles "The End of the Civil War" *(U.S. News and World Report)*, "The New Black Politics" *(Newsweek)*, and "Breakthrough in Virginia" *(Time)*.[7]

The state Democratic Party surely had much to celebrate from its sweep of statewide offices in the three 1980s elections. In large part this success could be attributed to the party's use of convention nominations, which led to the selection of electable centrist candidates. That stood in contrast to the party's poor showing in the 1970s, when such candidates as liberal populist Henry Howell prevailed in primary nominations. A string of statewide defeats convinced the party that it could nominate better candidates in conventions than in primaries—a judgment that proved correct.

Yet there was evidence of a Republican resurgence at the grass roots as the party worked vigorously to recruit good candidates for local offices. The Republicans in the 1980s had continued their steady, incremental gains in membership in the Virginia General Assembly, enough so that by 1989, party members could discuss with credibility the possibility of someday taking control of one or even both legislative chambers. In 1967 the Democrats controlled thirty-four of forty Senate seats and eighty-five of one hundred seats in the house of delegates. By the end of the 1980s the GOP had picked up four seats in the senate and twenty-five in the house, giving them ten of forty and thirty-nine of a hundred seats, respectively. It appeared that a few good election cycles could give the GOP control of at least one legislative chamber for the first time since Reconstruction (see table 7.1).

Aiding the GOP cause was the fact that Wilder had a troubled governorship during a period of economic recession. The era of state budget surpluses and economic growth had ended, and Wilder had to govern during a period of government retrenchment. State agencies and employees had become accustomed to better-than-usual government support from the Democratic administrations of Robb and Baliles and expected more of the same treatment from Wilder. With entirely premature thoughts of

Table 7.1
Partisan Composition of Virginia General Assembly, 1971–1997

	House			Senate		
	Dem.	Rep.	Ind.	Dem.	Rep.	Ind.
1971	73	24	3	33	7	0
1973	65	20	15	34	6	0
1975	78	17	5	35	5	0
1977	76	21	3	34	6	0
1979	74	25	1	31	9	0
1981	66	33	1	31	9	0
1983	65	34	1	32	8	0
1985	65	33	2	32	8	0
1987	64	35	1	30	10	0
1989	59	39	2	30	10	0
1991	58	41	1	22	18	0
1993	52	47	1	22	18	0
1995	52	47	1	20	20	0
1997	51	48	1	20	20	0

national office, Wilder committed his administration to a no-tax-increase pledge and vowed to cut government spending to keep the state budget balanced, as required by Virginia law. He consequently angered traditional Democratic constituency groups, especially in education and social services, as he promoted program cuts and state salary freezes.

As Wilder championed his fiscal conservatism and basked in the praises of such unlikely supporters of the former liberal as the *National Review* editorial board and the libertarian Cato Institute, he planned an ill-fated run for the presidency in 1992. The governor's frequent travels out of state to raise his national profile resulted in an angry Virginia electorate and a popular mocking bumper sticker that read "Wilder for Resident." Wilder further angered Virginians with an ongoing, very public feud with Senator Robb and with state legislators from the northern Virginia region who believed that his policies were slighting the area of the state that had delivered his election.

Indeed, the geographic base for statewide Democratic candidates is in the northern Virginia communities of Alexandria, Fairfax City, Falls Church City, and Arlington and along what is known as the "urban corridor"—a densely populated stretch of land from these northern Virginia communities south to Richmond and east along the coast in the Hampton Roads–Tidewater region. Excepting the far-southwest coal-mining communities, which have a strong labor union presence, the modern Republican base begins west of the urban corridor and covers many of the state's rural areas. On election night in 1989, television maps of voting showed a thin stretch of land along the urban corridor that voted for Wilder, while the vast portion of the state chose Coleman. Yet Wilder won with heavy urban support, and Coleman later quipped that he wished that Virginia had a statewide version of the electoral college.

Although Wilder left office with ebbing popularity, he could credibly claim some important accomplishments. He indeed kept the state budget balanced for four years and never raised the state income tax. He took the leadership in successfully promoting adoption by the general assembly of a bill that limited gun purchases to one gun per month. That he did so in a state with a strong pro-gun-rights tradition was no small feat (Wilson and Rozell 1998).

During Wilder's term, the Democratic-controlled state legislature and the state GOP feuded over redistricting proposals that ultimately resulted in the creation of a black-majority district. Consequently, in 1992, Democrat Robert C. Scott of Newport News became the first black elected to Congress from Virginia in over a century. Yet by early 1997 a panel of U.S. district court judges ruled that the district was unconstitutional because it had been drawn specifically to suit racial considerations (Nakashima 1997).

Wilder's governorship nonetheless proved a liability to state Democrats as they sought to extend their string of electoral victories in 1993. The Democrats nominated their two-term attorney general, Mary Sue Terry, for governor. The GOP nominated former state delegate and one-term congressman George Allen. The GOP campaign quickly seized on public disgust with the feud between Robb and Wilder, as well as the anger toward Wilder for how he conducted his governorship and more anger toward Robb for a series of scandalous allegations about his personal behavior while governor. In his nomination acceptance speech Allen introduced his theme of asking voters to send a message to the "Robb-Wilder-Terry" Democrats, a refrain repeated throughout the election season.[8] The refrain caught on so well that Terry actually ran television commercials reminding voters that her name was "Mary Sue, not 'Robb-Wilder.'"

Terry ran a spectacularly inept campaign, as she alienated her base by denouncing Clinton's economic policies, refusing to accept help from labor union groups, and waiting until the final days of the campaign to seek Wilder's support. She lacked presence and performed poorly in the media campaign and in debates with Allen. Terry lost in a GOP landslide that gave Allen 58 percent of the vote. In an extraordinary case of ticket splitting in a statewide election in Virginia, voters rejected GOP lieutenant governor nominee Michael Farris, a former Moral Majority leader. Farris ran 12 percentage points behind the top of the ticket, while the attorney general candidate, James Gilmore, easily won with 56 percent of the vote.[9] Perhaps more significantly to the GOP, for the first time in the twentieth century the party's candidates for the house of delegates won a majority of the votes statewide, although the Democrats retained control of a majority of the seats.

In the 1994 U.S. Senate campaign the GOP nominated Iran-contra figure Oliver North to challenge incumbent Chuck Robb. Because of widespread reporting of personal scandals, Robb appeared the most vulnerable incumbent Democrat in the nation at the beginning of the year. But because the GOP had nominated probably the only party figure who was even more tainted by scandal, Robb won reelection. What made the race particularly noteworthy was that because the two major parties had nominated controversial candidates, two major figures, Marshall Coleman and Doug Wilder, ran as independents. Ultimately, Wilder assured Robb's reelection by dropping out of the race, a decision made necessary by Wilder's disappointing polling numbers even among black voters. While Wilder was in the race, Robb astutely cultivated the support of key African American leaders in the state; as his efforts began to pay off, it became clear that

Wilder lacked a constituency. Coleman stayed in the race as the moderate GOP alternative to North and pulled 11 percent of the vote.

Also key to Robb's victory was the unrelenting effort of GOP senator John Warner to oppose North's candidacy. Warner acted as Coleman's benefactor and convinced the former attorney general to enter and stay in the race. Movement conservatives who backed North fumed that Coleman and Warner were "traitors" to the party and vowed to take revenge on the senator when he ran for reelection in 1996.

Exit polling by Mitovsky International found that North's base included white born-again Christians and gun enthusiasts. North received about 60 percent of the vote from either of those groups and 81 percent among churchgoing gun enthusiasts. Among the 57 percent who fell into neither category, Robb took 65 percent of the vote. Blacks were crucial to Robb's victory, giving him over 96 percent of their votes.

Although most of the rest of the nation underwent significant change with the 1994 "Republican Revolution," Virginia opted for the status quo, reelecting its senator and ten of its eleven House members. But in 1995 the Virginia GOP determined that the previous year's Republican strategy to nationalize congressional elections offered lessons for state legislative campaigns. Under the leadership of Governor Allen, early in the election season all but two of the GOP candidates for state legislative offices in 1995 met on the state capitol steps to unveil their ten-point "Pledge for Honest Change," modeled after the "Contract with America."

The goal of the pledge was to have the GOP candidates statewide adopt a unified message that included not only their policy commitments contained in the pledge but also their plea to the voters to give the governor legislative majorities in the general assembly. Governor Allen characterized the elections as a referendum on his leadership and staked his future conservative agenda on winning party control of the legislature (Rozell and Wilcox 1995). His effort failed, in large part, polls revealed, because the public perceived Allen as pushing too far to the ideological right and believed that legislative majorities would enable him to push such initiatives as easing gun ownership restrictions and limiting abortion rights. Yet the GOP did pick up two state senate seats to give them twenty of forty seats in the upper chamber, the GOP's best showing since Reconstruction.

The 1996 Elections

In 1990 Republican senator John Warner was such a strong candidate for reelection that the Democratic Party chose to let him run unopposed. His reelection made him the first Republican in Virginia history to win statewide three times. He did not get a free ride in 1996. He faced a serious intraparty challenge in the primary from a candidate backed by the Christian Right and then a historically well financed Democrat in the general election. Warner survived both challenges and earned a fourth term in the U.S. Senate.

That Warner faced a serious challenge for renomination is telling of the divisive nature of the modern Virginia GOP. The Christian Right currently dominates the leadership and activist base of the state GOP. Warner is very popular in the state, but most of the Christian Right despises him, largely because he refused to back Michael Farris's campaign for lieutenant governor in 1993 and because he openly opposed Oliver North in 1994 (Rozell and Wilcox 1996, chaps. 4 and 5).

Like the Democrats since the 1980s, the modern Republican Party in Virginia has relied on convention nominations to choose its statewide candidates. The GOP has held open primaries for statewide offices only three times in the modern era: in 1949, 1989, and 1997.[10] Dedicated party activists, who tend to be more conservative than rank-and-file voters who identify with the GOP, dominate these conventions. The party conventions have enabled a committed group of social movement activists to take control of party nominations away from Virginia's establishment Republicans, who tend to be more moderate and more like John Warner.

The most important event for Warner's 1996 reelection probably was a 16 April federal court decision upholding an obscure provision of a Virginia law that enables an incumbent to choose his preferred method of renomination. It was clear that Warner could not win renomination in a party convention dominated by the Christian Right. In fact, given the state party's loyalty rule—that only those who pledge to support the party's nominees and faithfully did so in the most recent elections could vote at the party's convention—it was questionable whether Warner would even be credentialed at his own party's nominating convention. When Warner invoked his right to choose a primary, the state party, led by the chair, challenged the constitutionality of the law that gave the senator that power. When the federal judge upheld Warner's right to an open primary, his renomination was nearly assured.

Former Reagan Office of Management and Budget director James Miller challenged Warner in the primary. Miller had unsuccessfully but credibly challenged North in the 1994 GOP convention. Because of strong Christian Right antipathy toward him, Warner had to take seriously the primary race. The state GOP lacked a tradition of primary nominations and no one knew what the turnout would be and who would show up. But most believed that Christian Right activists would mobilize against Warner.

Perhaps the best evidence of the divide between GOP activists and rank-and-file party voters was the dramatic difference between the results of a state party convention preference poll and the open primary vote. In the former, held just a little over a week before the primary, Miller bettered Warner by a three-to-one margin among the more than two thousand party delegates. But Warner won the primary nomination by a two-to-one margin.

In the general election Senator Warner faced Democrat Mark Warner, a former state party chair with a personal fortune of over $100 million. The Democratic nominee spent over $10 million of his own fortune to wage a credible campaign against a very popular incumbent. Virginians reelected the senator with 53 percent of the vote. Senator Warner garnered 19 percent of the black vote—a better-than-usual showing for a Republican. That blacks comprised only 15 percent of the voters in this election and that Mark Warner received a significantly lower percentage of black votes than other Democrats who have won statewide proved important to the senator's reelection. The Democrat Warner was unable to overcome the senator's 58 percent showing among whites.[11]

In the presidential campaign, given the state's record of voting in modern elections, Virginia should have been an easy win for Republican Bob Dole. Although he ultimately won Virginia with 52 percent of the vote, Dole evidenced his weakness as a candidate by devoting campaign resources to shore up his support in the state. Polls late in the campaign showed Clinton and Dole running even in the state. Therefore, unlike other recent GOP candidates, Dole made several visits to Virginia, including one very late in the campaign. The former senator's wife and daughter each made several trips to Virginia to campaign for him. That Dole had to divert precious campaign resources to a reliable Republican presidential state was good news to President Clinton's campaign.

The 1997 Elections

The 1997 elections continued the trend toward what seems to be inevitable GOP control of the state legislature. Although there were no elections for the state senate (they occur in 1999), the election of a Republican lieutenant governor held out the prospect for real GOP control of that chamber, as the lieutenant governor presides over that body and breaks tie votes.[12] The GOP came closer than ever to taking control of the house of delegates. At this writing in 1997, the Democrats have a slim

51–48 advantage (the independent member is a conservative who generally votes with the Republicans). One seat won by the Democrats by eight
votes is being contested, and there is some discussion in political circles of
possible party switching.

For the second straight election the GOP won a statewide landslide.
Former attorney general James Gilmore handily defeated Democratic
lieutenant governor Donald Beyer, and the GOP swept all three statewide
races. Gilmore won largely on the basis of a proposal to eliminate the
unpopular property tax levied primarily on automobiles.

For the first time, a Christian Right candidate won statewide office in
Virginia, largely on the strengths of the Gilmore landslide and the candidate's own unique ability to reach out to diverse constituencies. State
senator Mark Early, a Christian social conservative and the author of the
state's recently passed law requiring parental notification before teenage
abortions, won a landslide victory in the race for attorney general despite
Democratic charges that Early was an extremist on social issues.
Although a strong social conservative, after serving ten years in the senate, Early had compiled a credible record as a mainstream legislator with
credentials in various policy arenas. The GOP candidate had professed
support for affirmative action programs and some pro-labor-union sentiments, and he attracted the endorsements of the former head of the state
NAACP, several labor leaders, and the editorial page of the *Washington
Post*.

Conclusion: Prospects Ahead

The Virginia political landscape has undergone profound changes in the
modern era. As recently as the heyday of the Reagan era in the mid-1980s,
it was almost unimaginable to discuss the possibility of Republican control of the general assembly and the plausibility of a Democratic presidential candidate carrying the state. The reality today is that by picking
up merely one seat in the upper chamber and one or two in the lower
chamber, the GOP would take control of the Virginia legislature for the
first time in the modern era. That would also make Virginia the first
southern state with GOP control of both the legislative and the executive
branches. And with Bill Clinton's credible showing in the state in 1996, it
is now conceivable that a Democratic presidential candidate could win
Virginia in 2000.

Virginia has emerged as a truly competitive two-party state. Demographic changes, especially the phenomenal population growth of the

Washington, D.C., suburbs of northern Virginia, have altered state politics forever. Whereas rural legislators for years chaired crucial committees in the general assembly and routinely blocked legislation favorable to northern Virginia, today a bipartisan alliance of members representing the urban corridor exercises substantial influence over state policy and spending priorities. Much of this change is attributable to population shifts that have given a larger percentage of legislative seats to urban and highly populated suburban areas.

These changes have also created a political environment more conducive to minority-group interests than ever before, although most analysts of state politics would agree that much remains to be done. The black community now constitutes 17 percent of the state's population, and no Democrat is able to win statewide office without a very substantial percentage and turnout of black voters.

The modern GOP is making an increased effort in the state to reach the black community. When the state party chair in 1994 said that he didn't favor spending a lot of time cultivating black support for the GOP campaign because it was not "cost-effective," many party members openly criticized the comment and made it clear that they did not share this view. Although success has been minimal, the Christian Right movement in the state GOP has actively reached out to the black community to try to forge alliances on social issues where conservative white evangelicals and many blacks share similar views. In one successful endeavor, Christian Right and black church leaders throughout the state formed a coalition to fight a proposal to legalize riverboat gambling.

As in the rest of the South and the nation, black voters remain loyal to the Democratic Party. The increasingly progressive new state population and efforts by both parties to reach out to blacks are signs of the political evolution and maturation of a state with a poor historical record on racial issues. The civil rights era brought profound changes for blacks in Virginia in protecting their basic rights under the law in voting, education, employment, and housing.

Today much of the politically active black community is pursuing state policies that will help to alleviate vast disparities in spending in school districts and promote stronger social services and better educational opportunities at all levels. Despite much change, Virginia remains strongly committed to a view of fiscal conservatism that favors limits on spending programs. For now, leaders of both parties generally agree that, despite cutbacks in some federal domestic programs and more of the burden for services being placed on the states, Virginia should not adopt big-government approaches to solving public problems.

Notes

1. For an excellent biography of Byrd and analysis of his lasting impact on Virginia politics see Heinemann 1996.

2. For a detailed description of these events and of Wilder's campaign, see Yancey 1988, esp. 59, 103–4.

3. Press conference attended by author, 11 June 1988, Roanoke, Va.

4. Results provided by state board of elections.

5. The nation's only previous black governor was appointed to the office. Lieutenant Governor P. B. S. Pinchback of Louisiana, a Republican, held the office of governor for about four weeks while the elected governor underwent an impeachment trial.

6. Results provided by the state board of elections.

7. All three issues were 20 November 1989.

8. Republican nominating convention attended by author, 5 June 1993, Richmond, Va.

9. Results provided by state board of elections. For a detailed analysis of the 1993 statewide elections, see Rozell and Wilcox 1996, chap. 4.

10. In 1997, the state GOP held an open primary for the first time for the office of attorney general.

11. "Virginia Senate Exit Poll Results," (http://www.allpolitics.com), 6 November 1996.

12. At this writing, there will be one special election to fill the senate seat held by Mark Early, the attorney general elect. Should the GOP hold that seat, in 1998 the party will have effective control of one house of the state legislature for the first time in the modern era.

References

Atkinson, Frank. 1992. *The Dynamic Dominion: Realignment and the Rise of Virginia's Republican Party since 1945.* Fairfax, Va.: George Mason University Press.

Black, Earl, and Merle Black. 1987. *Politics and Society in the South.* Cambridge: Harvard University Press.

Heinemann, Ronald L. 1996. *Harry Byrd of Virginia.* Charlottesville: University Press of Virginia.

Hsu, Spencer C. 1997. "Fairfax Senator Decries Coeducation at VMI." *Washington Post,* 10 January, B1, 4.

Key, V. O., Jr. 1949. *Southern Politics in State and Nation.* New York: Knopf.

Nakashima, Ellen. 1997 "House District in Virginia Ordered Redrawn." *Washington Post,* 8 February, A1, 10.

Rozell, Mark J. 1991. "Local v. National Press Coverage of Virginia's 1989 Gubernatorial Campaign." *Polity* 24, no. 1 (Fall): 69-89.

Rozell, Mark J., and Clyde Wilcox. 1995. "Governor Allen's Big Chance." *Washington Post,* 29 October, C8.

————. 1996. *Second Coming: The New Christian Right in Virginia Politics.* Baltimore: Johns Hopkins University Press.

Sabato, Larry. 1977. *The Democratic Party Primary in Virginia: Tantamount to Election No Longer.* Charlottesville: University Press of Virginia.

————. 1983. *Goodbye to Goodtime Charlie: The American Governorship Transformed.* 2d ed. Washington, D.C.: Congressional Quarterly Press.

Wilson, Harry, and Mark J. Rozell. 1998. "Virginia: The Politics of Concealed Weapons." In *The New Politics of Gun Control,* edited by John Bruce and Clyde Wilcox. Lanham, Md.: Rowman & Littlefield.

Yancey, Dwayne. 1986. *When Hell Froze Over.* Dallas: Taylor.

8

North Carolina: Conservatism, Traditionalism, and the GOP

Thomas A. Kazee

For nearly half a century, students of southern politics have discussed, and often disagreed about, the essential nature of North Carolina politics. The Tar Heel State has enjoyed a reputation as a progressive exception to the reactionary politics of the South, a view given academic credence half a century ago with the publication of V. O. Key's *Southern Politics in State and Nation* (1949). Key concluded that North Carolina was a "progressive plutocracy," with a distaste for factionalism, corruption, and Jim Crow. He noted that the state had committed itself to public education for blacks at the turn of the century and had earmarked significant resources for improved public transportation and that its major university was regarded for its tolerance and academic freedom. With respect to race, the "state has a reputation for fair dealing with its Negro citizens" (206). Most important for our purposes, he argued that the good-government commitment of the majority Democrats was due to the presence of a small but important Republican minority: "The dominant faction of the Democratic Party, thanks to the Republicans, possesses a relatively high degree of discipline, and the party as a whole has a consciousness of being and of responsibility" (223). We thus see in Key's analysis the foundation stones of the prevailing view of North Carolina politics for the two decades following publication of *Southern Politics:* a strong and unusually disciplined (by southern standards) Democratic Party, a progressive character, and a well-entrenched but modest Republican Party.

Subsequent assessments of North Carolina politics have challenged this interpretation. Writing in 1975, Peirce described North Carolina as a state of "paradoxes," concluding, "behind every fact which can be cited as proof of its progressiveness lurks another which suggests just the opposite" (113). Bass and DeVries were less charitable in their 1976 book on southern politics, entitling the North Carolina chapter "The Progressive

Myth" (218). In it, they asserted that "good government . . . has come to mean government sympathetic to business interests" (226). Luebke's 1990 study echoes this theme, contending that the state's near-legendary investments in highways and public education "were serving the interests of a narrow economic elite" (2).[1] Many commentators have noted as well the pervasiveness of race as a feature of North Carolina politics. Willis Smith's victory over Frank Porter Graham in the 1950 Democratic primary for a U.S. Senate seat included a campaign in which Smith workers distributed thousands of handbills proclaiming, "White People WAKE UP Before It Is Too Late . . . Do you want Negroes working beside you, your wife, and your daughters in your mills and factories?" (Luebke 1990, 17). Republican Jesse Helms, who has won five U.S. Senate elections, is often accused of using thinly veiled racial appeals in his campaigns, the most famous of which was a 1990 television ad in his race against Harvey Gantt, an African American architect and former mayor of Charlotte. The ad managed to merge several anti-Gantt themes into a single image; it shows a white hand crumpling a rejection letter (ostensibly from a potential employer) as the text on the screen claims: "Harvey Gantt supports Ted Kennedy's racial quota law" (Jamieson 1992, 98). Helms's most recent reelection campaign emphasized Gantt's links with gay groups. Responding to Gantt's charges that he had received money from Taiwanese interests, Helms said, "I'll tell you what I'll do, I'll go to the bank and borrow that amount of money and give it back if Mr. Gantt will give back the money he's received from the homosexuals and the labor unions" (Monk and Leonnig 1996, 10A).

There are two North Carolinas, in fact, and it is in that division that we can begin to understand the most important development in the state's politics this century: the emergence of Republicanism and the creation of a competitive two-party system. North Carolina is committed simultaneously to "progress"—that is, to the politics of economic development—and to the maintenance of traditional values and political views, such as resistance to activist government. Politicians and community leaders advocating the pro-development view, whom Luebke calls "modernizers," believe that growth often requires an active government—one willing to raise taxes if necessary (Luebke 1990, 20–21). They see racial strife and a "deferential social structure" as obstacles to economic growth; accommodation, not resistance, is most likely to further the state's economic and political interests. Traditionalists, on the other hand, are skeptical of changes in the status quo, for such changes may create economic and social disruption (18). The modernizers, they argue, are far too willing to raise taxes and tolerate big government. Economically, traditionalism translates into support for tobacco farmers and related businesses and the textile and furniture industries. Traditionalists value Protestantism and are often threatened by movements advocating or protecting civil rights for blacks and gays, feminism, and labor.

North Carolina, in short, embraces both the traditional values of the Old South and the "entrepreneurial individualism" of the New South (Black and Black 1987, 29). In describing these New South values, Black and Black capture both their appeal and their potential costs:

> In the entrepreneurial version of individualism, pursuit of self-interest, primarily the making and keeping of wealth, is the cardinal value despite potentially disruptive consequences for the larger society. Such entrepreneurs promoted changes—particularly visible in the more advanced Peripheral South states—that brought about greater economic diversity, augmented state power structures, and established truly large cities. (29)

This entrepreneurial policy emphasis, though initially established within the context of one-party, Democratic dominance, has particular resonance for modern Republicanism. "The purpose of state action," Black and Black argue, "was not to subsidize or support have-nots or have-littles, but to subsidize the institutional and individual creators of wealth" (29).

The modernizer-traditionalist divide is not defined simply by partisanship. Indeed, modernizers and traditionalists are in both parties. Within the Democratic Party, for example, one could argue that the political clout of traditionalism has checked the modernizing (i.e., "progressive") tendencies of some of North Carolina's most prominent Democratic politicians, such as former governor Luther Hodges and governor and senator Terry Sanford, as well as current governor (elected four times) Jim Hunt. Hodges and Sanford were nationally regarded as moderate-liberals, owing in part to their associations with John F. Kennedy; Hodges served in Kennedy's cabinet and Sanford made an early commitment to Kennedy's 1960 presidential campaign. Both, however, though generally supportive of an economic development agenda, were very cautious in their support for the civil rights agenda. For his part, Hunt has loudly parted ways with the national Democratic leadership on the tobacco issue, supports the death penalty, and, one analyst argues, is perceived by the politically influential business sector in North Carolina "not as a liberal but as a hard-headed pragmatist who understood the economic underpinnings of the state" (Snider 1985, 46).

For the GOP, although Helms and other prominent Republicans, such as the late senator John East and former congressman David Funderburk, fit the traditionalist profile, the battle between the old guard and the new guard (more comfortable with a state government active in promoting economic development) has defined the party in the last thirty years. The Republicans have elected two governors since 1972: James Holshouser, who served one term, and James Martin, a former congressman who served consecutive terms from 1984 to 1992. Both were, Luebke argues, modernizers; indeed, Holshouser's gubernatorial primary win in 1972 came against former congressman Jim Gardner—who had endorsed George Wallace for president in 1968 and once described himself as an "early Jesse Helms" (Luebke 1990, 184). Martin is a former chemistry professor described in *The Almanac of American Politics, 1984* as "more interested in promoting free market economics than he is in the cultural agenda about which Jesse Helms is so concerned" (Grant and Ujifusa 1983, 890).

Conservatism and Traditionalism

In sum, North Carolina is a state that is struggling to accommodate change and resistance to change, a battle seen clearly in its recent political history and in today's inter- and intraparty divisions. This is not a battle between liberalism and conservatism, however, for conservatism—which may share some political goals but isn't the same as traditionalism—is without question the majority preference in the politics of the state, as it is in the South as a whole. "When southerners are queried about their ideological preferences," Black and Black conclude, "the collective thrust of their responses reveals a region in which conservatism flourishes and liberalism withers" (1987, 213).

The majorities won by recent Republican presidential candidates, especially nominees who unapologetically espouse a conservative philosophy, reveal North Carolina's conservative bent (see table 8.1). Liberal Democrats Hubert Humphrey and George McGovern won less than 30 percent of the North Carolina vote in 1968 and 1972, respectively, and Walter Mondale and Michael Dukakis did only marginally better. Notably, Republicans George Bush and Bob Dole carried the state against southern Democrat (and self-conscious moderate) Bill Clinton.

The most compelling evidence of the primacy of conservative ideology in the state's politics is the near complete rejection of liberalism as a label. Liberalism is certainly not dead in North Carolina, and coalitions of liberals and moderates can produce election victories in the state (though more often in county or district elections than in statewide races). In most of the

Table 8.1
Presidential Election Results in North Carolina, 1968–1996

	Democrat	%	Republican	%
1968	Hubert Humphrey	29.2	Richard Nixon	39.5
1972	George McGovern	28.6	Richard Nixon	69.8
1976	Jimmy Carter	55.3	Gerald Ford	44.2
1980	Jimmy Carter	47.2	Ronald Reagan	49.3
1984	Walter Mondale	37.9	Ronald Reagan	61.3
1988	Michael Dukakis	41.7	George Bush	58.0
1992	Bill Clinton	42.7	George Bush	43.4
1996	Bill Clinton	44.3	Bob Dole	49.0

Note: Third-party candidates not included. Significant third-party totals: 1968, George Wallace, 31.3%; 1980, John Anderson, 2.9%; 1992, Ross Perot, 13.7%; 1996, Ross Perot, 6.7%.

Sources: Mebane Rash Whitman, "The Evolution of Party Politics," *North Carolina Insight*, September 1995, 81–98; *North Carolina Manual*, North Carolina Department of the Secretary of State; North Carolina State Board of Elections.

state, however, candidates who successfully claim the conservative label are more likely to win than those who do not. Most candidates, Democratic and Republican, embrace conservatism—or at least avoid any association with liberals or liberalism. The problem for Democrats in statewide elections is to distance themselves from the national Democratic Party and to run as moderates and modernizers. This strategy can work but may become increasingly tenuous as Republican inroads at all levels of the state's politics penetrate more deeply. Such lower-level successes will generate a growing pool of Republican activists and would-be candidates for higher office, so that Democrats are likely to face higher-quality Republican opposition in the future. But even in today's politics, the moderate-modernizer Democrat has no guarantee of success when running against a rhetorically skilled Republican who can meld conservative and traditionalist ideas. Thus, Jesse Helms can win even when running against the otherwise invincible Jim Hunt.

But what is conservatism? Is it the modernizer conservatism of a Jim Martin, or is it the traditionalist conservatism of a Jesse Helms? The problem for the traditionalists is that many North Carolinians are turned off by what they see as the darker side of the traditionalist agenda (racial and sexual intolerance, most notably). Thus we see the challenge facing North Carolina Republicans today: can they put together the two pieces of the majority puzzle? The key to their success, it would seem, is to marry conservative economic philosophy, with its heavy emphasis on the free market and small government, with traditionalist political and social philosophy, with its suspicion of change and emphasis on traditional social and moral values.

This challenge is essentially the same problem Republicans have faced throughout the South, and the GOP's answer has been the development of their much discussed "Southern Strategy." Aistrup (1996) argues that the Republican Party's goal in the South, seen most clearly in the appeal of Ronald Reagan, is to bring together Old South voters committed to a traditionalist agenda of Christian fundamentalism and status quo maintenance and New South voters who favor small government, a strong military, and support for the free market. These voters see in Reagan's philosophy common ground on such issues as affirmative action, family values, deficit reduction, and welfare reform. "A major facet of the Reagan issue strategy," Aistrup concludes, "is that it presents a coherent economic philosophy to the southern voters" (42). The flip side of the strategy is to characterize the Democrats as the party of big government, tax-and-spend, and minority preference, ultimately to "make it seem socially unacceptable to be a Democrat" (42). This strategy is largely responsible for the ascendance of the GOP throughout the South, and it has produced in North Carolina, for the first time this century, real and sustained party competition. Will this translate to Republican dominance? Perhaps not, for the marriage of the traditionalist and conservative/modernizer comes at some cost. Blacks are likely to see little in the coalition that benefits them, and women may also be uncomfortable in a coalition that rejects abortion rights and guarantees of gender-blind policies. In addition, some voters, regardless of race or gender, may be offended by a politics that is perceived to be exclusionary and intolerant. Nonetheless, the Big Story in North Carolina politics in the latter third of the twentieth century is the emergence of the Republican Party.

Republican Growth in North Carolina, 1972–1996

The most distinctive aspect of Republican expansion in North Carolina is its breadth. Republican candidates have enjoyed some success at every level, from presidential to local races. The improvement in GOP fortunes, which started in the 1960s, gradually began to reverse a pattern of Democratic hegemony that dated to Reconstruction. Until 1968, for example, Democratic presidential candidates had carried the state in every election this century, save one. In 1928, legendary governor Furnifold M. Simmons led a so-called Hoovercrat revolt against Al Smith, New York's "wet" (i.e., anti-Prohibition) Catholic governor. In 1968, however, Richard Nixon won a three-way contest against Hubert Humphrey and American Independent Party candidate George Wallace, who finished second in the state. Since then, Republicans have won North Carolina six of seven times. Only in 1976, when former Georgia governor Jimmy Carter defeated Republican Gerald Ford, have the Democrats won the Tar Heel State's electoral votes. Bill Clinton twice lost the state by relatively narrow margins—demonstrating that even a southern Democrat with arguably moderate credentials has a difficult time cracking what has become a solid Republican preserve in presidential contests.

In congressional elections, Republican successes have been less sweeping but no less significant. The GOP has won seven of nine U.S. Senate races since 1972, with Jesse Helms winning five times. Two other Republican candidates have won: Helms protégé John East defeated incumbent Robert Morgan in 1980, and Lauch Faircloth upset incumbent Democrat and former governor Terry Sanford in 1992. North Carolina Senate elections are remarkably competitive; no candidate since 1972 has won more than 54.5 percent of the vote, and the mean vote for GOP Senate candidates during that time has been 50.2 percent.

U.S. House elections in North Carolina are also closely contested. As table 8.2 shows, Republicans held between two and five House seats from 1972 to 1992 but gained an eight-to-four majority with the Republican takeover of the House in 1994.[2] During the last decade, the North Carolina delegation has undergone especially rapid changes; only four of the members of the delegation serving in the 105th Congress were serving ten years ago in the 100th Congress—and one of those members, Democrat David Price, lost his seat in 1994 and regained it in 1996. The present six-to-six split is tenuous, for four of the incumbents, all Democrats, won by 55 percent or less of the vote in 1996.

Control of the governor's mansion has mirrored the competitive state of North Carolina politics. It would be accurate, though probably misleading, to say that the Democrats win only as long as they nominate Jim Hunt. Hunt has won four times, in 1972, 1976, 1992, and 1996, struggling a bit only in 1992 when he defeated Jim Gardner 53 percent to 43 percent. In every other election since 1972 the Republican candidate for governor has won. In 1972, James Holshouser became the first Republican to win in this century, and Jim Martin followed with relatively easy wins over Rufus Edmisten in 1984 and Bob Jordan in 1988. Hunt, Holshouser, and Martin all fit Luebke's modernizer profile, so it seems reasonable to conclude that North Carolina's voters prefer state executives who will push an aggressive economic agenda, perhaps leaving articulation of a social

Table 8.2
North Carolina Seats in the U.S. House, 1972–1996

	Total Seats	Democratic	Republican	Republican Vote Percentage
1972	11	7	4	45
1974	11	7	4	35
1976	11	9	2	35
1978	11	9	2	40
1980	11	9	2	44
1982	11	9	2	45
1984	11	6	5	48
1986	11	8	3	43
1988	11	8	3	44
1990	11	8	3	46
1992	12	8	4	48
1994	12	4	8	57
1996	12	6	6	52

Sources: Mebane Rash Whitman, "The Evolution of Party Politics," *North Carolina Insight,* September 1995, 81–98; W. Lee Johnston, "North Carolina: V. O. Key's Progressive Plutocracy, Almost Fifty Years of Janus-Faced Politics" (paper presented at the Southern Political Science Association Meeting, Atlanta, Ga., November 1996).

agenda to House and Senate incumbents. This pattern is consistent with Black and Black's contention that federal elections in the South "provide the Republican far right with more targets and symbols to deploy against their opponents than do the more mundane and practical agendas of state politics" (1987, 316). The rhetoric of North Carolina's recent Senate races underscores this ideological emphasis. In 1980, for example, John East blasted incumbent Democrat Robert Morgan for the Panama Canal "giveaway." In 1984, Jim Hunt's television ads attempted to link Jesse Helms with right-wing death squads in El Salvador. And in 1996, Helms complained about the media's role in the Senate campaign: "the self proclaimed media sit in their ivory towers and virtually manage the campaign of my opponent. . . . I long ago became accustomed to the liberal dogma that they spout forth" (Monk and Leonnig, 1996, 10A).

Since elections for national office and the governorship provide voters with sufficient information to cast votes on grounds other than partisanship, perhaps the most valid measure of Republican strength in North Carolina is the party's success in capturing state legislative and local offices. Table 8.3 reveals a pattern of relatively gradual Republican growth in the 1974–1992 period, followed by a dramatic jump in 1994—an election in which the Republicans gained control of the state house and were within two votes of the Democratic majority in the senate. The Democrats recaptured seven house seats and eight senate seats in 1996, though the Republicans retained their house majority by two votes.

The Republicans have also made gains at the local level. In the 1994 elections, the GOP won 39 percent of county commission seats across the state and gained control of forty-two of one hundred county boards of commissioners—up from twenty-seven boards controlled after 1992 (Whitman 1995, 88).

Finally, Republican Party registration has continued an upward movement that began to accelerate in the 1980s (see table 8.4). By the mid-1990s, roughly one-third of voters registered as Republicans. It is difficult to overestimate the significance of Republican registration in a region in which Democratic affiliation was, until relatively recently, the ticket to participation in the Democratic Party primary—which was the only meaningful election for most offices.

Table 8.3
Partisan Distribution of North Carolina State Legislative Seats, 1972–1996

	House				Senate			
	Democratic	%	Republican	%	Democratic	%	Republican	%
1972	85	71	35	29	35	70	15	30
1974	111	93	9	7	49	98	1	2
1976	114	95	6	5	46	92	4	8
1978	105	88	15	12	45	90	5	10
1980	96	80	24	20	40	80	10	20
1982	102	85	18	15	44	88	6	12
1984	83	69	37	31	38	76	12	24
1986	85	71	35	29	40	80	10	20
1988	74	62	46	38	37	74	13	26
1990	82	68	37*	32	36	72	14	28
1992	78	65	42	35	39	78	11	22
1994	52	43	68	57	26	52	24	48
1996	59	49	61	51	30	60	20	40

Sources: Mebane Rash Whitman, "The Evolution of Party Politics," North Carolina Insight, September 1995, 81–98; W. Lee Johnston, "North Carolina: V. O. Key's Progressive Plutocracy, Almost Fifty Years of Janus-Faced Politics" (paper presented at the Southern Political Science Association Meeting, Atlanta, Ga., November 1996).

*1 independent member

Table 8.4
Registration of North Carolina Voters, 1974–1996 (in percent)

	Democratic	Republican	Unaffiliated
1974	73	24	3
1976	72	24	4
1978	73	23	4
1980	71	25	4
1982	70	24	6
1984	70	26	4
1986	69	27	4
1988	65	30	5
1990	64	31	5
1992	61	32	7
1994	59	33	8
1996	56	34	10

Sources: W. Lee Johnston, "North Carolina: V. O. Key's Progressive Plutocracy, Almost Fifty Years of Janus-Faced Politics" (paper presented at the Southern Political Science Association Meeting, Atlanta, Ga., November 1996); *North Carolina Manual,* North Carolina Department of the Secretary of State.

The Political Geography of North Carolina

The data presented above draw with broad brush strokes the picture of Republican Party growth. A more complete understanding of that growth is possible by looking carefully at the patterns of partisan support across the state, for North Carolina is divided into relatively distinct political regions. Key, for example, described the sectional character of the state's politics, noting that factions within the Democratic Party roughly corresponded to an east-west division and that Republican support was largely concentrated in the mountainous west. These divisions were of more than symbolic importance; for many years the Democrats semiformally rotated U.S. Senate seats and the governorship between the east and the west (Key 1949, 219).

Various analysts have defined the regions within North Carolina in slightly different ways (Key 1949; Edsall and Williams 1972; Lamis 1990; Luebke 1990).[3] For purposes of this analysis, I use a formulation that best captures the most important political and economic divisions. By this construction, North Carolina is composed of four areas: the East, Western Piedmont, Urban Piedmont, and Mountains (see figure 8.1).[4]

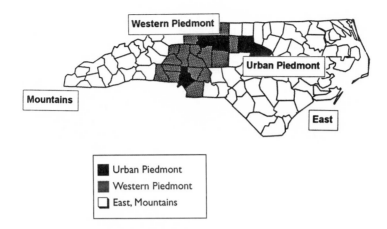

Fig. 8.1. North Carolina Political Regions

The East contains fifty-three counties and, in 1995, 33 percent of the state's registered voters. It is the state's least Republican region, with 20 percent of eastern voters registering with the GOP. The region is distinctive for its relatively large black population (average county percentage: 36 percent) and agricultural economy, much of which is tobacco related. Luebke reports that in 1984 the East contained the ten top-ranking counties in terms of farm income (1990, 67). The region has also had considerable out-migration of blacks (Peirce 1975, 125–26) and is the most economically stressed region of the state.

The Western Piedmont's eighteen counties, in which reside 22 percent of the state's registered voters, differ from their eastern cousins. Counties in this region have an average black population of 12 percent, and agriculture is less prominent; indeed, Luebke refers to this region as North Carolina's "industrial heartland" and notes its relatively diversified manufacturing base (1990, 67). The Western Piedmont, with 42 percent GOP registration, is the most Republican region in the state.

The Urban Piedmont (shown in black in figure 8.1) is a collection of noncontiguous counties that contain all of North Carolina's major cities. The region is economically, politically, and culturally powerful within the state and has been a magnet for attracting nonmanufacturing employers, including banks and insurance companies. Its six counties hold 31 percent of the state's registered voters, with an average Republican percentage of 32 percent. The average black percentage in Urban Piedmont counties is 26 percent. The region is politically diverse, ranging from the mainstream Republicanism of Charlotte to the overt liberalism of university communities such as Chapel Hill. As such, it reflects well the divisions in the state between traditionalist and modernist politics. Charlotte's congressional district, for example, has elected a Republican House member since 1952, yet the city gave President Ronald Reagan a cold reception on a 1994 visit when he criticized court-ordered school busing. Charlotte had implemented a busing plan in the early 1970s and prided itself on its relative success in dealing with a racially charged issue.

The Mountain region, with twenty-three counties, holds 14 percent of the state's registered voters. These counties are more Republican and white than the norm in North Carolina, averaging only 7 percent black population and 41 percent GOP registration. The Mountain region's affinity for Republicanism can be traced historically to its lack of slaves, non-cotton economy, and discomfort with secession. Like the East, the Mountain counties could be in better shape economically; a large number of workers are in low-wage industries, the region has a relatively low per capita income, and unemployment has been higher than in most other parts of the state (Luebke 1990, 68).

The Geography of Republican Growth

Partisan change can be measured by analyzing fluctuations in psychological identification with parties, party registration, and electoral support for candidates. Though party identification and formal party registration are important indicators of party strength, these measures are somewhat problematic in the South. Party registration may be slow to change, as southerners are reluctant to abandon long-held commitments to the "Democracy" or to forfeit their opportunities to vote in Democratic primaries. Moreover, the erosion of party identification, or dealignment, weakens the link between self-professed party preference and voting behavior. Ticket splitting and partisan defection make declarations of partisan affinity less valid measures of party strength (Fleer, Lowery, and Prysby 1988, 109–10). For our purposes, the success of a party's candidates in the best measure of party vitality (Bullock 1988, 220).

To measure regional changes in support for the GOP in North Carolina, the focus here is on four types of elections: presidential, gubernatorial, U.S. Senate, and the Council of State. The latter set of offices includes North Carolina's attorney general, treasurer, auditor, secretary of state, and the commissioners of agriculture, labor, and insurance. The performance of Republican candidates running for these positions is an especially useful measure of party strength, for voters' knowledge of Council of State nominees is likely to be less than their knowledge of candidates for high-profile offices. The measure used here is an average of county support for Republican candidates for attorney general and auditor; these offices were selected because the resulting county averages closely approximate the overall level of support for all Council of State positions in the two years selected for analysis.

For each county, the overall measure of support for the Republican Party is measured as an average of the Republican vote received by the GOP candidates for president, governor, U.S. Senate, and Council of State in 1976 and 1996.[5] These years were selected because (1) in both 1976 and 1996, presidential, gubernatorial, U.S. Senate, and Council of State elections were held (with one exception: no Senate election was held in 1976; the 1978 election is used to calculate the 1976 average); (2) both years include the most prominent Democratic (Jim Hunt) and Republican (Jesse Helms) politicians in the recent history of the state; and (3) in both elections the Democrats nominated moderate southern governors for president, minimizing the distortion produced by northern liberals on the ticket and, as in 1984, a landslide Republican victory.

Figure 8.2 presents the geographic distribution of Republican support in North Carolina in 1976 and 1996. The heavily shaded counties are those

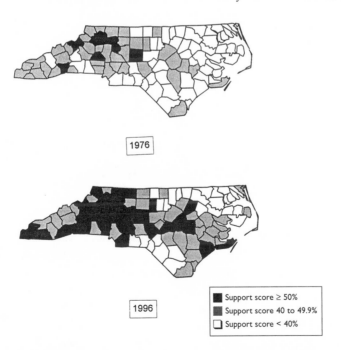

1976

1996

■ Support score ≥ 50%
■ Support score 40 to 49.9%
☐ Support score < 40%

Fig. 8.2. Support for the Republican Party by County, 1976 and 1996

in which the Republican Party support score exceeded 50 percent, and the unshaded counties are those in which Republican support was less than 40 percent. Lightly shaded counties are those in which the party support score ranged from 40.0 to 49.9 percent. The 40 percent and 50 percent demarcation points were selected because a party's ability to compete seriously depends on winning a substantial proportion of the vote, on average, in important elections. The 50 percent division recognizes that competing seriously and winning are two different things; a support score in excess of 50 percent reveals a county in which the Republicans are winning at least some, if not most, elections.

In the mid-1970s the Republicans were clearly in a subordinate position, with a party support score of 50 or more in only eight of one hundred counties; in sixty counties, the GOP had a support score of less than 40, despite the fact that one component of the measure, U.S. Senate voting, had produced a Republican winner during that period (see table 8.5).

Table 8.5
Republican Party Support Scores by North Carolina Region, 1976 and 1996

	East	Urban Piedmont	Western Piedmont	Mountains	Entire State
			1976		
Less than 40%	81	33	61	17	60
	(43)	(2)	(11)	(4)	(60)
40.0% to 49.9%	19	67	17)	65	32
	(10)	(4)	(3)	(15)	(32)
50% or more	0	0	22	17	8
	(0)	(0)	(4)	(4)	(8)
Overall region	32	42	45	46	38
support score	(53)	(6)	(18)	(23)	(100)
			1996		
Less than 40%	45	33	0	0	26
	(24)	(2)	(0)	(0)	(26)
40.0% to 49.9%	42	67	11	35	36
	(22)	(4)	(2)	(8)	(36)
50% or more	13	0	89	65)	38
	(7)	(0)	(16)	(15)	(38)
Overall region	40	41	57	52	46
support score	(53)	(6)	(18)	(23)	(100)

Note: The first entry in each instance is the percentage of counties in each region with specified support scores. The number in parentheses is the actual number of counties in that category.

Note also the distinctive regional character of Republican support. In no county in the East did the GOP have a support score higher than 50, and the party's score reached 40 in only ten of the region's fifty-three counties (19 percent). The Urban Piedmont counties were slightly more Republican, though in all counties in the region support remained below 50 percent. Even in the regions of greatest GOP success, the Democratic Party dominated most elections. Republican support scores reached 50 percent in only four Western Piedmont counties and four Mountain counties. Overall GOP scores for the four regions reflected this partisan division, with the East's 32 score considerably lower than the scores for the other regions, which ranged from 42 to 46.

The partisan picture in 1996 was much different. GOP support fell below 40 percent in only twenty-six counties, all in the East, and in a plurality of thirty-eight counties the Republican score topped 50 percent. Even Democratic hegemony in the East had been broken, as Republican penetration in the East neatly subdivided areas of greatest Democratic strength into a northern segment of counties mostly bordering Virginia and a southern segment of counties on the South Carolina state line. The western regions have become an area in which the Republican Party is, at worst, competitive in most elections and, at best, dominant. This is especially true of the Western Piedmont; fully 89 percent of its counties had support scores over 50 in 1996. The overall regional scores testify to the dramatic improvement in Republican fortunes in the Tar Heel State. The party support percentage jumped 8 points in the East, 12 in the Western Piedmont, and 6 in the Mountains; only in the Urban Piedmont did the GOP fail to expand, as support scores for these counties fell by 1 point.

Molding a Successful Electoral Coalition

The substantial increase in Republican voting in North Carolina during the last two decades demonstrates the power of a modernist-traditionalist Republican coalition. At the presidential level, for example, Ronald Reagan's potent combination of economic and social conservatism carried the state in both 1980 and 1984, winning more than 61 percent of the vote in the latter election. George Bush and Bob Dole, less able to articulate convincingly the social conservative message, also won in the state, but by more modest margins.

Below the presidential level, the victories of modernizer governors and traditionalist U.S. senators—sometimes in the same election year—reveal the ideological ambivalence at the core of North Carolina politics. At the gubernatorial level, successful Republican candidates James Holshouser and Jim Martin, both modernizers committed to expanding business and attracting new industries to the state, won in part because they took traditionalist positions on key issues that resonate with socially conservative Tar Heel voters. Martin, for example, voted against the Martin Luther King holiday while a member of Congress and opposed North Carolina funding of abortions for poor women (Luebke 1990, 32–33). Indeed, Jim Hunt nicely demonstrates the power of assuming a pro-business but socially traditional image. Four-time winner Hunt, a modernizer to the core, nonetheless personally opposes abortion and touts his teetotaling image (28).

In U.S. Senate and House elections, traditionalist Republicans have won their share of elections, including victories by Jesse Helms, John East, David Funderburk, and Lauch Faircloth. The closeness of their wins (Funderburk, in fact, lost a U.S. Senate primary in 1986 and in 1996 lost his House seat) suggests that voters otherwise willing to vote for Republicans are dismayed by the perceived stridency of traditionalist appeals.

The characteristics of GOP growth are perhaps best revealed by taking stock of regional differences in party success. As table 8.5 shows, Republicans have made major gains since 1976 in the East, Western Piedmont, and Mountains. The East was an area of strength for George Wallace in 1968. White voters in this socially conservative region have supported traditionalist candidates, regardless of party, like Wallace and Helms. For example, in 1968, Wallace won 79 percent of the counties where blacks were more than 25 percent of registered voters (Luebke 1990, 163).[6] Helms's emphasis on social issues, maintenance of the racial status quo, and support for tobacco appeals to traditionalist eastern Democrats; counties there gave Helms 50 percent of the vote, on average, in 1996. These voters, often called "Jessecrats," have known Helms since his Tobacco Network commentaries in the 1960s and early 1970s (Fleer, Lowery, and Prysby 1988, 100; Snider 1985). This support doesn't necessarily transfer to other Republicans, however; GOP gubernatorial candidate Robin Hayes won, on average, only 35 percent of the vote in the eastern counties in 1996, and Bob Dole won only 42 percent.

The most solid area of GOP support in North Carolina is the Western Piedmont, an area with well-developed Republican organizations and a history of voting for traditionalist candidates. On average, Western Piedmont counties gave Ronald Reagan 70 percent of the vote in 1984 and turned out in large numbers in Jesse Helms's contentious reelection contest against Jim Hunt in the same year. Helms's strategists worked hard to produce a large blue-collar vote for their candidate in this region heavily dependent on manufacturing. Their efforts were apparently successful, as Helms won over 60 percent of the vote in seven of the Western Piedmont counties that had above-average turnout (Luebke 1990, 152).

Historically the most reliable, if no longer the most substantial, area of Republican support has been the Mountains. Support for the GOP in this region is a historical legacy of the nonplanter economy of western North Carolina, and the party has a well-developed organizational infrastructure in most Mountain counties. This region has become more competitive as modernizers and traditionalists battle for a public that is often attracted to populist appeals—appeals that don't fit neatly into the modernist or traditionalist camps. The Eleventh U.S. House District, the westernmost district in the state, changed hands four times in the 1980s.

The region of the state least attracted to traditional candidates is the Urban Piedmont. Its six counties are certainly not monolithic with respect to ideology or partisanship; the Ninth District, which includes Charlotte and Mecklenburg County, has elected a Republican House member for almost half a century, while the Twelfth District—a majority-black district running through much of the Urban Piedmont—has elected Mel Watt, an African American liberal. The battle in this region is largely over the nature of modernism, however; Republicans from this region tend to be relatively moderate and committed to a pro-business, expansionist philosophy. In *Dixie Rising,* Peter Applebome offers an apt characterization of Charlotte, the largest city in the Urban Piedmont: "God and Mammon— a desire to do good and a desire to do well—are knitted together in Charlotte like threads in an intricate pattern" (1996, 155). Jesse Helms ran more poorly in this region against Jim Hunt in 1984 than in any other area.

Helms and the Limits of Traditionalist Appeals

To ensure continued growth and to consolidate gains already made, North Carolina Republicans must maintain the precarious alliance between traditionalism and modernism. Keeping the ideological peace is necessary not only to ensure the support of the growing number of registered Republicans in the state but also, more critically, to appeal to registered Democrats and independents who are, for the most part, politically conservative. The GOP wants also to attract the large number of new residents in the state, many of whom are conservative and Republican but have moved to the state from parts of the country less attracted to a socially conservative agenda (Morrill and Leonnig 1996, 9B).

Maintaining the peace is difficult, however, for modernizers and traditionalists disagree on important core issues. With respect to race, for example, "modernizers came to see segregation as impeding the influx of capital that could reduce North Carolina's dependence on textiles and tobacco" (Luebke 1990, 28). Traditionalists, on the other hand, oppose governmental intervention aimed at remaking the racial status quo and resent preferential policies such as affirmative action. Republican officeholders such as Jim Martin may successfully negotiate this narrow ideological line, or they may, as in the case of Jesse Helms, eschew entirely the modernist approach and celebrate a traditional, socially conservative ideology.

In at least one key respect, Helms has been successful because he understands the fundamental nature of North Carolina politics: a majority of North Carolinians are conservative, and a traditionalist will, all other things being equal, win an election if he or she is seen as the conservative standard-bearer. As Charlie Black, a Republican consultant and adviser to Helms in his recent win over Harvey Gantt, said, "In a Helms-Gantt race you've got a pretty classic confrontation between a liberal and conservative, and the history that does matter is the conservative almost always wins" (Morrill and Leonnig 1996, 9B). Though Black oversimplifies the ideological clarity of the choice presented to voters, the basic truth of his statement is supported strongly by evidence from the 1984 Hunt-Helms race. This rare clash of state political titans pitted a Democratic modernizer with one foot in the traditionalist camp against an assertive and unequivocal conservative traditionalist. Many Tar Heel voters liked both candidates, as indicated by election outcomes preceding and subsequent to the 1984 race. When confronted with this clear choice, most of these voters opted to support Jesse Helms.

Table 8.6 compares the vote by region for each candidate in his last election preceding the 1984 Senate contest. Jesse Helms had defeated John Ingram, 54.5 percent to 45.5 percent, in 1978, and Jim Hunt had convincingly defeated I. Beverly Lake, 62.3 percent to 37.7 percent, in 1980. Helms largely held his own against Hunt in the East, where his average county percentage dropped off 4 points, and improved over his 1978 performance in the Western Piedmont (by 4 points) and the Mountains (by 2 points). Only in the Urban Piedmont, with its commitment to modernist government (and the relative liberalism of its university communities) did Helms's percentages decline substantially. Support for Jim Hunt, on the other hand, dropped precipitously in the two areas of deepest traditionalist sentiment, the East and the Western Piedmont, and also lost ground, though to a lesser degree, in the Urban Piedmont and Mountains. It is not surprising, of course, that both candidates were unable to maintain their previous election performance levels in a race against much

Table 8.6
Regional Vote for Helms and Hunt in 1984 and Preceding Election (in percent)

	Helms			Hunt		
	1978	1984	Change	1980	1984	Change
East	51	47	-4	70	53	-17
Urban Piedmont	53	43	-10	69	57	-12
Western Piedmont	57	61	+4	55	39	-16
Mountains	53	55	+2	54	45	-9

Note: Entries for each election year are averages of the percentage of the vote received by each candidate in all counties in the region. For Jesse Helms, the preceding election was the 1978 Senate race; for Jim Hunt, the preceding race was the 1980 gubernatorial election.

tougher opposition. Helms's appeal, however, was simply more resilient than Jim Hunt's. William Snider, the former editor of the *Greensboro News and Record*, said of Helms after his most recent reelection win, "I think Jesse is like an old badger. He's up in a hole and you can't get at him" (Christensen and Krueger 1996, 20A).

The 1984 campaign typified the kinds of appeals Helms has used to attack his Democratic opponents in each of his contests. His opponents, he reminds Tar Heel voters, are too liberal, not sufficiently committed to North Carolina (i.e., traditional) values, and too willing to promote the interests of African Americans and to ignore the interests of whites. In 1972, a Helms ad declared, "He's one of us"—suggesting that his opponent, Nick Galifianakis, a liberal Democratic congressman of Greek American heritage, was not (Luebke 1990, 26). In 1978, Helms described Democratic nominee John Ingram as the "handpicked candidate of the AFL-CIO" and appeared on the *PTL Evangelical Hour* to describe his reliance on prayer to give him strength in the campaign (Snider 1985, 50–51). During a 1984 debate, Helms expressed opposition to the Martin Luther King national holiday and the "so-called voting rights act extension" by asking Hunt, "Now which is more important to you, governor, getting yourself elected with the enormous black vote, or protecting the Constitution and the people of North Carolina?" (Snider 1985, 160). And in his two races against Harvey Gantt, various television ads charged that Gantt supported racial quotas and same-sex marriages, benefited financially from racial preference policies, and, in sum, was "more liberal than Bill Clinton—too liberal for North Carolina" (Leonnig and Morrill 1996, A9). A majority of voters apparently agreed.

Notable about Helms's success as well, however, has been his inability to expand his electoral base and secure a comfortable reelection constituency. In his five Senate wins he has never received more than 54.5 percent of the vote, despite facing candidates greatly varying in experience, appeal, and financial backing. John Ingram, for example, was a maverick Democratic candidate who spent only $264,088; Helms spent $7,460,966. He has twice narrowly defeated Harvey Gantt, receiving less than 53 percent in each race, though Gantt was an African American candidate with no previous legislative or statewide officeholding experience.

Helms hasn't been able to cultivate a larger electoral base because, as an avowed and controversial traditionalist, he alienates many voters even as he attracts just enough votes to win. Modernizer Republicans and some economically conservative (and moderate) Democrats are ambivalent about supporting a candidate who so assertively promotes a socially conservative agenda. This is a problem the GOP continues to face in North Carolina, and it limits the ability of the party to make significant additional inroads into groups usually voting Democratic.

Politics, Race, and Redistricting

The development of a strong Republican Party in North Carolina is, as Aistrup (1996) argues for the South as a whole, at least partly due to the association of the Democratic Party with the interests of African Americans. In the 1996 U.S. Senate campaign, for example, the North Carolina Republican Party mailed out five hundred thousand flyers with photographs of Harvey Gantt and, in various versions of the flyer, different members of the state's congressional delegation; two of the three House members pictured, Mel Watt and Eva Clayton, are black. The version with Watt was headed, "Mel's bad enough. Do you want Harvey, too?" (Morrill 1996, 1A). The racial character of the Tar Heel vote has worked to the advantage of the GOP in many recent elections. With the North Carolina electorate roughly divided four-fifths white and one-fifth black, even the predictable black vote for Democratic candidates—usually on the order of 90 percent—can be overcome by Republicans if they win 60 percent of the statewide white vote (Luebke 1990, 156). The key to the modernizer-traditionalist Republican coalition, therefore, is to appeal to white voters on modernist grounds of limited government (e.g., welfare reform) and economic development, and on traditionalist grounds of opposition to change in the social order and racial preference policies (e.g., quotas).

Race has emerged as a dominant feature of North Carolina politics in yet another way: the redrawing of congressional district boundaries to make more likely the election of African Americans. In a 1986 North Carolina case, *Thornburg v. Gingles,* the U.S. Supreme Court ruled that a minority group can sue for discrimination if "its preferred candidates are usually defeated as a result of bloc voting by a white majority" (Canon, Schousen, and Sellers 1994, 24). The 1965 Voting Rights Act requires the U.S. Department of Justice to "preclear" state legislative action affecting minority voting rights. The Justice Department, citing the *Gingles* case, ordered the state legislature to create black-majority districts as a remedy for this "discriminatory effect" (24). The Democratic state legislature's first attempt at redrawing the congressional map in 1991 produced a single black-majority district in eastern North Carolina that looked to some observers like "a bug splattered on a windshield" (25). The convoluted district reflected the problem faced by North Carolina mapmakers: African Americans in the state live in widely scattered areas, and only creative cartography can piece them together in numbers sufficient to produce a black majority. An unlikely alliance then formed between the National Association for the Advancement of Colored People, the American Civil Liberties Union, and the North Carolina Republican Party, all of which argued that, since the black population of the state is 22 percent, the legislature should have created two majority-black districts. The GOP, of course, felt that it would benefit from concentrating blacks, who were overwhelmingly Democratic, into two districts, thus making Democratic white incumbents in the surrounding districts more vulnerable.

The Justice Department refused to preclear the proposed redistricting plan. A special legislative session of the Democratic-dominated state legislature then drew a new map that created two black-majority districts, one of which was the now famous Interstate 85 district. This district, which brought together blacks in an area stretching from Durham in the north central part of the state to Gastonia in the southwest, was only as wide as one lane of the freeway in some places. *Politics in America* called it "the mother of all gerrymanders" (Duncan 1993, 1155). Black state legislator Mickey Michaux commented, "I love this district. I can drive down I-85 with both car doors open and hit every person in the district" (29).

Although the redrawn districts were used in the House elections in 1992, 1994, and 1996, the U.S. Supreme Court, in *Shaw v. Reno* (1993), ordered the federal district court in North Carolina to review the new map to ensure that its districts were not drawn solely to increase black representation. The Court eventually found, in *Shaw v. Hunt* (1996), that the Twelfth District had been created primarily to elect a black representative and ordered the state legislature to redraw the boundaries again. The state legislature, this time with Republicans controlling the house and Democrats the senate, produced in early 1997 a new map not dramatically different from the map rejected by the Court.[7] The new map has met the approval of at least two incumbents, white Republican Sue Myrick and black Democrat Mel Watt, perhaps because it makes likely their reelection. "I had long ago said that I thought it was a reasonable way to configure this district," Watt told the *Charlotte Observer.* Myrick concurred, saying, "I think overall the plan is fair for everybody" (Morrill and Gibbs 1997, 1C).

The lessons of North Carolina's redistricting wars may remain unclear, but the short-term impact is evident. In the three elections held using the now-defunct map, North Carolina has elected two African American legislators—the first blacks to represent the state in Congress since 1901—while Republicans increased their number of U.S. House seats from three (of eleven) in 1990 to an average of six (of twelve) seats during the 1992–1996 period. Of concern for Democrats, however, is that all four of the white Democratic winners in 1996 won 55 percent of the vote or less. If the old map had been retained, in other words, a strong Republican election year could have conceivably produced a ten-to-two Republican House delegation, supporting the claims of many observers that majority-black districts work to the advantage of the GOP.[8]

A Tale of Two Parties

The complicated nature of North Carolina politics is frequently on display for intrigued observers. In April 1997 the Mecklenburg County Commission voted 5-4 to kill $2.5 million in public funding for the local arts and sciences council in order to "protect children from exposure to perverted forms of sexuality" (Batten 1997, 1A). The arts and sciences council had, among other things, helped to fund a recent production of *Angels in America,* a play that deals with AIDS and homosexuality. Carroll Gray, president of the Charlotte Chamber of Commerce, lamented the vote: "We now have another obstacle to overcome in recruiting business, and frankly it runs counter to the message we've been using for over a decade that Charlotte is an open and progressive city" (1A).[9] The largest city in the state, committed to economic development and entrepreneurial promotion, keeps one foot firmly planted in the socially conservative soil of the Old South.

Can the Republicans in North Carolina manage the tensions between the two philosophies and emerge as the dominant party in the state? Perhaps they can; the evolution of the Southern Strategy in other states, especially during the Reagan years, suggests that GOP candidates can articulate a coherent philosophy of free-market economics that at least pays lip service to the agenda of social conservatives (Aistrup 1996). By muting ideological differences between the party's factions, Republican modernizers like former governor Jim Martin or Congresswoman Sue Myrick of the Ninth District (a close associate of Newt Gingrich) can build durable bases of party support. More strident conservatives like Helms, however, threaten to disrupt the intraparty peace that the GOP needs to forge a truly dominant coalition. The limits of Helms's appeal, seen clearly in the narrow victories he fashions against opponents weak and strong, suggests that ultimately the fortunes of North Carolina Republicans, perhaps more so than in the Deep South states, are not well served by an overzealous commitment to a socially conservative agenda.

The evidence of a substantial and consequential North Carolina party realignment is clear. Although the most commonly used measure of realignment, changes in party identification, shows only gradual growth of Republican affiliation (Johnston 1996, 16), the success of GOP candidates in offices across the board (especially at the local and state legislative levels) indicates that the state has moved beyond a simple dealignment. It is true, as Luebke noted in the aftermath of the 1994 elections, that "many North Carolina whites have lost their commitment to the Democratic Party but have not yet transferred their loyalty to the Republicans" (Whitman 1995, 85). However, these voters, a majority of whom describe themselves as conservatives, are more attracted to the appeals of Republican candidates than Democratic candidates, an attraction that appears to have increased in the 1990s. A betting man or woman would probably be wise to wager that the GOP is on the verge of creating a durable majority, but the vicissitudes of politics, the fervor of the social conservatives, and the willingness of Democratic moderates like President Bill Clinton to move with the voter, suggest that predictions of Republican dominance in the short term, at least, are premature. In the long term, however, absent a definitive move of the national Democratic Party to the center of the political spectrum—which would offer a refuge for New South conservatives offended by Helms-like rhetoric—the creation of a solid Republican majority in the Tar Heel State seems likely.

Notes

1. To be sure, Key recognized the dominant role of business interests in the state, describing them as a "plutocracy" that largely controlled policymaking. "Progressive, forward-looking, yes," he described them, "but always sound, always the kind of government liked by the big investor, the big employer" (214).

2. North Carolina had eleven House seats from 1972 to 1990 but gained a twelfth seat in 1992 following the 1990 reapportionment—which, as discussed below, produced a major political fight along partisan and racial lines.

3. Key referred to the Highlands, Piedmont Plateau, Coastal Plain, and Tidewater (221). Edsall and Williams combine the latter two regions into one region that they refer to simply as the East but break out of the Piedmont a twelve-county region containing almost all of the state's major cities, which they refer to as the Piedmont Crescent (397).

4. These divisions roughly correspond as well to topographical differences. The three major physical regions of the state are the mountains, piedmont, and coastal plain. The formulation used here combines the coastal plain and the eastern portion of the piedmont into a single region that, while somewhat varying in terms of terrain, is remarkably similar in many political and economic respects.

5. For assessments of Republican Party performance in years preceding the 1970s, see Edsall and Williams (1972), Peirce (1975), and Bass and DeVries (1976).

6. One must be careful about the "ecological fallacy," of course; that is, imputing individual characteristics and behaviors to voters based on aggregate data. Absent individual-level survey data, for example—data that are often unavailable at the state level—the analyst must proceed with caution, suggesting relationships between variables only when supported by logic and other corroborating empirical evidence.

7. The black population of the new Twelfth District falls from 57 percent to 47 percent but retains its serpentine shape and I-85 character.

8. This estimate is based on House races using the map since declared unconstitutional by the Supreme Court. The vulnerability of incumbents in the newly created districts remains to be seen. At the state level, redistricting appears to have contributed to a significant increase in the number of African American state legislators. The number of blacks in the state house and senate has increased from six in 1975 (4 percent of all legislators) to twenty-four in 1975 (14 percent of all legislators) (Whitman 1995, 95).

9. The tensions between modernism and traditionalism are particularly pronounced in Charlotte and other Urban Piedmont cities. Applebome says that Charlotte, "second perhaps only to Atlanta, stands for the degree to which the New South troops in pinstripes, starched white shirts, and spit-shined wing tips finally succeeded" (1996, 153). The city, he writes, "may edge out Dallas and Atlanta as home to the purest strain ever discovered of the Southern booster gene" (153).

References

Aistrup, Joseph. 1996. *The Southern Strategy Revisited.* Lexington: University of Kentucky Press.

Applebome, Peter. 1996. *Dixie Rising.* New York: Random House.

Barone, Michael, and Grant Ujifusa. 1983. *The Almanac of American Politics, 1984.* Washington, D.C.: National Journal.

Bass, Jack, and Walter DeVries. 1976. *The Transformation of Southern Politics.* New York: Basic Books.

Batten, Taylor. 1997. "Vote Could Hurt City, Some Fear." *Charlotte Observer.* 3 April. 1A.

Black, Earl, and Merle Black. 1987. *Politics and Society in the South.* Cambridge: Harvard University Press.

Bullock, Charles S., III. 1988. "Creeping Realignment in the South." In *The South's New Politics,* edited by Robert H. Swansbrough and David M. Brodsky. Columbia: University of South Carolina Press.

Canon, David T., Matthew M. Schousen, and Patrick J. Sellers. 1994. "A Formula for Uncertainty: Creating a Black Majority District in North Carolina." In *Who Runs for Congress?* edited by Thomas A. Kazee. Washington, D.C.: Congressional Quarterly.

Christensen, Rob, and Bill Krueger. 1996. "Helms Does It Again." *Raleigh News and Observer,* 7 November, 20A.

Duncan, Phil, ed. 1993. *Politics in America.* Washington, D.C.: Congressional Quarterly.

Edsall, Preston W., and Oliver J. Williams. 1972. "North Carolina: Bipartisan Paradox." In *The Changing Politics of the South,* edited by William C. Havard. Baton Rouge: Louisiana State University Press.

Fleer, Jack D., Roger C. Lowery, and Charles L. Prysby. 1988. "Political Change in NorthCarolina." In *The South's New Politics,* edited by Robert H. Swansbrough and David M. Brodsky. Columbia: University of South Carolina Press.

Jamieson, Kathleen Hall. 1992. *Dirty Politics.* New York: Oxford University Press.

Johnston, W. Lee. 1996. "North Carolina: V. O. Key's Progressive Plutocracy, Almost Fifty Years of Janus-Faced Politics." Paper presented at the Southern Political Science Association Meeting, Atlanta, Georgia, November.

Key, V. O., Jr. 1949. *Southern Politics in State and Nation.* New York: Knopf.

Lamis, Alexander P. 1990. *The Two Party South.* 2d ed. New York: Oxford University Press.

Leonnig, Carol D., and Jim Morrill. 1996. "Ad Watch: U.S. Senate Campaign." *Charlotte Observer,* 7 April, A9.

Luebke, Paul. 1990. *Tar Heel Politics.* Chapel Hill: University of North Carolina Press.

Monk, John, and Carol D. Leonnig. 1996. "What Helms Says." *Charlotte Observer,* 11 November, 10A.

Morrill, Jim, and Stephanie Gibbs. 1997. "Remap Hits 25% of Voters." *Charlotte Observer,* 26 March, 1C.

Morrill, Jim, and Carol D. Leonnig. 1996. "Racial Attitudes Could Determine Senator." *Charlotte Observer,* 7 April, B1.

North Carolina Manual. (Various editions.) North Carolina Department of the Secretary of State.

Peirce, Neal R. 1975. *The Border South States.* New York: Norton.

Snider, William D. 1985. *Helms and Hunt.* Chapel Hill: University of North Carolina Press.

Whitman, Mebane Rash. 1995. "The Evolution of Party Politics: The March of the GOP Continues in North Carolina." *North Carolina Insight,* September, 81–98.

9

Tennessee: Genuine Two-Party Politics

David M. Brodsky

During the past half-century, two-party politics in Tennessee has moved from politics characterized by Key (1949) as "two one-party systems" to politics described by Bass and DeVries (1976) as a "genuine two-party politics." This chapter first sketches the historical roots of contemporary politics in Tennessee. It then traces the "modern" evolution of politics in the Volunteer State, focusing on the competitive balance between Democrats and Republicans and on the impact of race in the state's political life. Finally, the chapter considers what the future may hold for politics in the state.

Background

A full appreciation of contemporary politics in Tennessee requires an understanding of how the past gave shape to the present. As Key (1949, 76) put it,"the consequences of the projection of the past into the present for Tennessee politics are great."

Geography, the Civil War, and Reconstruction

Tennessee stretches over five hundred miles from its eastern border with North Carolina to its western edge along the Mississippi River. The state's topography varies from mountains in the east to rolling hills in the middle and flatlands in the west, and Tennessee's economics, history, and politics frequently have reflected these geographic divisions. For example, when Tennessee held two secession votes in 1861, the largely slave-owning plantation counties in the west twice voted for secession, the largely nonslave counties along the western Highland Rim and in the

mountainous east twice voted to remain in the Union, and the slavehold-
ing counties of Middle Tennessee ultimately provided the second ballot
margin for secession (Majors 1986). The votes on secession and the later
conflicts between unionists and secessionists during the war and during
Reconstruction served as the catalysts that gave form to the partisan
attachments of Tennessee's voters. The eastern mountain and western rim
counties that rejected secession became the bedrock of Tennessee Republicanism, while the Middle and West Tennessee counties that voted for
secession became the Democratic Party's base (Key 1949; Green, Grubbs,
and Hobday 1982).

Factional Strife

Tennessee Democrats and Republicans have periodically suffered from
the effects of factional conflict described by Key (1949) as "having a character all its own." The sources of these factional battles varied over time.
Sometimes they resulted from conflicts between ambitious politicians and
their followers. Other times they resulted from differing conceptions of
how (and whether) to build an effective political party. And sometimes
they resulted from differences on questions of public policy.

Between 1932 and 1954, Tennessee Democrats routinely divided into
two factions: supporters of Mayor E. H. Crump and his Memphis-based
political machine, and a loose coalition of anti-Crump politicians and
activists. Following Crump's death in 1954, factional strife among Democrats took one of two forms: a *personality-based factionalism* centered around
strong individuals (e.g., Frank Clement, Estes Kefauver, and Buford
Ellington) who appeared on Tennessee's political stage; or an *ideologically
based factionalism* centered on competing conservative and progressive
policy agendas (Parks 1966). More recently, the Democrats have suffered
from the competing interests of its legislative caucuses and its candidates
for statewide office.

The sources of factional conflict among Tennessee Republicans have
also varied over time. For example, in the 1940s Key (1949) found a conservative, pro-business, and patronage-oriented faction willing to accept
Democratic dominance of politics outside of the GOP's East Tennessee
redoubt and a more populist antiorganization faction interested in expanding the party's base and in challenging the Democrats across the state. In
the mid-1960s, Parks (1966) described a strongly conservative pro-business
and anti–civil rights faction led by Goldwater supporters from Memphis
and the state's other metropolitan areas and a less conservative "moderate" faction centered in traditionally Republican East Tennessee. Since

1964, when conservatives dominated the state convention, moderates and conservatives have struggled for control of the party, most recently in the aftermath of the party's poor performance in 1992 (Brodsky 1997).

Race

Historically, Tennessee placed few obstacles in the path of potential African American voters. Unlike most southern states, Tennessee lacked a literacy test and moved to repeal its poll tax in 1953, prior to the 1964 passage of the Twenty-fourth Amendment (Green, Grubbs, and Hobday 1982). Key (1949) speculated that the relative ease of access to the ballot, especially in the cities, resulted in a "Negro community . . . rife with factionalism." Indeed, despite the importance of black votes to the success of the Memphis-based Crump machine, Key concluded that "Negroes, as a group, play no important role in state politics."

Party Competition

The Republicans Break Out

For most of the period between the end of Reconstruction and the early 1950s, the leadership of the Tennessee Republican Party accepted its minority status in the Volunteer State. The party's leaders chose to forgo any effort to build a statewide party. They opted instead to maintain their dominance in East Tennessee and to trade GOP support for the pro-business, conservative candidates fielded by the Democratic Crump machine for a share of federal patronage coming into the state and for freedom from serious Democratic challenges. Consequently, while East Tennessee regularly sent Republican representatives to Washington and to the state legislature, the party won only three statewide races (the 1910 and 1920 gubernatorial contests and the 1928 presidential contest) prior to 1952.

Between 1952 and 1972, Tennessee Republicans accomplished four seemingly impossible tasks. First, they built a party organization capable of competing with the Democrats across the state. Second, they recruited attractive candidates who could appeal to traditionally Democratic voters. Third, they expanded the Republican electorate to include voters outside the party's traditional East Tennessee and Highland Rim strongholds. And finally, they put together an unprecedented string of electoral successes across the Volunteer State.

The Republican "breakout" in statewide elections began at the presidential level and spread to victories in contests for the U.S. Senate and for governor. Dwight D. Eisenhower's 1952 presidential win marked the beginning of a string of victories interrupted only in 1964 by Lyndon Johnson's defeat of Barry Goldwater. The Republican winning vote totals ranged from a low of 38 percent in Richard Nixon's narrow 1968 victory over George Wallace and Hubert Humphrey to a high of 68 percent in 1972 when Nixon defeated George McGovern. In 1966, Howard H. Baker Jr. became the first Republican since Reconstruction to represent Tennessee in the U.S. Senate when he scored a one-hundred-thousand–vote victory over Frank Clement, the favored Democratic candidate. Four years later, in 1970, the Republicans gained their second U.S. Senate seat when Congressman Bill Brock defeated Albert Gore, the incumbent Democrat, in a bitterly fought contest. Also in 1970, Winfield Dunn, a West Tennessee dentist, became the first Republican since the 1920s to occupy the governor's mansion.

The two decades between 1952 and 1972 also saw Republican gains in the state legislature and in the state's congressional delegation. The GOP's share of seats in the state house increased from fewer than one in five at the beginning of the period to a short-lived working majority in the 1969–1970 legislative biennium, while the party's share of seats in the state senate grew from less than one in five in 1952 to two in five seats by 1972. The expansion of the Republican presence in Tennessee's congressional delegation began in 1962 when William E. Brock III took advantage of a divided Democratic Party to capture the Third Congressional District seat once held by Estes Kefauver. The GOP later captured two additional seats, including one in traditionally Democratic West Tennessee. Thus, by 1972 the Republicans held five of Tennessee's eight congressional seats.

The Democrats Get Up off the Mat

Although 1972 ended with Tennessee's Democrats flat on their backs, the party struggled to its feet and by 1974 had taken the first steps on the road to recovery. At the polls, Ray Blanton, a former Democratic congressman from West Tennessee, defeated East Tennessee Republican Lamar Alexander, a onetime aide in the Nixon White House, in the 1974 gubernatorial contest. The Democrats also regained two U.S. House seats, scoring upset victories in the Eighth Congressional District (Memphis) where Harold Ford, an African American candidate, defeated the Republican incumbent, Dan Kuykendall, in a district with a white majority; and in the Third Congressional District (Chattanooga), where Marilyn Lloyd, a political novice who replaced her deceased husband on the ballot, recaptured a seat held by the Republicans since Bill Brock's 1962 win (Bass and DeVries 1976). In 1974, the Democrats also managed to stanch the Republican tide in the state legislature as the GOP lost ground in both the house and the senate.

Slugging It Out in the Center of the Ring

Between 1976 and 1994, Tennessee's Democratic and Republican Parties continued to fight it out in national and state elections with first one party and then the other apparently delivering a knockout punch only to find itself put on the defensive by an effective counterpunch. In 1976 the Democrats appeared to have the Republicans on the ropes. First, Jimmy Carter became only the second Democrat since Harry Truman (Lyndon Johnson was the first) to carry the Volunteer State. Second, Jim Sasser, the Democratic challenger, upset incumbent Republican senator Bill Brock. And finally, the Democrats maintained their five-to-three advantage in the state's congressional delegation.

The Republicans staggered, but they quickly countered these Democratic blows. In 1978, Republican senator Howard Baker easily defeated Jane Eskind, his Democratic challenger, and Republican candidate Lamar Alexander bounced back from his 1974 defeat at the hands of Ray Blanton to capture the gubernatorial contest with millionaire banker Jake Butcher. 1980 saw Ronald Reagan carry the state's electoral votes in a three-way contest with Jimmy Carter and John Anderson.

The elections between 1982 and 1994 continued the pattern of punch and counterpunch. The Republicans scored points in 1982 when Governor Lamar Alexander won reelection in an easier-than-expected contest with Knoxville mayor Randy Tyree and in 1984 when Ronald Reagan and George Bush buried the Mondale-Ferraro ticket, carrying seventy-two of Tennessee's ninety-five counties. The first Democratic counterpunch came in 1984 when Tennessee's voters split their tickets to give Middle Tennessee's Democratic congressman Albert Gore Jr. an easy win in the contest to fill the U.S. Senate seat left vacant when Republican Howard Baker Jr. retired. The Democrats landed a second blow in 1986 when Ned Ray McWherter, the former speaker of the Tennessee House of Representatives, gained the governor's mansion.

In 1988 the Reagan-Bush team again knocked out the Democratic presidential contenders, and the Republicans scored additional points when they expanded, albeit slightly, their delegations in both houses of the state legislature. The Democrats also scored points when Senator Jim Sasser carried all but one of Tennessee's ninety-five counties in his bid for reelection and when they managed to hold on to their share of the state's congressional delegation.

Both parties added to their point totals in 1990. The incumbent Democratic governor, Ned Ray McWherter, won a second four-year term when he earned two of every three votes, while Democratic U.S. senator Albert Gore Jr. received seven of every ten votes as he defeated his Republican challenger. Nothing changed at the congressional level, where the Democrats maintained their six-to-three advantage. Although the statewide results looked bad for the Republicans, they also scored some points as they increased the size of both delegations in the Tennessee General Assembly, to forty-two representatives and thirteen senators.

After the polls closed in 1992, it looked as if the Democrats had put the Republicans on the canvas for a ten count. The Clinton-Gore ticket carried sixty-six of Tennessee's ninety-five counties, a total that included Davidson County (Nashville) and Shelby County (Memphis), the state's two most populous counties. The Democrats also maintained their six-to-three advantage in the Tennessee congressional delegation and, with the help of a creative reapportionment plan, managed to reduce the Republican presence in the Tennessee House of Representatives to thirty-six representatives. The only bright spot for the Republicans came in the state senate, where they defeated the senate majority leader and managed a net gain of one seat.

The Republicans Land Some Devastating Combinations

Like the Democrats two decades earlier, Tennessee's Republican Party got up off the canvas after 1992's near-death experience. When the dust cleared after election day 1994, the Republicans found themselves standing over a Democratic Party stunned by punches thrown in devastating combinations. In a one-two punch, political newcomer Bill Frist, a Nashville heart surgeon, stunned U.S. Senator Jim Sasser, who was seeking a fourth term; and lawyer, lobbyist, and occasional actor Fred Thompson defeated Fourth District congressman Jim Cooper in the contest for the remaining two years of Vice President Al Gore's unexpired Senate term. The Republicans landed another one-two punch when GOP candidates captured formerly Democratic open seats in the Third (Zack Wamp) and Fourth (Van Hillary) Congressional Districts. The GOP also held on to the open Seventh District seat (won by Ed Bryant) vacated by Don Sundquist, the successful GOP gubernatorial candidate, and maintained control of East Tennessee's First and Second District seats. And in a final one-two punch, the Republicans increased their presence in the Tennessee

House of Representatives and gained, with the help of Democratic defections, a majority in the Tennessee Senate.

Up Off the Canvas Again

The 1996 elections afforded Tennessee Democrats yet another opportunity to demonstrate their ability first to take a punch and then to begin counterpunching. The election results indicate that some blows landed. The Democrats scored when their presidential ticket carried the Volunteer State (despite failing to win a statewide popular-vote majority), gaining majorities of the popular vote in Middle and West Tennessee, the party's traditional strongholds, and holding down the Dole-Kemp ticket's margin in historically Republican East Tennessee. The Democrats also scored, although not as well as they hoped, when they managed to retain their four congressional seats. The Democratic victories included a narrow victory by Sixth District incumbent Bart Gordon. Despite these successes, the Democrats delivered their most effective counterpunches in the state legislative contests, where they reclaimed majority status (17-15) in the senate and increased their majority in the house of representatives to sixty-one seats.

Holding On in the Clinches

Despite the Democrats' success in the presidential and state legislative contests, 1996 saw the Republicans build on their 1994 gains. Senator Fred Thompson easily defeated his Democratic opponent, attorney Houston Gordon, in the contest for a full six-year term. Thompson carried all thirty-three counties in traditionally Republican East Tennessee, twenty-nine of forty-one counties in normally Democratic Middle Tennessee, and fifteen of twenty-one counties in West Tennessee. Although the Republicans failed to gain any additional congressional seats, freshman incumbents in the Third, Fourth, and Seventh Congressional Districts improved on their 1994 performances, while candidate Bill Jenkins retained the First Congressional District seat left open when seventeen-term congressman Jimmy Quillen retired.

Partisan Change

The election returns clearly point to a transformation in the competitive balance between Tennessee's Democratic and Republican Parties. Four factors—changes in legislative apportionment, changes in the party preferences expressed by Tennessee voters, changes in historically fixed regional voting patterns, and changes in the structure and effectiveness of the state and local party organizations—seem to account for the increased competition between the parties.

Changes in Legislative Apportionment

Two U.S. Supreme Court decisions compelling legislative reapportionment (*Baker v. Carr* in 1962 and *Reynolds v. Sims* in 1964) had a profound impact on the partisan balance in Tennessee. These decisions required state legislatures, including Tennessee's, to create legislative districts with roughly equal populations. The resultant reapportionment dramatically increased the number of legislative seats given to previously underrepresented urban and suburban areas, with many of these seats going to such emerging Republican strongholds as the Shelby County suburbs surrounding Memphis and the Knox County suburbs around Knoxville (Green, Grubbs, and Hobday 1982). Although the Republicans gained some seats following the first efforts at reapportionment, their gains came after the legislature changed the method of election for both representatives (in 1966) and senators (in 1968) from at-large, countywide, multimember districts to single-member districts (McGinnis 1985). In the elections immediately following the change to single-member districts, the Republicans' share of seats in the state house increased from 24 percent to 49 percent, and their senate delegation increased from 24 percent to 36 percent.

Changing Partisan Preferences

The data presented in table 9.1 indicate that changes in the partisan preferences of Tennessee voters have accompanied the transformation of electoral politics in the Volunteer State. Between 1981 and 1996, the proportion of Tennesseans who identified themselves as Democrats gradually declined from two in five to three in ten. During the same period, the proportion of Republican identifiers increased from one in four to three in ten. Thus, the Democrats found 1981's 17-percentage-point advantage transformed into 1996's virtual dead heat.

Data from a series of statewide surveys conducted in 1981, 1985, and 1989 (Brodsky and Swansbrough 1990) point to several possible explanations for the changes in the partisan preferences reported by Tennessee voters (see table 9.2).

Table 9.1
Partisan Identification of Tennessee Voters (in percent)

	Democrat	Republican	Independent
1981	42	25	32
1984	37	29	30
1985	32	29	39
1989	33	28	29
1996[a]	31	30	35

Sources: 1996 data from preelection poll conducted by the University of
Tennessee Social Science Research Institute, Knoxville, 20–24 October
1996. 1984 data from ABC News Poll 1984 "Yearend Wrap-up" (New
York: ABC News). 1981, 1985, and 1989 data from statewide polls of
registered voters conducted by Professor Robert H. Swansbrough of
the University of Tennessee at Chattanooga.
[a]1996 data omit respondents with no partisan preference.

First, the proportion of white voters who identified with the Democratic Party declined from 39 percent in 1981 to 29 percent in 1989, while the percentage of whites who identified themselves as Republicans increased from 28 percent to 42 percent. At the same time, the proportion of African American Democrats remained above 65 percent. Second, while the proportion of voters in the youngest age group (eighteen to twenty-nine) who identified with the Democrats remained virtually unchanged over the three surveys, the percentage of young Republican identifiers increased from 28 percent in 1981 to 44 percent in 1989. Third, even though Democratic identification among the oldest voters (fifty-five and older) decreased from 60 percent to 40 percent, this group remained the most Democratic age group. Finally, and perhaps most important, voters who described themselves as either moderates or conservatives moved away from the Democrats and toward the Republicans. Thus, the proportion of Democratic conservatives declined from 34 percent in 1981 to 23 percent in 1989, while the proportion of Republican conservatives increased from 34 percent in 1981 to 54 percent in 1989.

Softening Regional Voting Patterns

A softening of Tennessee's historically determined regional voting patterns (Republican in East Tennessee and the Western Highland Rim counties, Democratic in Middle Tennessee and West Tennessee) also accompanied the rise in interparty competition. More important, the erosion of

Table 9.2
Partisan Identification of Tennessee Voters by Selected Characteristics
(in percent)

	1981		1985		1989	
	Dem.	Rep.	Dem.	Rep.	Dem.	Rep.
Race						
African American	65	9	68	9	71	13
White	39	28	28	31	29	42
Age						
18–29	28	28	31	38	31	44
30–54	38	27	30	22	30	41
55 and older	60	21	37	31	40	30
Ideology						
Liberal	60	8	46	15	60	18
Moderate	42	20	36	20	30	32
Conservative	34	34	23	43	23	54

Source: Data are from statewide polls of registered voters conducted by Professor Robert H. Swansbrough of the University of Tennessee at Chattanooga in 1981 (N = 461), 1985 (N = 620), and 1989 (N = 541).

traditional voting patterns occurred not only in presidential elections but also in U.S. Senate and gubernatorial contests.

At the presidential level, the Democratic share of the popular vote in East Tennessee climbed above 40 percent in 1976, 1980, 1992, and 1996, with the Democratic ticket gaining a majority of the region's votes in 1976 and 1992 and a 49 percent plurality of the votes in 1996 (see table 9.3). The Democrats failed to carry any East Tennessee counties in 1988 but carried ten counties in 1992 and eight counties in 1996. In tradition-ally Democratic Middle Tennessee, the Republicans received popular-vote majorities in the presidential elections of 1972, 1984, and 1988. Although the GOP ticket won twenty-three of the region's forty-one counties in 1988, the party carried only two Middle Tennessee counties in 1992 and seven counties in 1996. West Tennessee also became less reliably Democratic in presidential elections. The region gave popular-vote majorities to Nixon in 1972, Ronald Reagan in 1984, and George Bush in 1988. While 1988's Bush-Quayle ticket captured eighteen of the twenty-one counties in the region, the GOP won only four West Tennessee coun-ties in 1992 and five counties in 1996.

The four U.S. Senate elections involving Jim Sasser vividly illustrate the declining dependability of each party's traditional regional base. In 1976 when Sasser challenged the incumbent, Republican Bill Brock, the

Table 9.3
Democratic Presidential Vote by Tennessee Region (in percent)

	East	Middle	West
1972	27	39	33
1976	50	66	57
1980	42	60	54
1984	34	46	48
1988	35	45	47
1992	52	63	58
1996	49	57	57

Sources: Compiled by the author from certified election returns provided by the Tennessee Secretary of State and from selected editions
of the *Tennessee Bluebook,* published by the Tennessee Secretary of
State.

customary regional voting patterns held firm. The challenger captured
popular-vote majorities in usually Democratic Middle and West Tennessee while the incumbent gained 56 percent of the vote in traditionally
Republican East Tennessee (see table 9.4). In 1982 and 1988, Middle and
West Tennessee remained true to form, delivering substantial majorities to
Sasser. However, East Tennessee voters broke with the past, favoring the
Democratic incumbent in both elections. In 1994, when Sasser faced an
unexpectedly tough, and ultimately successful, challenge from political
novice Bill Frist, a majority of voters in East Tennessee returned to the
Republican fold. Unfortunately for Sasser, electoral majorities in usually
Democratic Middle and West Tennessee left the fold and voted for Frist,

Table 9.4
Democratic Senatorial Vote by Tennessee Region (in percent)

	East	Middle	West
1976	44	61	54
1982	56	67	64
1988	58	68	71
1994	37	46	45

Sources: Compiled by the author from certified election returns provided by the Tennessee Secretary of State and from selected editions
of the *Tennessee Bluebook,* published by the Tennessee Secretary of
State.

Table 9.5
Democratic Gubernatorial Vote by Tennessee Region
(in percent)

	East	Middle	West
1970	37	57	45
1974	45	67	55
1978	40	46	47
1982	29	48	54
1986	49	58	57
1990	57	68	62
1994	36	54	46

Sources: Compiled by the author from certified election returns provided by the Tennessee Secretary of State and from selected editions of the *Tennessee Bluebook,* published by the Tennessee Secretary of State.

sending the three-term incumbent down to defeat.

The willingness of Volunteer State voters to abandon established voting patterns also affected the outcome of recent gubernatorial contests (see table 9.5). For example, in 1970 when Winfield Dunn became Tennessee's first Republican governor since 1921, he carried normally Democratic West Tennessee (perhaps because he lived in the region) as well as the GOP bastion in East Tennessee. In 1978 and 1982, another Republican, Lamar Alexander, captured popular-vote majorities in Middle Tennessee while Democrat Ned Ray McWherter carried East Tennessee in 1990 (he almost carried the eastern grand division in 1986, winning 49 percent of the vote). Finally, in 1994 Republican Don Sundquist, who gave up his seat as a U.S. representative from West Tennessee's Seventh Congressional District, won a popular-vote majority in his home region, carrying sixteen of twenty-one counties in the process, on his way to the governor's mansion.

Developing Party Organizations

Tennessee Republicans took the early lead in developing modern and effective state and local party organizations. In 1964, Goldwater supporters from Memphis, Nashville, and Chattanooga, three of the state's four major metropolitan centers, spearheaded a largely successful effort by ideological conservatives to gain control of the state party organization and to build party organizations across the Volunteer State (Parks 1966). By 1966 the Republicans had a staff operating from Nashville and organizations in approximately seventy-five Tennessee counties (Bass and DeVries 1976). These "modernized" state and local party organizations contributed substantially to the electoral successes enjoyed by GOP candidates in races for state and national offices, including Howard Baker Jr.'s 1966 Senate victory, Winfield Dunn's successful 1970 gubernatorial campaign, and Bill Brock's upset win in his 1970 U.S. Senate contest with Albert Gore.

It took Tennessee Democrats almost seven years (until 1973) to begin, in earnest, an effort to slow the Republican juggernaut. Backed by legislative leaders, the state party managed to retire its debt and to increase its efforts to recruit attractive candidates (Bass and DeVries 1976). By 1992 the party had an organizational presence in all Tennessee counties and a fund-raising capability that enabled it to raise more than one million dollars (Brodsky 1997). These and other improvements in the party's organizational capabilities fueled the Democratic resurgence between 1974 and 1992.

Race and Politics

Key (1949) concluded that African Americans had little influence on Tennessee politics. Nevertheless, race played a prominent role in Tennessee's transformation from two one-party systems to a state with two statewide parties.

Race as a Political Issue

Disaffection with the national Democratic Party's position on civil rights issues led many white Tennesseans to reconsider their support for Democratic candidates. In 1948, Memphis mayor and political boss E. H. Crump endorsed the Dixiecrat ticket. Although the Dixiecrat rebellion failed in Tennessee, the 1948 election marked the start of a gradual erosion of the Democratic Party's West Tennessee base (Bass and DeVries 1976). This decay in Democratic support continued through the civil rights era and, when taken in conjunction with the growing Republican presence in the rapidly expanding Memphis suburbs, created a Memphis–East Tennessee axis that provided the base for the GOP's statewide successes (Phillips 1969).

Race also figured prominently in the 1964 emergence of a statewide Republican Party. According to Parks (1966, 153), the conservative activists who spearheaded the 1964 organizational effort agreed "on the necessity to reconstitute the Republican party as a lily-white, solidly conservative, business-oriented organization." The Republicans took a significant step in the direction of building support among whites disenchanted with the Democratic Party's position on civil rights when, for the first time in history, the state convention sent an all-white delegation to the GOP's national convention. These actions and the general thrust of the Goldwater campaign accelerated two trends: the movement, especially in West Tennessee, of formerly Democratic-leaning white voters to the Republican Party; and a concomitant shift of African American voters to the Democratic Party.

The 1970 senatorial contest between Democrat Albert Gore and William E. Brock III, his Republican challenger, marked a change in the politics of race. Although the race issue played a central role in the Brock campaign's strategy, the strategists handled the issue in a more subtle manner than usual in southern politics (Lamis 1990). Nevertheless, the election results indicate that the strategy worked, as Brock captured a majority of the votes in West Tennessee (Swansbrough 1985).

More recently, race, although still an important predictor of how Tennesseans vote, has not played a highly visible role in statewide political contests. Instead, candidates and their campaigns have placed more emphasis on issues like economic policy and the proper role of government that have traditionally divided Democrats and Republicans (Lamis 1990). Examples of contests where class and economic issues played an important role include the Blanton-Alexander gubernatorial contest in 1974, the Sasser-Brock battle for a U.S. Senate seat in 1976, the Clinton-Bush struggle in 1992, and the Clinton-Dole contest in 1996.

Race and Political Office

The same changes in election methods and legislative apportionment plans that increased the Republican delegation in the Tennessee legislature also contributed to an African American presence in the house and senate. The first "modern" African American representative entered the house in 1964. The African American delegation in the legislature now includes twelve representatives and three senators, all Democrats who, for the most part, represent the state's four largest urban counties.

In Memphis, former congressman Harold Ford, an African American, built a formidable political organization, one reminiscent of the legendary Crump machine that dominated Memphis and Tennessee politics for nearly two decades. Ford and his organization have provided a valuable base of support for Democratic candidates in statewide races. The organization has also proved effective at electing African American candidates to state and national office, most recently (1996) helping Harold Ford Jr. replace his father as the Ninth Congressional District's representative to Washington.

Race and Voting

The civil rights movement and the Goldwater movement galvanized Tennessee's African American voters to support Democratic candidates at the same time many whites shifted their votes to Republican candidates, especially in statewide elections (Parks 1966). Exit poll data for several recent elections confirm the persistence of these voting tendencies. Between 1980 and 1992, the Democratic presidential ticket averaged less than two of every five white votes but received more than nine of every ten African American votes. In 1996 the Clinton-Gore team captured 92 percent of African American votes but only 41 percent of white votes (www.Allpolitics.com 1996). Although Democratic candidates in other statewide contests (i.e., U.S. Senate and governor) have sometimes captured a majority of white votes (e.g., McWherter for governor in 1986 and Gore for senator in 1988), Democratic victories in statewide contests generally depend on high turnout among African American voters.

Conclusion

The challenge confronting students of southern politics, according to Lamis (1990, 304), "is not to see something change and to shout at it: There is change! Rather one must try to understand the nature of the change, explain why it is happening, and analyze its antecedents and likely direction." Clearly, much has changed in the politics of the Volunteer State. First, the Republican Party has established itself as a formidable presence across Tennessee's three grand divisions. The spread of Republicanism began slowly but then accelerated rapidly. Although the Republicans achieved their first statewide success in the presidential election of 1952, the "party" really didn't begin until the 1966 U.S. Senate race, when the GOP claimed its first down-ticket victory in a statewide contest. The Republicans followed up this success in 1970 when they captured another U.S. Senate seat and the governorship. The GOP began to expand its share of the state's congressional delegation in 1962, when it captured its first seat outside traditionally Republican East Tennessee. By 1972 the party held five of Tennessee's eight congressional seats. The GOP ended 1972 with two U.S. Senate seats, the governorship, a majority of Tennessee's congressional delegation, and substantial minorities in both houses of the state legislature. Second, the Tennessee Democratic Party has repeatedly demonstrated an ability to respond to the expanded Republican presence, an ability manifested by the party's 1974 successes in the gubernatorial and congressional district contests and in the 1976 presidential and U.S. Senate contests. Third, historic party ties have eroded, making election outcomes more dependent on such factors as candidates, issues, and campaigns and less dependent on party loyalty and tradition. Fourth, Republican and African American gains in the state legislature have resulted from court decisions shifting the balance of power away from the traditionally Democratic rural areas of the state to its suburban and urban areas. Finally, despite its declining importance as a highly visible political issue, race remains an important consideration, with the Democrats increasingly dependent in statewide races upon supermajorities of African American voters.

Taken together, these changes have produced a more volatile political environment. The parties have battled back and forth, with first one and then the other gaining an advantage. The future promises more of the same, indicating that a "genuine two-party politics" has replaced the "two one-party systems" that emerged from the Civil War and Reconstruction.

References

Bass, Jack, and Walter DeVries. 1976. *The Transformation of Southern Politics.* New York: Basic Books.

Brodsky, David M. 1997. "Tennessee." In *State Party Profiles,* edited by Andrew M. Appleton and Daniel S. Ward. Washington: Congressional Quarterly.

Brodsky, David M., and Robert H. Swansbrough. 1990. "The Changing Composition of Tennessee's Democratic and Republican Parties." Paper presented at the Citadel Symposium on Southern Politics.

Green, Lee S., David H. Grubbs, and Victor C. Hobday. 1982. *Government in Tennessee,* 4th ed. Knoxville: University of Tennessee Press.

Key, V. O., Jr. 1949. *Southern Politics in State and Nation.* New York: Knopf.

Lamis, Alexander P. 1990. *The Two-Party South.* New York: Oxford University Press.

Majors, William R. 1986. *Change and Continuity: Tennessee Politics since the Civil War.* Macon, Ga.: Mercer University Press.

McGinnis, H. Coleman. 1985. "The Tennessee General Assembly: Incumbency, Competition, Experience, and Institutionalization." In *The Volunteer State: Read-*

ings in Tennessee Politics, edited by Dorothy F. Olshufski and T. M. Simpson. Knoxville: Tennessee Political Science Association.

Parks, Norman L. 1966. "Tennessee Politics since Kefauver and Reece: A 'Generalist' View." *Journal of Politics* 28: 144–68.

Phillips, Kevin P. 1969. *The Emerging Republican Majority.* New Rochelle, N.Y.: Arlington House.

Swansbrough, Robert H. 1985. *Political Change in Tennessee.* Knoxville: University of Tennessee, Bureau of Public Administration.

www.allpolitics.com. 1996. All-Politics–CNN Time. *The Vote '96.* 6 November.

10

Arkansas: Electoral Competition in the 1990s

Gary D. Wekkin

> Perhaps in Arkansas we have the one-party system in its most unde-
> filed and undiluted form.
> —V. O. Key Jr., 1949

Known fifty years ago as V. O. Key's prototypical southern one-party Democratic state, Arkansas was the last state of the old "Solid South" to fall to a Republican presidential candidate, waiting until 1972 to be swept along in the Nixon landslide. Consistent with that resistance to change at the top of the ticket, the spread of Republicanism at the level of the statehouse and the courthouse has been exceedingly slow. Only a decade ago Blair and Savage (1986) maintained that despite recent Democratic slippage in vote share, both behavioral evidence and affective evidence suggested that Arkansas's true second political party consisted of independent voters, not Republicans. Even political humor suggested that the Democratic Party's former grip on the state had given way to dealignment, not realignment: "Show me a state that can be represented by Dale Bumpers and Tommy Robinson at the same time, or choose Rockefeller for governor, Fulbright for senator, and Wallace for president on the same day, and I'll show you a state with a personality disorder." Scholars speculated why the breakthrough election of Winthrop Rockefeller as governor had not resulted in Republican growth in Arkansas, as breakthrough elections in other one-party states had done (Appleton and Ward 1994).

In the 1990s, however, slow but steady Republican growth of the "top-down" variety is finally occurring in Arkansas. This growth is all the more impressive for its incremental pace, which proceeded unabated during 1992, 1994, and 1996 despite a set of in-state electoral disturbances. In 1992, native son Bill Clinton's presidential candidacy, which raised $4.5

million in Arkansas[1] (Brummett 1993; White 1992), effectively dried up the state's political money supply. Of course, Clinton's candidacy also monopolized state media attention, as well as elicited a larger-than-usual turnout of the state's Democratic base. In 1994, Clinton's troubled presidency dominated the public square in his home state, to the detriment of candidates competing for lesser offices. In 1996, the conviction of Clinton's 1990 running mate and successor, Governor Jim Guy Tucker, during the first Whitewater trial, headlined a parade of scandals that thinned the ranks of the state's Democratic establishment and seemed to open several windows of opportunity for Arkansas Republicans. But at the top of the Democratic ticket once again stood Arkansas's Clinton, this time as the incumbent president. Arkansas Republicans working in Clinton's shadow can verify the significance of Miroff's (1982) work on the problems that the presidency poses for others trying to compete for public attention.

Yet the number of offices contested by state Republicans, and the vote shares won by Republicans, grew during each election cycle in the 1990s. A pattern of steady partisan change is likely to mature into stable Republican growth and contains positive implications for the growth of two-party competition in Arkansas.

"Left Waiting at the Altar": The Arkansas GOP in the 1980s

The 1980s began full of hope and promise for Arkansas Republicans. Longtime incumbent Republican representative John Paul Hammerschmidt, entrenched in the Third District since Rockefeller's breakthrough election of 1966, had help from a copartisan alliance in the state congressional delegation for the first time in his career. Ed Bethune, a talented Republican attorney, had been elected to Wilbur Mills's old Second District seat in 1978. Also that year, the state GOP had contested a record forty-one of one hundred seats in the Arkansas House of Representatives, as well as two of eighteen seats in the Arkansas Senate (Whistler, forthcoming, chap. 3). Then, when Frank White upset Governor Bill Clinton in 1980 and Arkansas returned to the Republican column in the electoral college as well, the future looked very bright indeed for the state GOP.

But it was not to be. White had only been the accidental beneficiary of an electoral "spanking." Many had voted for White with the intent of scaring, not defeating, their bright young rising star. Chastened by defeat, Clinton told the state's voters that he had "gotten the message" and would learn from his mistakes, and he bent the full power of his campaign skills to the task of sweeping the less appealing White from office in 1982. After Clinton secured passage of his education reform package, the GOP could not find a good candidate in 1984, recycled Frank White in 1986, and turned to Sheffield Nelson in 1990. Clinton won no less than 57.3 percent of the vote in any of these races.

Meantime, Ed Bethune loosened his sure grip on the Second District seat for an ill-advised run against incumbent U.S. senator David Pryor in 1984 and lost by a 15 percent margin. His seat reverted to Democratic hands for the duration of the 1980s, until its occupant, Tommy Robinson, switched parties. There would be no more electoral gains for Arkansas Republicans at the top of the ticket. They would end the 1980s without the governor's mansion, and they would regain their grip on two of the state's four congressional seats only through serendipity.

Nor were there any down-ticket GOP gains in legislative or court-house races as a result of top-down Republican growth similar to that experienced during the 1980s in other southern states such as South Carolina and Georgia (Bullock 1988, 1991a, 1991b). Instead, Republicans were able to contest an average of only 15.2 out of 100 seats in the Arkansas House of Representatives across the 1980–1988 elections, 2.0 out of 17 or 18 seats in the 35-member state Senate across the 1980 and 1984–1988 elections, and 11 out of 35 seats in the postreapportionment election of 1982. In contrast, during the three elections of the Rockefeller years (1966–1970), the GOP fielded candidates for an average 35.0 of the 100 seats in the lower house and 7.67 of the 35 seats in the state senate (Whistler, forthcoming, chap. 3). Since that time (1968), Arkansas has had the fewest contested legislative races of any state in the South (Hamm and Anderson 1992, 5).

The "Reagan Revolution" had nowhere near the impact on the fortunes of Arkansas Republicans of the Rockefeller breakthrough of 1966. Therefore, it is difficult to dispute Blair and Savage's (1986) characterization of independent voters as Arkansas's true "second party." Not only was this characterization true even during the Reagan era, it was true especially during the Reagan era.

"Lovelier the Second Time Around": The GOP in the '90s

The 1990s, in contrast, thus far suggest a new era of Republican growth in Arkansas. Republicans at present control 50 percent of the state's congressional delegation plus the offices of governor and lieutenant governor. And although the Democrats continue to dominate the state legislature, both the number of two-party contests for seats in the Arkansas

General Assembly and the size of Republican vote shares in statewide
and legislative races are as high in the 1990s as they were in the Rockefeller years.

Statewide Contests

Table 10.1 updates Blair and Savage's (1986) study to include the
results of major statewide races from 1988 through 1996. As the data suggest, the Democratic vote share in Arkansas presidential, gubernatorial,
and senatorial contests declined as a whole between 1976 and 1996. In the
1992 and 1996 presidential contests, for example, Bill Clinton's 53 percent
shares are unimpressive for a favorite-son candidate, even when one
takes into consideration the presence of Perot on the ballot. Indeed, even
with Perot on the ballot, Bush probably would have carried Arkansas in
1992 against almost any Democrat except Clinton, or perhaps Al Gore.
Despite Perot's declining stock between 1992 and 1996, Clinton's 1996
Arkansas vote share remained stuck at 53 percent, which was only 4 percent higher than his 1996 national vote share, whereas in 1992 Arkansas
had given its favorite son a margin 10 percent higher than his share of the

Table 10.1
Democratic Voting for President, Governor, and U.S. Senator
in Two-Party Contests, 1976–1996

	President	Governor	U.S. Senator
1976	65.0	83.2	
1978		63.4	76.6
1980	47.5	48.1	
1982		54.7	
1984	39.6	57.3	57.3
1986[a]		63.9	62.2
1988	42.2		
1990		57.5	—[b]
1992	53.2		60.1
1994		59.8	
1996	53.7		47.2

[a]Arkansas shifted from two-year to four-year gubernatorial terms
beginning with the 1986 election.

[b]Incumbent David Pryor did not have a Republican opponent in 1990
and won 99.7 percent of the vote versus an independent.

national vote. Thus, in 1996 as well, one cannot help being impressed by the competitiveness of the Republican presidential ticket in Clinton's home state and cannot but wonder if the favorite-son factor was again the only thing keeping the state out of the Republican column.

In the other major statewide race in 1992, incumbent Democratic senator Dale Bumpers was reelected to a fourth term over Mike Huckabee. However, Huckabee, a Baptist clergyman and accomplished speaker, performed so impressively during the campaign that he was dubbed a rising political star. Unlike Sheffield Nelson, the 1990 and 1994 Republican gubernatorial nominee, whose wooden campaigns were fashioned from the national party boilerplate of the 1980s, Huckabee adroitly invoked the moderate Winthrop Rockefeller as well as Ronald Reagan and established himself as being in or near Arkansas's political mainstream.

Half a year later, in the special election held to replace Lieutenant Governor Jim Guy Tucker, Huckabee narrowly defeated Nate Coulter. In 1994, Huckabee retained the office with 58.6 percent of the vote against state senator Charlie Cole Chaffin (D-Benton), even while Governor Tucker was defeating Nelson by a wide margin. The rest, as they say, is history: Tucker's conviction in the first Whitewater trial in early 1996 catapulted Huckabee into the governor's office in such rapid succession following Tucker and Clinton that Arkansans could be pardoned for thinking that the governorship still carries a two-year term.

Tucker's conviction not only netted the GOP the governorship but also altered the race for the retiring David Pryor's U.S. Senate seat. Huckabee had announced his intention to run for the vacant Senate seat, but Tucker's conviction forced the lieutenant governor to reconsider. Huckabee was the clear favorite, but he decided that the state's need for orderly succession should take precedence over his own career and announced that he would give up the nomination. Representative Tim Hutchinson announced that he would seek the GOP Senate nomination.

At the last minute, however, Tucker tried to withdraw his resignation and nearly altered the ballot for the senatorial race once again. Having already demonstrated his spite by making 310 appointments after his conviction[2] and spending most of the funds in the Governor's Emergency Fund, Tucker announced at Huckabee's swearing-in ceremony that he was rescinding his resignation, pending appeal, because of the discovery that one of the twelve jurors who had voted for his conviction had become an in-law of an old political enemy during the course of the trial. Everyone present for the transition-of-power ceremony was shocked. Attorney General Winston Bryant, who had won the Democratic nomination, was apoplectic. Both his present office and his future ambition were jeopardized by Tucker's announcement, which would have freed Huckabee to resume his own pursuit of Pryor's Senate post. Amid the furor, wiser heads prevailed, and Tucker was convinced by his own party's legislative leaders that they would not back him (Wekkin 1996, 1997; O'Neal 1996).

The Republicans not only captured the governorship by default but also held on to Huckabee's vacated office and gained Pryor's Senate seat, as well. Winthrop Paul Rockefeller, son of the late governor, ran a weak race for lieutenant governor and barely won. In contrast, Representative Tim Hutchinson defeated Attorney General Bryant, who had never lost in seven previous statewide races. County returns in this race along with those of other statewide contests during the 1990s show that Hutchinson, a Christian conservative, not only piled up huge victory margins in his home district base but also fared comparatively well in the "Delta Democrat" strongholds of east and southeast Arkansas. In the seventeen counties between Crowley's Ridge and the Mississippi River, Hutchinson averaged 42.6 percent of the vote, where Nelson in 1994 had pulled only 33.7 percent, Huckabee in 1992 had pulled only 29.0 percent, and Bush in 1992 had averaged only 28.9 percent. As an open-seat race, this contest attracted huge amounts of coordinated expenditures and soft money transfers for get-out-the-vote (GOTV) and attack ads from both national party organizations. The state GOP received more than $700,000 in soft money transfers from national party committees, $350,000 to $375,000 of which was spent on state-party-sponsored "issue ads" admonishing Attorney General Bryant for requesting a large budget increase for his office and suggesting that voters call and ask Bryant to stop wasting their money. Although the state party spent the rest of this money on advertising attacking the Democratic opponents of its nominees in the First, Second, and Third District races, the National Republican Senatorial Committee and allied groups spent additional funds on issue ads attacking Bryant. In turn, the Arkansas Democratic Party received well over $1 million in soft money transfers for its advertising campaign seeking to link Tim Hutchinson to Newt Gingrich and imploring voters to call Hutchinson and "tell him to stop listening to Newt and start listening to us." Another $1 million was spent on Democratic telephone banks and "walking around" money.

Congressional District Contests

As the 1990s started, the Arkansas congressional delegation was so stable and, in most cases, so senior that candidate emergence in federal races was at best stunted. Hammerschmidt had held the Third District seat since 1966. Democrat Bill Alexander, probably the most liberal politician who has ever represented Arkansas in Washington, had held the First District seat since 1968. Bumpers had served in the U.S. Senate since 1974, where David Pryor joined him in 1978, the same year that Democrat Beryl Anthony was elected to represent south Arkansas. Among Arkansas's federal seats, only the Second District seat could be considered a high-turnover district (five have held the seat since Wilbur Mills retired in 1976),[3] and even it acquired instant stability when former congressman Ray Thornton took it over in 1990.

Such stability did not seem to permit much outlet for higher ambitions (Veasey and Wekkin 1993). Then the floodgates of competition suddenly opened. Hammerschmidt announced his retirement in 1992, putting the Third District in play for the first time in twenty-six years. Hutchinson held the district for the Republican Party despite a strong Democratic challenge. Blanche Lambert, a former member of Bill Alexander's staff, who had taken note of Democrat Jim Wood's strong primary challenge to the liberal Alexander in the late 1980s and Republican Terry Hayes's respectable showing against Alexander in 1990, filed against her former boss, defeated him in the 1992 primary, and then dashed Hayes's soaring hopes with a 69 to 30 percent beating. Democratic secretary of state Bill McCuen ran against Fourth District incumbent Beryl Anthony and pulled off an upset victory. Thinking the district safely Democratic, McCuen then coasted through the summer months, mounted a desultory fall campaign, and was beaten by his Republican opponent, Jay Dickey. Only the Second District's Thornton had a walkover in 1992.

In 1994 the political equilibrium of the state's U.S. House delegation was somewhat restored, insofar as all four incumbents won. Signs of change afoot, however, included fairly close competition in all four races, which was more of a positive for state Republicans than for Democrats. In the First District, Warren Dupwe had a surprisingly strong showing against incumbent Blanche Lambert Lincoln. In the Second, conservative radio talk show host Bill Powell ran well in losing to Thornton. In the Third District, Tim Hutchinson strengthened his grip, and the Republicans', with a solid margin. In the Fourth, Republican Jay Dickey defeated state senator Jay Bradford.

In 1996, until midautumn it looked as if the Arkansas GOP might sweep all four congressional districts. Warren Dupwe, who had run so well in 1994 against Blanche Lambert Lincoln in the First District, appeared to have enough of a head start to beat the odds in the traditionally Democratic district when the young congresswoman announced that she was expecting a multiple birth and would not run for reelection. Ray Thornton's decision to seek a seat on the Arkansas Supreme Court opened up the Second District again, and vigorous primaries, culminating in June runoffs, ensued on both sides. When it was all over, Republican Bud Cummins had vanquished several other Republicans for the right to face Democratic state senator Vic Snyder. In the GOP's Third District stronghold, Hutchinson's decision to seek Pryor's Senate seat left the district's GOP nomination in the very capable hands of his older brother, Asa Hutchinson. A former U.S. attorney under Reagan, Asa Hutchinson had run a creditable campaign against Dale Bumpers in 1986, had lost even more narrowly to Winston Bryant in the attorney general race in 1990, and remained in the political spotlight thereafter by cochairing the state GOP. Sources in Governor Huckabee's office expressed confidence in the summer of 1996 that Asa Hutchison "could mail it in" in the Third—a sentiment that spread more widely when Democratic primary winner Boyce Davis withdrew from the race in late summer. Finally, in the Fourth District, Jay Dickey was regarded by both parties as well entrenched.

The Democratic nominees proved just too competitive for such a Republican sweep to occur. In the First District, where the numerous African Americans are of course Democrats and the delta whites are just as likely to be "yellow-dog Democrats" as conservatives, Democratic votes just seemed to materialize for Warren Dupwe's little-known Democratic opponent, Marion Berry, who won with 52.7 percent of the vote. State-party-financed "issue ads" linked Dupwe to Newt Gingrich and frightened elderly voters by saying that cuts in Social Security and Medicare were in store. Extensive GOTV efforts aimed at the African American vote also probably played a role in retaining the seat in the Democratic column. In the usually competitive Second District, the race between former law school classmates Bud Cummins and Vic Snyder turned into an ugly brawl. Negative ads painted Snyder as too liberal for the district, which was easy to do because Snyder had championed same-sex marriage and repeal of the state's sodomy laws, among other liberal causes, while in the state senate. The state and national Democratic parties in turn ran a countercampaign attacking Cummins as a religious right extremist. Snyder's own ads took the high road by stressing his service in Vietnam and as a caring doctor and community servant, but each candidate felt smeared by the other because of the political parties' issue ads. Ironically, some Cummins backers claim that the negative ads highlighting Snyder's liberalism were working and, given two more weeks or so, would have put Cummins ahead; but many voters less liberal than Snyder claim to have pulled the lever in sympathy for him because of the GOP attack ads.

In the Third District, the race became much more competitive than anyone could have predicted, especially after Boyce Davis withdrew after winning the Democratic nomination. Many in the party tried to persuade Lu Hardin, a state senator who had run unsuccessfully but impressively against Bryant for the U.S. Senate nomination, to pick up the reins. But Hardin, who had said no to a race in the Third in 1992 (Veasey and Wekkin 1993), demurred once again for the very realistic reason that there was not enough time left to raise money or campaign. Then University of Arkansas-Fayetteville professor Ann Henry, a Democratic activist and close personal friend of the Clintons, was nominated to run for the seat. Henry loaned herself $130,000 and, with the help of a Hillary Clinton–hosted $500-a-plate fund-raiser in Washington, managed to outpace Asa Hutchinson in fund-raising during the month of September (Whiteley 1996b). Betsy Wright, who had been Clinton's chief of staff in the state capital, was sent in to manage Henry's campaign. The national party committees pitched in with issue ads seeking to link Asa Hutchinson to Newt Gingrich. Henry put a bit of a scare into Hutchinson but ultimately had to settle for 41.8 percent of the vote.

It could well be that a better Democratic strategy might have been to leave the Third District uncontested after Boyce Davis dropped out. Henry's strong run in a traditional bastion of the opposing party appears to have served to stir up and turn out Republican voters in the Third District. A Republican official who did fieldwork in the First and Third District races maintains that the national Democratic Party's standard "cookie-cutter" ads linking Asa Hutchinson to Newt Gingrich and scaring elderly voters " backfired because a lot of voters up there like Newt Gingrich." Another effect of the Henry race was to make Asa Hutchinson work harder at turning out his votes, which also worked to the advantage of his brother's up-ticket race. Indeed, students of party candidate recruitment have pointed out that Republican strategists in some southern states recently have tried to discourage would-be GOP candidates from challenging really strong incumbents in down-ticket races, because the incumbents then work hard at turning out their supporters, which works to the advantage of the Democrats' up-ticket candidates (Cassie 1994).

Finally, in the Fourth District, incumbent Jay Dickey's attentive homestyle continued to pay dividends as he easiy won reelection against Vincent Tolliver, a young African American candidate. The state Republican Party, which spent heavily on issue ads in the First, Second, and Third District races, spent no advertising funds against Dickey's opponent.

Table 10.2
Average Republican Vote Share in Contested Races for the Arkansas General
Assembly, 1992–1996

	No. of Contested Races		% Voting Rep.[a]	
	House	Senate	House	Senate
1990	22	6	35.7	37.2
1992	25	7	42.8	52.7
1994	33	9	42.7	38.3
1996	34	6	44.3	42.5

[a]The averages shown are not calculated by adding up the total Republican vote in all legislative races. Rather, they are calculated as the average of the vote shares won by the
respective GOP candidates contesting seats. The latter is a better measure of the progress
of Republican competitiveness in races all across the state than the former average, which
can be influenced by the larger turnouts in some of the state's higher-growth areas, as well
as the larger GOP margins in the state's northwest Republican stronghold.

State Legislative Competition

As table 10.2 shows, Arkansas Republicans registered steady growth in
the number of seats contested in the state legislature during the 1990s. The
34 House seats contested in 1996 represent a greater than 50 percent
increase over the number of seats contested in each house in 1990 and a
greater than 100 percent increase relative to the average of 15.2 seats contested in the house across the five Reagan-era elections of 1980 through
1988. A similar progression in Republican challenges is not seen in the
senate; the number of seats contested in 1996 was the same as in 1990. Two
points, however, should be kept in mind. First, the number of seats contested did grow in 1990, 1992, and 1994, only to drop from 9 to 6 in 1996.
Second, the drop in 1996 shows that the measure used can have the effect
of disguising Republican successes: some Republican legislators are not
being challenged by Democrats for reelection. Tables 10.2 and 10.3 show
that in 1996 Republicans contested 34 races in the house of representatives
and won 14 seats. Yet, when we look at the results of those 34 house races,
we find that Republicans won only 5 of them. Obviously, then, the
remaining Republican house members had no Democratic challengers in
1996 (although one has been elected in a special election since November).

A similar progression in the size of the average vote share won by
Republican legislative candidates during the 1990–1996 elections is
shown in the right-hand columns of table 10.2. The average vote share
across all house races grew from 35.7 percent in 1990 to 44.3 percent in
1996, and that for the senate races grew, despite a precipitous drop fol-

Table 10.3
Partisan Division of the Arkansas General Assembly in the
1990s

	House[a]		Senate[b]	
	Rep.	Dem.	Rep.	Dem.
1991–1992	9	91	4	31
1993–1994	10	90	5	30
1995–1996	12	88	7	28
1997–1998	14	86	7	28

[a]100 seats total
[b]35 seats total

lowing 1992, from 37.2 percent in 1990 to 42.5 percent in 1996. These averages are calculated as the average of the percentage of the vote won by each GOP candidate.

Not only has the number of contested races risen; the percentage of what Hamm and Anderson (1992) term "two-party competitive contests"—that is, contests in which the minority party wins at least 40 percent or more of the vote—has risen as well during the 1990s. In Arkansas during the 1990s, 17.5 percent of all house races and 19.5 percent of all state senate races qualify as two-party competitive. In contrast, from 1968 through 1990, only 3.2 percent of all races for the Arkansas House and 6.6 percent of all races for the Arkansas Senate met the two-party "competitive" criterion of a 60-40 or smaller split of the total vote (Hamm and Anderson 1992, 6–7 and tables 3–4).

Finally, table 10.3 shows that Republican fortunes in Arkansas legislative elections have slowly risen during the 1990s. The number of house seats occupied by Republicans has grown from nine during the seventy-eighth legislature (1991–1992) to fourteen during the eighty-first legislature (1997–1998), and the number of senate seats held by Republicans grew from four to seven during the same period. Again, the pattern is one of slow, steady Republican growth during the political turmoil in Arkansas in the 1990s.

Explaining Republican Growth in Arkansas

What accounts for this pattern of Republican growth? The theories are numerous. Some authors argue, in keeping with Key's (1949) belief that race and the racial-political equilibrium of the South are important factors structuring the politics of the region, that the evolving issue of race has transformed American politics in general and is the driving force behind the partisan-change process. Davison and Krassa (1991) posit a "white flight" theory of partisan change that has conservative whites in "black-belt" areas leaving the Democratic Party for the Republican Party after the 1965 Voting Rights Act increased the political presence of African Americans in the Democratic Party coalition by some 3 million voters in the South. A second theory holds that Republicanism began spreading in the South, at the level of presidential politics, before the civil rights movement turned from litigation to nonviolent collective action—indeed, even before *Brown v. Board of Education*, not to mention the Voting Rights Act and affirmative action—and has been percolating downward slowly ever since, as Key's "presidential Republicans" succumbed to the habit of supporting down-ticket Republicans as well (Bullock 1988, 1991a, 1991b; see also Sundquist 1973). Others regard two-party competition as one of the products of development, which concentrates both capital and labor in a locale, giving rise to parties representing each, as well as to urbanism. Sundquist's southern "metropolitan Republicans" (1973), Havard's (1972) urban and suburban southern "Whigs," Bass and DeVries's (1976) work on southern "transformation," and Mackey's (1991) study of the relationship between industrialization and the rise of Republicanism and two-party competition in the South all exemplify this approach. Still others cite the influx of sun-seeking or opportunity-seeking migrants with previously formed partisan attachments (Bass and DeVries 1976; Blair 1988, chap. 4).

All of these explanations are easily tested by comparing county election returns for the various races with county demographics from the 1990 census. Regression of Republican vote shares in each county against the percentage of African Americans in the county should enable us to test the racial hypothesis: if black-belt whites are indeed fleeing to the Republican Party, then a significant relationship should obtain between these variables. Regression of down-ticket Republican vote shares in each county against Republican vote shares in up-ticket races is a way to test the top-down hypothesis; again, the expected direction of the relationship is positive. Regression of GOP vote shares against the counties' percentages of urban population, per capita incomes, and high school graduation rates should enable us to test the development hypothesis. The direction of the relationship between all three of these variables and the dependent variable should be positive, and one or more should be significant. Finally, regression tests using county net population change since the last census as an independent variable should enable us to test the migration hypothesis. The elections data are from *Arkansas Elections*, a biennial publication of the Elections Division of the Arkansas Secretary of State's Office, and from returns for the 1996 election.[4] The demographic data are from Bell's *Arkansas Statistical Abstract, 1996* and, except for county per capita incomes, which are from 1992, are from the 1990 census.

Table 10.4 shows that in the statewide races since 1990, the Republican vote share in the 1992 presidential contest interacts significantly with the Republican vote share in all other statewide contests (as the 1988 presidential vote does, obviously, with the 1992 vote). It also achieves the greatest beta weight in every case except the 1996 Senate race, where it is nudged out by Percentage Urban, and the relationship always lies in the expected direction. Percentage African American does achieve significance in two statewide races (the 1994 gubernatorial and the 1996 presidential), but the coefficients are neither very large nor in the expected direction. Not surprisingly, this suggests that the Democratic Party does best where African Americans are most numerous. Percentage Urban is significant in the 1990 gubernatorial race, the 1994 lieutenant governor's race, and in the 1996 presidential race, as well as in that year's Senate race. However, in the 1990 case, the valence of the relationship is counterintuitive. Thus, its performance is only somewhat more impressive than that of Percentage African American, which itself is only marginally better than that of Population Change, which is significant only in the 1996 presidential contest.

Turning to the state general assembly election test results (table 10.5), the county Republican vote share in the 1992 and 1996 presidential contests proved to be a positive predictor of Republican vote shares in 1992 and 1996 races for the state house of representatives, but there were no significant correlates in 1994. The only other variable to achieve significance, this time in the anticipated direction, is the county percentage of African Americans during the 1996 state house elections.

In order to perform these tests on the races for the state house of representatives, some modification of the independent variables was necessary. Because several of the house districts contain portions of more than one county (sometimes as many as five), it was necessary to create demographics weighted to reflect the percentage of the district's total vote that each county contributed. Because the latter percentages varied to some degree as turnout changed from 1992 through 1994 to 1996, the results in table 10.5 should not be viewed with the same confidence as those in table 10.4. The evidence suggests that GOP growth in Arkansas in the 1990s is of the top-down variety and has less to do with race or modernization or population shift than is frequently supposed.

Table 10.4

Multiple Regression Correlates of Republican Vote Share in Statewide Contests, 1992–1996

Contest	Variable	B[a]	SE B[b]	Beta[c]	Sig T[d]
President					
1992	Bush's '88 %	.750	.055	.977	.000
	(adj. R^2 = .832; sig F = .000; N = 75)				
1996	Bush's '92 %	.834	.059	.711	.000
	% Urban	.042	.017	.140	.015
	% African American	-.082	.026	-.198	.002
	Population change	.120	.053	.175	.027
	(adj. R^2 = .892; sig F = .000; N = 75)				
Senator					
1992	Bush's '92 %	.963	.135	.645	.000
	(adj. R^2 = 650; sig F = .000; N = 75)				
1996	Bush's '92%	2.412	1.153	.310	.040
	% Urban	.662	.335	.328	.052
	(adj. R^2 = .069; sig F = .090; N = 75)				
Governor					
1990	Bush's '88 %	.716	.076	.738	.000
	% Urban	-.178	.025	-.543	.000
	(adj. R^2 = .801; sig F = .090; N = 75)				
1994	Bush's '92 %	.713	.078	.659	.000
	% African American	-.078	.035	-.203	.028
	(adj. R^2 = .775; sig F = .000; N = 75)				
Lt. Governor[e]					
1994	Bush's 92 %	.659	.092	.646	.000
	% Urban	.067	.027	.253	.015
	(adj. R^2 = .648; sig F = .000; N = 75)				
1996	Bush's 92 %	.751	.121	.582	.000
	(adj. R^2 = .624; sig F = 000; N = 75)				

Note: Correlates are obtained by regressing GOP candidates' vote shares in the 75 counties against county demographics and county returns for other statewide races.

[a]Slope coefficient.

[b]Standard error of slope coefficient.

[c]Standardized regression coefficient.

[d]Statistical significance of slope coefficient.

[e]The 1990 lieutenant governor's race was excluded from the analysis because it was felt that the race of one of the candidates could influence the findings, and data for the 1993 special election to fill the vacancy when Tucker succeeded Clinton were not obtained from the secretary of state's office.

Table 10.5

Multiple Regression Correlates of Republican Vote Share in State House of Representatives Races, 1992–1996

Year	Variable	B[a]	SE B[b]	Beta[c]	Sig T[d]
1992	Bush's '92 %	2.160	.825	.965	.017
	(adj. R^2 = .361; sig F = .023; N = 25)				
1994	No significant correlates				
	(adj. R^2 = .189; sig F = .959; N = 33)				
1996	Dole's '96 %	1.321	.626	.630	.044
	(adj. R^2 = .340; sig F = .006; N = 34)				

[a]Slope coefficient.

[b]Standard error of slope coefficient.

[c]Standardized regression coefficient.

[d]Statistical significance of slope coefficient.

Conclusion

Clearly, there has been movement toward Republicanism in Arkansas since 1990. Indeed, Arkansas has become a two-party state for purposes of federal and statewide offices. Furthermore, there is slow movement toward the Republican Party in state legislative elections. Republican rates of contesting and competitiveness in legislative races are double what they were during the Reagan era; in fact, they are the highest they have been since the Rockefeller elections of 1966–1970 and also match the rates achieved in that period. Indeed, other measures indicate that there is even slow movement toward the GOP in local races. Howard (1997) reports that the number of GOP candidates for local offices in Arkansas jumped from 66 in 1994 to 231 in 1996 and that the number of GOP victors grew during that time span from 21 to 65. After thirty years in the wilderness, Republicans may once again have an opportunity for a breakthrough.

To be sure, such rates of contesting and competitiveness also mean that Arkansas is still a one-party Democratic state as far as substate contests are concerned. After all, the GOP is no further along in this regard than it was in 1966. Remembering that the electoral shock of that year prompted Arkansas Democrats to come together and meet the Rockefeller challenge, the possibility that 1996 could energize them in a similar manner must be admitted. Contrasting the sizes of the respective parties' state legislative delegations, the Democrats still have an enormous pool of officeholders from which to groom a new generation of viable up-ticket candidates, whereas the Republicans, who are fielding candidates for only a third of the legislative offices, could find it hard to grow from the top down if there are no down-ticket GOP options for voters to choose. Indeed, many Republicans still run for office as independents, which in itself suggests that the party has not yet achieved a truly competitive footing.

Furthermore, measurements of partisan affect do not back up the behavioral measurements that suggest the growth of two-party competition. A statewide random digit-dialed Computer Assisted Telephone Interviewing (CATI) sample of 411 Arkansans conducted 10–19 February 1997 by the University of Central Arkansas Citizen Poll found that only 19 percent of the respondents considered themselves national Republicans, whereas 35 percent called themselves national independents and 40 percent were national Democrats.[5] Such findings are very consistent with the 1980s-era findings reviewed by Blair and Savage (1986). Moreover, the 25 percent of the sample who identified themselves as having different partisan/independent orientations at different levels of government also bring to mind the characterization of independents as Arkansas's "second political party."[6]

Ultimately, however, the objective electoral context suggests that Republicans may fare better than they did after 1966. In Huckabee, the Hutchinson brothers, Dickey, and Winthrop Paul Rockefeller, the Arkansas GOP has several stars, not just one, who might inspire other Republicans to file for office or prompt those who are merely ambitious for office to file as Republicans. Although one of these stars is again named Rockefeller, he neither tries to be nor is the leader of the party, and his family's fortune is not as threatening to copartisans in the more developed Arkansas of the 1990s as it was in the 1960s. Indeed, the state GOP has little need of such a patron; thanks to its own foresight in hiring experienced list-development specialists to build its contributor base to over twenty-six hundred, and thanks to state campaign finance reforms that lowered the limits from $1,000 to $300 on individual and PAC gifts to candidates, the party was able to raise over $1.5 million in 1996 (Howard 1997), in addition to the more than $1 million in soft money it received in transfers from national Republican committees.

Two other election reforms helped the Arkansas GOP to be more competitive in 1996 and will help it even more hereafter. First of all, Arkansas finally has joined the other forty-nine states in mandating state financing (as opposed to party financing) of primary elections, which means that participation in Republican primary contests will be as accessible to voters as Democratic primaries have been.[7] Second, the state's recently enacted term limits will begin pushing entire electoral classes (fifty house members and seventeen or eighteen senators) out of state offices, beginning in 1998. It also seems likely that Dale Bumpers may vacate his U.S. Senate seat in 1998. So many open-seat races should encourage more Republican filings and create a more level playing field thereafter. Under such objective conditions, it is hard not to forecast the emergence of real two-party competition on most levels in Arkansas.

However, the Arkansas GOP tripped during the Rockefeller era over the stumbling block of factionalism, and more recent political events suggest that factionalism could emerge to brake the party's progress again. In 1990, political brawling between GOP gubernatorial primary rivals Sheffield Nelson and Tommy Robinson hurt the party's image during the general election and necessitated a negotiated cochairmanship of the state party thereafter. And now one of the peacemakers in that 1990 episode, Asa Hutchinson, has been a target for those worried about the appearance of a Hutchinson "dynasty." Only time will tell whether Arkansas is ready for the Republicans, and whether the Republicans themselves are ready.

Notes

1. Most of this money was raised very early, in advance of the first presidential primaries.

2. According to Governor Huckabee's press secretary, Rex Nelson (1996), not one vacancy in state government existed when Huckabee took his oath of office.

3. Since Mills, the Second District has been represented by Democrat Jim Guy Tucker (1977–1978), who ran unsuccessfully for the Democratic nomination to replace Senator John McClelland in 1978; Republican Ed Bethune (1979–1984), who ran unsuccessfully against incumbent senator David Pryor in 1984; Tommy Robinson (1985–1990), who switched to the Republican Party in 1989 after the House Democratic Caucus stripped him of his committee assignments for supporting an Illinois Republican colleague for reelection and then lost the 1990 GOP gubernatorial nominaton to Sheffield Nelson in a bitter contest; Ray Thornton (1991–1996), who probably returned to Congress so he could complete the ten years of service needed to qualify for the generous congressional pension and then ran successfully for the Arkansas Supreme Court in 1996; and Vic Snyder (1997–).

4. Until publication of the 1996 volume of *Arkansas Elections*, these data can be obtained as a Microsoft Excel 5.0 file (PREC.ZIP) by sending $1 to the Secretary of State's Office, State Capitol, Little Rock, AR 72201.

5. The author wishes to thank the University of Central Arkansas Foundation and the chair of its grants committee, John Ward, for their financial support of the UCA Citizen Poll.

6. Interestingly, however, the percentage of Arkansans calling themselves *state* Republicans in the February 1997 poll was higher, at 20 percent, compared to

33 percent state independents and 40 percent state Democrats. In previous measurements taken by the author in Arkansas and nationwide, the percentage of respondents calling themselves state Republicans has never come close to, much less exceeded, the percentage calling themselves national Republicans.

7.   Until 1996, primary elections in Arkansas were financed by the county parties out of filing fees determined by three-person county election commissions controlled by the party that enjoyed majority control of the Arkansas General Assembly. (Prior to Rockefeller's 1966 gubernatorial victory, however, Arkansas law had specified that the party controlling the governor's mansion would enjoy majority control of the county election commissions.) Under this arrangement, the paucity of Republican candidates meant that most county GOP units could not afford to staff more than one or two voting precincts in the entire county, discouraging voter participation.

References

Adcock, Robert H. 1997. Telephone interview by author, 5 February.

Appleton, Andrew M., and Daniel S. Ward. 1994. "Party Organizational Response to Electoral Change: Texas and Arkansas." *American Review of Politics* 15: 191–212.

Bass, Jack, and Walter DeVries. 1976. *The Transformation of Southern Politics.* New York: Meridian.

Bearden, Richard. 10 February 1997. Telephone interview by author.

Bell, Jerry L., ed. 1995. *Arkansas Statistical Abstract, 1996.* Little Rock: Arkansas Census State Data Center.

Benham, Terry. 1997. Telephone interview by author, 18 February.

Blair, Diane D. 1988. *Arkansas Politics and Government.* Lincoln: University of Nebraska Press.

Blaire. Diane D., and Robert L. Savage. 1986. "The Appearance of Realignment and Dealignment in Arkansas." Pp. 126–40 in *The South's New Politics: Realignment and Dealignment,* edited by Robert H. Swansbrough and David M. Brodsky. Columbia: University of South Carolina Press.

Brummett, John. 1993. Telephone interview by author, January.

Bullock, Charles S., III. 1988. "Regional Realignment: An Officeholding Perspective." *Journal of Politics* 43: 662–82.

———. 1991a. "Southern Partisan Changes: When and How." *Midsouth Political Science Journal* 12 (Spring): 23–32.

———. 1991b. "Republican Strength at the Grass Roots: An Analysis at the County Level." *Midsouth Political Science Journal* 12 (Autumn): 80–99.

Cassie, William E. 1994. "More May Not Always Be Better: Republican Recruiting Strategies in Southern Elections." *American Review of Politics* 15: 141–55.

Davison, Donald L., and Michael A. Krassa. 1991. "Blacks, Whites, and the Voting Rights Act." *Midsouth Political Science Journal* 12 (Summer): 3–22.

Hamm, Keith E., and R. Bruce Anderson. 1992. "State Legislative Elections,

1968–1991: Patterns of Contestation and Competitiveness." Paper presented at the annual meeting of the Southern Political Science Association, Atlanta, Ga.

Havard, William C. 1972. *The Changing Politics of the South.* Baton Rouge: Louisiana State University Press.

Howard, Tom. 1997. "Trends toward a Two-Party System in Arkansas: An Analysis of Republican Party Progress, 1984 to 1996." Paper presented at the annual meeting of the Arkansas Political Science Association, Fayetteville, Ark., 21 February.

Key, V. O., Jr. 1949. *Southern Politics in State and Nation.* New York: Knopf.

Mackey, Eric M. 1991. "Industrialization and Two-Party Democracy." *Midsouth Political Science Journal* 12 (Autumn): 100–112.

Miroff, Bruce I. 1982. "Monopolizing the Public Space: The President as a Problem for Public Politics." In *Rethinking the Presidency,* edited by Thomas I. Cronin. Boston: Little, Brown.

Nelson, Rex. 1996. Telephone interview by author, 10 August.

O'Neal, Rachel. 1996. "Tucker Ousted." *Arkansas Democrat-Gazette,* 16 July, 1A.

Sundquist, James L. 1973. *Dynamics of the Party System.* Washington: Brookings Institution.

Veasey, R. L., and Gary D. Wekkin. 1993. "Ambition and Perspective in Postmodern Politics: The Arkansans Who Stayed Home." Conway: University of Central Arkansas.

Wekkin, Gary D. 1997. "Arkansas Politics after Jim Guy Tucker." In *Arkansas Politics: A Reader,* edited by Richard Wang and Michael Dougan. Fayetteville, Ark.: M & M Press.

———. 1996. "Whitewater, Arkansas Politics, and Election '96." *Comparative State Politics* 17: 28–35.

Whistler, Donald E. Forthcoming. *The Modern Arkansas General Assembly.* Conway: University of Central Arkansas.

White, Frank. 1993. Telephone interview by author, February.

——— 1997. Telephone interview by author, 7 February.

Whiteley, Michael. 1996a. "Armey Takes Bite Out of 'Cookie Cutter' Ads." *Arkansas Democrat-Gazette,* 17 October, B1.

———.1996b. "Henry Contributions Outpace Hutchinson's." *Arkansas Democrat-Gazette,* 17 October, B1.

11

Oklahoma: GOP Realignment in the Buckle of the Bible Belt

Ronald Keith Gaddie and Scott E. Buchanan

The Expatriate Southern State

Oklahoma has often stood at the fringe of the South, both in the study of southern politics and in its mind-set. While Oklahoma was not a state at the time of the Civil War, many of the events and cultural factors that structure Oklahoma politics are distinctly southern. As in many southern states, the GOP has enjoyed a dramatic growth in adherents and electoral success in contests for major offices. What is so intriguing about the Republican growth in Oklahoma is the catalyst of growth. In most southern states studies have shown that Republican growth can be linked to race (Lamis 1988; Carmines and Stimson 1989; Black and Black 1992). Race is not such a divisive issue in Oklahoma. Only 6.7 percent of the state population is black (Morgan, England, and Humphreys 1991). Instead, religion—the growth of the Christian Right—appears to be a major catalyst in the GOP upswing.

Oklahoma was originally part of the Louisiana Purchase. Most of present-day Oklahoma was set aside from the purchase as Indian territory. During the 1820s the Five Civilized Tribes (the Cherokees, Chickasaws, Choctaws, Creeks, and Seminoles) were forcibly removed from Florida, Georgia, and Alabama to the Indian Territory. Once there, the tribes established five Indian nations that ruled as republics under written constitutions (Morgan, England, and Humphreys 1991). During the Civil War some Indian tribes, most notably the Cherokees, sided with the Confederacy. Many tribes owned slaves, and the potential costs of abolition to the tribes were great. The Oklahoma tribes sent delegates to the Confederate Congress and served in the southern armies.

As early as the 1840s, white settlers were anxious to take the lands of Oklahoma. The federal government attempted to keep settlers out. After the end of the Civil War, the Five Civilized Tribes underwent a reconstruction as harsh as that of the rest of the South. Indian participation in the rebellion gave the federal government sufficient cause to seize the central and west Oklahoma lands from the tribes and then to open the territory to white settlement. In the remaining Indian territories, tribes were forced to free their slaves and to offer the freedmen membership in the tribes. In response to the emancipation of the blacks, the tribes passed segregation laws that created all-black townships and placed limitations on the black freedmen that resembled the Jim Crow laws.

In the 1880s, the Bureau of Indian Affairs declared the tribal reservation system to be an abysmal failure. This evaluation was reached by the Dawes Commission, apparently under some influence from development interests that sought to open the Indian Territory to white settlement. The lands of the Civilized Tribes were broken up, and each tribal member was granted a 160-acre homestead. The territory was partitioned into two territories: Oklahoma Territory, which took in the northern and western parts of the state; and the Indian Territory, which covered an area roughly below a line running from the northeast corner of the state, through Tulsa and Oklahoma City, and on east to the Texas border. This partition is reflected in the settlement patterns and subsequent political behavior of the state. White settlers in the Indian Territory were largely expatriate southerners from Texas, Arkansas, and Mississippi. A journey through the southeast corner of the state reveals that many of the towns and counties take their names directly from Mississippi locales.

The Democratic Party dominated state politics from the first state elections in 1907 until the 1990s. The only exceptions to Democratic hegemony were the two Republicans elected governor in the 1960s and 1980s and the brief Republican control of the state legislature from 1920–1922. At the presidential level, the Democrats faded more quickly; Lyndon Johnson is the only Democrat to carry Oklahoma since 1952.

The reputation of Oklahoma politics is conservative. This reputation is not altogether accurate. In the early days of statehood the Democrats rode to dominance on a progressive platform, following the southern Democratic habit of coopting the Populists. Soon after statehood a series of economic depressions hit Oklahoma. Many Oklahomans supported socialist candidates, and by 1914 there were numerically more socialists in Oklahoma than in New York State. The Socialist candidate for governor pulled nearly 20 percent of the vote. This socialist presence cost the Democrats control of the state legislature in 1920, as well as a U.S. Senate seat and three congressional districts. The Democrats regained control of the legislature in 1922, and by the time of the New Deal realignment the GOP was thoroughly devastated. In the late 1950s over half the legislative seats in the state still went to Democrats without contest (Hale and Kean 1996).

The 1950s were a difficult time for the Oklahoma Republican Party. Despite the successive Eisenhower victories in 1952 and 1956, the state political scene was still thoroughly dominated by the Democrats. The 1958 GOP gubernatorial candidate won only 19 percent of the vote and lost every county. While the GOP was politically frustrated, Oklahoma was confronting difficulties with segregation. As we noted above, Oklahoma has a relatively small black population. Nonetheless, the state had maintained the Jim Crow laws inherited from the tribes and the territorial government. Unlike the Deep South states, Oklahoma did not get caught up in massive resistance and instead quietly complied with the *Brown* decision.

The 1960s were a better time for the GOP. In 1962, Henry Bellmon was elected the first Republican governor of Oklahoma. As the decade proceeded, Republicans won a congressional seat; Goldwater ran ahead of his national average, although Johnson carried the state for president. In 1966, Republican Dewey Bartlett succeeded Bellmon as governor (at that time Oklahoma governors were limited to a single term). Bellmon was subsequently elected to the Senate in 1968, where he was joined by Bartlett in 1972.

Below the level of major statewide offices, success by the GOP was at best fleeting. Like many southern states, Oklahoma was forced to reapportion the state legislature and congressional districts to accommodate the one-man, one-vote standards set in *Baker v. Carr* and *Westbury v. Sanders*. Rural interests had traditionally been overrepresented in the legislature owing to guarantees of representation for each county. This malapportionment helped to perpetuate the Democratic domination of both chambers. Since reapportionment the Democrats have continued to hold substantial majorities, especially in the rural areas, while Republicans are elected almost entirely from the populous metropolitan counties.

As in much of the South, the GOP suffered setbacks after Watergate. The governorship and one of the Senate seats were lost to the Democrats, and the GOP lost seats in the House. In the 1980s the Republicans embarked on another era of expansion. Republican registration surged, and the GOP won more seats in the legislature. Henry Bellmon, retired from the Senate in 1980, returned for another term as governor in 1986. Don Nickles, a thirty-one-year-old Republican businessman from Ponca City who ran with evangelical support, succeeded Bellmon in the Senate. The GOP held two U.S. House seats from 1986 forward, when James

Inhofe was elected to represent the House district surrounding Tulsa. The extent of GOP electoral expansion then stagnated, to be followed by a flood of success in 1994.

A systematic electoral eradication of Democrats started in 1994. Entering the election year, the GOP held one Senate seat, two House seats, and no major state office. After the November election, Republicans held both U.S. Senate seats and five of six U.S. House seats and had recaptured the governor's mansion. In 1996 the last Democratic congressional seat was captured by the Republicans, after incumbent Bill Brewster retired and was succeeded by party-switching former incumbent Wes Watkins.

The Geography of Oklahoma Partisanship

The most direct evidence of changing allegiances in the electorate is in the voter registration figures. Oklahoma uses a partisan registration system with a closed party primary, which allows us to examine the expressed preferences of voter allegiance. With the exception of a brief falloff of support from 1974 to 1978, the Republican proportion of registered voters has increased steadily from less than 20 percent of voters in 1964 to about 36 percent in January 1996 (see figure 11.1). Most of this growth occurred between 1980 and 1990, and the change in partisan balance appears to be related to the falloff in registered Democrats, as well as to gains in registered Republicans. Oklahoma has traditionally gained and lost population with the cycles of sudden economic boom and long, drawn-out decline. The most recent of these cycles did not distribute its impact

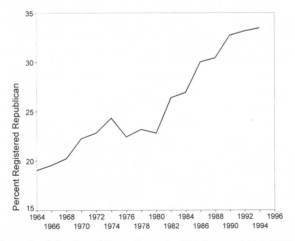

Fig. 11.1. Growth of the Republican Party in Oklahoma, 1964–1996

evenly across parties. A general decline in registrants occurred at the depth of the oil bust and reduced the number of Democratic registrants from 1.4 million to just over 1.1 million, a loss of 300,000 voters. Since the oil collapse in 1986, the number of GOP registrants has hovered around 600,000. The net number of registrants gained by Republicans since 1980 is roughly twice that gained by Democrats.

The geographic settlement patterns of Oklahoma play a prominent role in explaining the politics of the state. After the Oklahoma Territory was opened to white settlement, the western and northern tiers of counties were settled by midwesterners and plainsmen, especially those steeped in the Jayhawker traditions of Kansas. The southern and eastern counties, especially in Indian territory, were settled by southerners from Texas, Mississippi, and Arkansas. Democrats dominated politics in the state after co-opting the progressive and socialist movements. The west and north continued as a Republican redoubt.

As the urban centers of Oklahoma grew, the political geography of the state took on the tripartite shape now familiar to Oklahomans. If a line were drawn from the northeastern corner of the state to the southwestern corner, it would pass through the urban centers of Tulsa, Oklahoma City, and Lawton. The area to the north and west of this line and outside these cities is predominantly Republican and contains about 10 percent of the state population. To the south and east of the line is predominantly Democratic, the "Little Dixie" region that contains about 20 percent of the state's population. The remaining 70 percent of Oklahomans live in the urban corridor that encompasses the major cities of the state (Morgan, England, and Humphreys 1991).

The growth of the suburban corridor has not altered the partisan differences between the two major urban counties (Oklahoma and Tulsa) and the rest of the state. Kirkpatrick, Morgan, and Kielhorn (1977) observed that, in the 1960s, the major urban counties voted substantially more Republican than the rest of the state in major statewide elections. As indicated in table 11.1, the average urban-rural difference in gubernatorial elections is 12.9 percentage points. The GOP has won a majority of the urban core counties' vote on six of nine occasions but has not carried the rural vote since 1966. The urban vote constituted the margin of victory for the last three Republican governors, none of whom won an outright majority of the vote. The difference in the rural-urban vote was 10 to 14 points for every election since 1966, although in 1994 the margin was substantially larger—almost 19 points—because of the very large urban GOP vote.

The urban-rural split in Oklahoma is less pronounced in presidential races. Republican presidential candidates have won Oklahoma's electoral

Table 11.1
The Cities and Republican Success

	Statewide	OKC/ Tulsa	Out State	Difference
	Vote for Governor			
1962	55.2	61.2	52.5	+8.7
1966	55.7	65.3	51.0	+14.3
1970	48.1*	57.9	43.3	+14.6
1974	36.1	45.5	31.4	+14.1
1978	47.2	53.9	43.9	+10.0
1982	37.6	47.5	32.6	+14.9
1986	47.5*	54.5	44.0	+10.5
1990	36.2	43.0	32.9	+10.1
1994	46.9*	59.0	40.3	+18.7
	Vote for President			
1964	44.3	51.3	40.7	+10.6
1968	47.7*	52.9	44.9	+8.0
1972	73.7	76.3	72.2	+4.1
1976	49.9*	58.8	45.1	+13.7
1980	60.5	66.1	57.5	+8.6
1984	68.6	72.3	66.6	+5.7
1988	58.4	64.0	54.6	+9.4
1992	42.6*	48.9	39.1	+9.8
1996	48.2*	54.1	45.1	+9.0

Sources: Samuel A. Kirkpatrick, David R. Morgan, and Thomas Kielhorn, *The Oklahoma Voter* (Norman: University of Oklahoma Press, 1977); and David R. Morgan, Robert E. England, and George G. Humphreys, *Oklahoma Politics and Policies* (Lincoln: University of Oklahoma Press, 1991). Figures for years since 1990 computed by authors from data provided by the Oklahoma State Board of Elections.

*GOP plurality win

votes in every election since 1968, and even in 1964, Goldwater ran six points ahead of his national showing. As in many southern states, Republican presidential candidates run ahead of other Republicans in rural, traditionally Democratic counties. Aistrup (1996) observed that the persistence of Republican success up the ticket in rural localities eventually leads to GOP success down-ticket in those areas. Southern voters have usually found it far easier to break first with the Democratic Party at the national level, where the policy stands and personal values of the party candidates are often at odds with southern tradition and values. The breaking of the southern-Democratic linkage at the state and local level requires greater effort, especially if the values of Democratic candidates comport with the beliefs and values of the Democratic electorate. When those linkages are broken and the Democratic Party is lost as an avenue of expression for conservatives, the opportunity for GOP growth is greatest (Heard 1952).

Some evidence of a down-ticket shift is illustrated in the recent political career of J. C. Watts, congressman from the Fourth District. Watts, a former football star and minister, first won elective office in 1990 in a statewide campaign for corporation commissioner. Watts then sought the open Fourth Congressional District seat in 1994, when incumbent Democrat Dave McCurdy tried to advance to the U.S. Senate. Watts advanced to the national stage with a close victory over Democrat David Berryhill (Bednar and Hertzke 1995), and he subsequently defended his seat against a well-funded Democratic challenger in 1996.

Watts's growing appeal to rural Oklahoma voters is evident in his performance across successive elections. When the county-level vote for Watts in the fourteen-county Fourth District is plotted against the GOP registration percentage for each county for the 1990, 1994, and 1996 elections, the Watts vote tracks closely with the percent GOP registration. However, change in his support is nonetheless evident. Watts ran slightly stronger in 1990 than 1994, and his 1996 performance tracks somewhere between the two. Watts's vote is stable (around 60 percent) for the more Republican, metropolitan counties of Cleveland (Norman) and Oklahoma (Oklahoma City) across all three elections. In the most rural, Democratic counties of the district, Watts's performance improves dramatically. In Cotton, Jefferson, and Tillman Counties (which all have GOP registration of less than 10 percent), Watts's vote share in 1996 improved by over 10 points over 1990 and 1994. Bivariate regression estimates of the Watts vote as a function of GOP registration indicate that in 1990 and 1994 the Watts vote was more closely associated with GOP registration (R^2 = .94 for both elections), while this relationship was weaker in 1996 (R^2 = .64). The intercept for the Watts vote increased from 31 percent of the vote in 1990 and 1994 to 47.5 percent in 1996. In the absence of any registered Democrats, Watts still pulled nearly a majority of a county's vote.

The areas where the GOP expects its greatest opportunities are in the suburban and exurban counties outside Oklahoma City and Tulsa that have strong, conservative Democratic traditions. The persistence of the electoral geography of the state since the 1960s is evident from figure 11.2. The most Republican counties in the state are in the north and west above

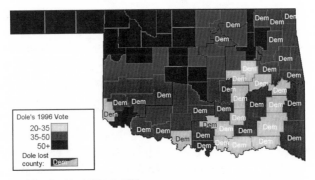

Republican Presidential Vote in 1996

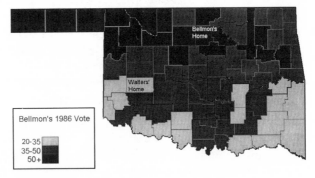

Republican Gubernatorial Vote in 1986

Fig. 11.2. The Partisan Political Geography of Oklahoma

the urban corridor. The other areas of GOP competitiveness are in the metropolitan counties around Tulsa and Oklahoma City. The center-city counties are the most solidly Republican. The only Democratic stronghold appears to be the southeastern part of the state.

The extent of GOP electoral success and the long-term stability of the voting patterns stand in contrast to the overwhelming Democratic registration in the state. The percent Republican registered stands at an all-time high of 36 percent. The analysis of support for Watts in the Fourth Congressional District indicates that the GOP registration base is a good predictor of the GOP vote. However, that analysis also indicates that anywhere from 30 to 40 percent of registered Democrats might defect in a given election. Certainly there is Democratic defection going on to sustain the competitive pattern of statewide elections.

The last three gubernatorial elections illustrate the stability of the partisan vote patterns and the role of campaigns in Oklahoma elections. The

1986, 1990, and 1994 elections exhibit a similar pattern, with Republicans running stronger to the northwest of the urban corridor and in the core urban counties of Tulsa and Oklahoma than in the in rural, Democratic counties in Little Dixie. Still, even in Little Dixie, where some counties can count their registered Republicans on one hand, the GOP consistently pulls 30 to 35 percent of the vote.

The Parties

"I don't belong to an organized political party; I am a Democrat.
—Will Rogers

The Democratic and Republican Party organizations in Oklahoma are decidedly different in their degree of organization and unity and in their relationships with the national parties. The state Democrats resemble the Democratic parties of so many southern states: fractured, rent by internal conflict, and loosely linked to the Democratic National Committee. The Oklahoma Republican Party has been centrally organized since the 1960s, and the state party has sought to follow the "grassroots" development model advanced by former Republican National Committee chairman Haley Barbour. More recently the Christian conservatives have firmly established themselves in the party.

For years Oklahoma was what Austin Ranney called a "modified one-party state" (Kirkpatrick, Morgan, and Kielhorn 1977; Hale and Kean 1996). However, as we have noted, Republicans have shown consistent national-election strength for almost forty years, even as the Democrats dominated state and local politics. Henry Bellmon, the first Republican governor of Oklahoma, sought to overcome the political anemia of the GOP in the 1950s by actively organizing the party at the county level. Bellmon's "Operation Countdown" emphasized candidate recruitment and voter mobilization. He even ventured into the Little Dixie region of the state. Bellmon's grassroots efforts won him the governorship in 1962, as well as the moniker of "father" to the modern Oklahoma GOP. In the 1980s, Republicans reinvigorated this strategy, using sophisticated data analysis and polling to target campaigns outside of the GOP strongholds. Grassroots mobilization of Republicans, especially evangelicals, has further invigorated the GOP.

For years the state Republican Party was characterized by a bifactionalism between "moneybags" elements from Tulsa (also called country-club Republicans) and "grassroots" elements from the small towns of the western plain and panhandle (Hale and Kean 1996; Jones 1974). Bellmon typified the country-club GOP, advocating smaller government and lower taxes; it is widely acknowledged that he has no patience for social-issue conservatives. The emergence of the Christian Right as a force in the party has therefore reoriented this factionalism to set traditional Bellmon Republicans against the Christian Right. For the present, intraparty disputes have been muted by the success enjoyed by the GOP.

The Oklahoma Democrats are decidedly less organized. Until 1990, the state party did little to organize with the national party. There is no paid staff. The Democratic National Committee does not see Oklahoma as a critical state, and consequently national party funds and support are not readily forthcoming. As Hale and Kean put it, "Oklahoma is simply not a priority for the [Democratic] national party" (1996, 303).

The decentralized state Democrats are hamstrung by internal divisions. A mix of urban liberals and unionists, Little Dixie state legislators, and county elected officials compose the principal factions. The struggle between legislators and county officials for control of local projects in part underlies this division, as do the continued efforts of urban liberals and union officials to change the state's right-to-work law. The large number of local and state legislative Democrats means that there are a variety of ambitious officeholders who are all seeking political advancement, in the face of a rising Republican tide. Again, quoting Hale and Kean (1996) "with so many elected officials . . . seeking the spotlight, it is difficult for any one person to energize or direct the [Democratic] party." In contrast, a series of strong, insightful Republican state chairs—Tom Cole, Clinton Key, and Quineta Wylie—have taken advantage of the organizational groundwork laid by Henry Bellmon to develop a set of grassroots organizations and strategies that exploit the division among Democratic voters. Mobilizing the religious right and targeting congressional and state legislative races have paid electoral dividends.

The Legislature

Democrats dominate the Oklahoma state legislature. GOP gains in the legislature roughly correspond to the gains by the party among registered voters. The growth of Republicans in the legislature is indicated in table 11.2. In 1962, the last election preceding the court-ordered reapportionment of state legislative seats to comply with the one-man, one-vote standard, the GOP held 24 of 129 house seats (18.5 percent) and 5 of 44 senate seats (11.3 percent). The reapportionment of seats produced a loss of 2

Table 11.2
Party and Race in the Oklahoma Legislature

	Republican (%)		Black (%)	
	House	Senate	House	Senate
1965	17.2	18.5	2.5	2.0
1967	24.8	18.8	2.9	2.0
1969	22.8	18.8	2.9	2.0
1971	20.8	18.8	2.9	2.0
1973	25.7	20.8	2.9	2.0
1975	24.8	18.8	2.9	2.0
1977	24.8	18.8	2.9	2.0
1979	25.7	18.9	2.9	2.0
1981	27.7	22.9	2.9	2.0
1983	24.8	29.2	2.9	2.0
1985	31.7	35.4	2.9	4.2
1987	30.7	31.3	2.9	4.2
1989	31.7	22.9	2.9	4.2
1991	31.7	22.9	2.9	4.2
1993	32.7	22.9	2.9	4.2
1995	35.6	27.8	2.9	4.2
1997	35.6	31.3	2.9	4.2

Note: There were 101 members of the Oklahoma House and 48 members of the Oklahoma Senate as of 1997.

Sources: Oklahoma Department of Libraries, *The Oklahoma Almanac, 1995–1996* (Oklahoma City: Oklahoma Department of Libraries, 1995); National Conference of State Legislatures (1996), www.ncsl.org/public/about.htm.

seats in the house and a gain of 5 in the senate. By 1991 the GOP house caucus had increased to 32 of 101 seats, with a pair of modest setbacks after Watergate and during the 1982 recession. The current GOP house caucus is 36 seats.

Republican success in the state senate has been more fleeting. Oklahoma state senators serve four-year terms, and those terms are staggered so that only half of the chamber comes up for reelection every two years. From 1964 to 1980, the GOP senate caucus cycled between nine and eleven senators out of forty-eight. GOP representation peaked at seventeen senators in the 1986 elections but fell off to eleven seats following the 1990 election. After the 1996 elections the GOP caucus in the senate stood at fifteen senators. Despite the use of staggered terms, the state senate is more vulnerable to the recent state and national political tides than the house. The peak of GOP senate representation came in the wake of Reagan's successful reelection and the return of Republican Henry Bellmon to the governor's mansion. The subsequent loss of four seats in the 1990 election came in the disastrous 26-point defeat of Republican Bill Price.

Despite the limited level of GOP representation, Republican gains have made an impact on lawmaking in Oklahoma. In the past, Republican governors found themselves largely at the mercy of the Democratic leadership in the legislature; when unified, Democrats had more than enough votes to override Republican gubernatorial vetoes. Frank Keating's election as governor in 1994 was accompanied by the first contemporary GOP caucus to exceed one-third of the membership in a chamber. Republicans can now sustain any gubernatorial veto, which enhances the limited powers of the governor.

Oklahoma Democratic legislators are primarily from rural districts. After the 1994 election, all fourteen senate districts that lie completely outside the five Oklahoma standard metropolitan statistical areas (SMSAs) were represented by Democrats. Thirteen GOP senators were elected from the two principal SMSAs of Oklahoma City and Tulsa.

The Democratic domination of rural districts is not so complete in the state house. About 45 percent of representatives are elected from outside SMSAs, but 58.4 percent of the Democratic caucus is elected from rural districts. By comparison, Republicans were elected from eleven of the twenty-three districts in the Tulsa SMSA and seventeen of twenty-seven districts in the Oklahoma City SMSA.

There has been little variation in black representation in Oklahoma. Currently, the state has five black state legislators: three state house members and two state senators (Congressman J. C. Watts is the other major black officeholder). All are elected from predominantly urban, center-city Tulsa and Oklahoma County districts.

Congressional Representation

The more dramatic change in Oklahoma politics has been the partisan turnover of the congressional delegation in the 1990s. Throughout its history the state sent overwhelmingly Democratic delegations to Congress. For a brief period in the 1970s the GOP held both U.S. Senate seats; however, only one majority-GOP House delegation had been elected since statehood, and that was in 1920. In the 1980s Oklahoma sent three Republicans to Congress: Senator Don Nickles (elected in 1980) and Representatives Mickey Edwards (elected 1976) and James Inhofe (elected 1986). This alignment continued into the 1990s. Then, after the 1992 election, the partisan balance of the state started to spin precipitously away from the Democrats. In early 1994 Democrat Glenn English resigned his west Oklahoma Sixth District seat. The subsequent special election pitted Republican state representative and rancher Frank Lucas against Democrat Dan Webber, a political aide and protégé of Democratic senator David L. Boren. This race was one of several such contests in 1994 that were closely watched as referenda on the presidency of Bill Clinton. Republican Lucas defeated Webber, despite the tremendous campaigning and fund-raising efforts by Democrats such as David Boren on behalf of his protégé. Bednar and Hertzke (1995) argue that Lucas's success was a product of the political activism of conservative Christians. Relying heavily on flyers and handbills distributed in evangelical churches, the Christian Coalition mobilized conservative voters to support Lucas's bid. This technique of contrasting the policy stands and beliefs of the candidates in terms of "acceptability" to the Christian Coalition became a hallmark of later congressional and state senate campaigns in 1994 and 1996.

Subsequent GOP congressional gains followed in the general election of 1994, largely as a consequence of the actions of Senator David L. Boren, the three-term Democratic senator and former governor of Oklahoma. Boren had enjoyed a mercurial political career. Elected to the state legislature while he was still in law school at the University of Oklahoma, Boren subsequently was elected governor in 1974 at age thirty-three with 64 percent of the vote, and in 1978 he advanced to the U.S. Senate. Boren enjoyed two successful reelections, including a massive 83 percent win in 1990 in which he carried all but two voting precincts in the state. Despite his electoral security and the respect and seniority accrued during his tenure in the Senate, by 1994 Boren was publicly discussing his dissatisfaction with the Senate and how he was "tired" of the Washington game. He resigned in early 1994 after publicly courting (and receiving) the presidency of the University of Oklahoma. Boren's departure prompted two congressmen, Dave McCurdy (D-4th) and James Inhofe (R-1st) to seek the open Senate seat. McCurdy's resignation presented an opportunity for another GOP gain in the House, and both elections proved to be heavily influenced by the activities of the Christian Right (Bednar and Hertzke 1995).

An unexpected opportunity for a GOP gain occurred in the east Oklahoma Second District. Incumbent congressman Mike Synar (D-2d) had survived a bitter primary and runoff in 1992 to gain reelection to an eighth term in office with a 56-41 win. In 1994, Synar again faced primary opposition, this time from a lightly regarded seventy-one-year-old retired schoolteacher who was backed by the Christian Coalition. Synar lost his fall bid for renomination. The GOP nominee, local obstetrician Tom Coburn, was also considered acceptable by the Christian Coalition and won election by 4 points.

In the two open House seats, a Christian Coalition–backed Republican retained the Tulsa First District vacated by Republican James Inhofe, and, as we noted previously, Republican evangelical minister and state corporation commissioner J. C. Watts won the previously Democratic Fourth District. The defeat of Democrat Dave McCurdy by Republican James Inhofe for the open Senate seat and the election of Republican Frank Keating in a three-cornered gubernatorial contest completed the stunning GOP victory in the major elections of 1994. At the beginning of 1994, five of the eight members of Oklahoma's congressional delegation and the governor had been Democrats. By 8 November, only one Democrat held major office in Oklahoma: Representative Bill Brewster (D-3rd), who would soon retire for reasons unrelated to politics. His departure in 1996 created an opportunity for the GOP to complete its sweep of the major elective positions in Oklahoma. Brewster's Little Dixie district was historically the most traditionally Democratic part of the state and might have proved a tough nut for the GOP to crack given the popularity of the moderate incumbent.

The Fall of the Last Redoubt: Little Dixie, 1996

The southeastern corner of Oklahoma, known as Little Dixie, starts at the edge of the Gulf Coast Plain in the western foothills of the Ozarks and runs west along the Texas border. Of all the parts of Oklahoma, Little Dixie displays the most quintessential (or stereotypical) southern character. Here business is conducted in small towns where nineteenth-century-style courthouses dominate the town square along with monuments to the honored war dead and forgotten founders. The largest city in the region, Ardmore, counts fewer than twenty-five thousand residents. The region is hillier than the rest of the state, bearing a close resemblance to the piney-wood regions of Arkansas, Mississippi, and Georgia. This is the most heavily Democratic part of the state; Bill Clinton won the district in 1992 and 1996. With one exception (1908), Little Dixie never elected a Republican to Congress. This is the part of the state where recent Democratic statewide candidates have sought to offset the Republican-voting northern tier of counties and the emergent GOP suburbs around Tulsa and Oklahoma City. *Congressional Quarterly* columnist Phil Duncan observed that "Republicans occasionally travel through [Little Dixie] but they seldom settle there" (in Barone, Ujifusa, and Matthews 1977).

The most distinguished political resident of Little Dixie is Carl Albert. Still politically active in his late eighties, "Mr. Carl" represented Little Dixie for thirty years after World War II and ascended to become Speaker of the U.S. House of Representatives in 1971. He continued as Speaker until his retirement in 1977 (Albert 1990). Upon his retirement, a six-man field emerged in the Democratic primary, including Albert's chief aide, Charlie Ward, and Ada state senator Wes Watkins. The district voters did not defer to the preferences of Albert, who publicly supported his aide in the primary. Ward trailed Watkins in the initial primary by ten thousand votes and almost 8 percentage points and lost the runoff by a decisive margin. Watkins went on to carry the Third District by an 83-17 margin, running 20 points ahead of Democratic presidential candidate Jimmy Carter. Watkins held the seat as a Democrat until 1990.

Watkins left the Third District to seek the open governor's seat in 1990. He narrowly led the initial primary with just under 33 percent of the vote; the second-place finisher, 1986 Democratic nominee David Walters, who narrowly lost to Henry Bellmon in 1986, won 32 percent of the vote. Walters won a narrow 51-49 victory in the runoff. In the initial primary and runoff, Watkins's strongest support was in Little Dixie. Watkins broke with the Democratic Party after the 1990 election. In 1994, he sought the governorship as an independent. Watkins pulled almost 24 percent of the vote in a three-cornered race that saw him finish just 5 points behind the Democratic nominee but 20 points behind Republican Frank Keating. If we examine the patterns of the county vote in figure 11.3, we see that Watkins pulled his strongest support in the Little Dixie region. In 1996, Watkins won the Third District as a Republican, with 52 percent of the vote.

The partisan change of the Third District might have been a continuation of the Christian realignment we described above (see Bednar and Hertzke 1995). This explanation goes further in explaining partisan change than the other conventional explanation for partisan change in the South— the racial threat hypothesis. Little Dixie is one of the most lily-white congressional districts in the South. In fact the racial threat hypothesis is of relatively little use in explaining Oklahoma politics in general—nowhere is there a significant concentration of blacks who are positioned to wield majority power. Even in the major urban counties, blacks constitute less than 15 percent of the population. The dynamic of black threat is far less likely because the prospects for majority-black government are nil. However, Little Dixie does contain some of the most heavily evangelical counties in the state. Republicans can appeal to the social conservatism of these voters. The Protestant basis for opposing large government and tolerance

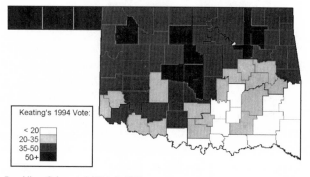

Republican Gubernatorial Vote in 1994

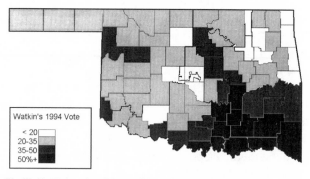

Wes Watkins' Independent Gubernatorial Vote in 1994

Fig. 11.3. Regionalism and Democratic Defection in 1994

of moral equivocation melds nicely with the southern opposition to social and economic programs for which blacks are high-profile recipients (Giles and Buckner 1993; Giles and Hertz 1994). While the racial dimension of Democratic defection is removed, the underlying social and cultural mores that facilitate that defection are present.

Most voters in the region supported both Watkins's 1990 primary bid and his 1994 independent gubernatorial campaign. In his independent bid he drew heavily on voters who usually cast Democratic ballots. As figure 11.3 indicates, in the core Democratic counties along the Texas and Arkansas borders, Watkins carried a majority of the votes and often held the Democratic nominee to under 30 percent. Republican Keating was held to under 20 percent in much of Little Dixie.

There has been speculation that Watkins's decision to run as a Republican served as a catalyst to move Democrats away from their party. As an independent, Watkins carried approximately 47 percent of the Third

District; as a Republican he won 51.4 percent of the vote. Are these elections drawing on the same bases of support? When we look at Watkins's vote at the county level and compare his 1994 and 1996 elections to a "normal" GOP candidacy—the 1996 Dole vote—we see that Watkins wins Little Dixie in back-to-back elections by drawing on disparate sets of voters. In figure 11.4, the 1994 and 1996 Watkins votes are plotted against the 1996 Dole vote for the twenty-one counties in the Third District. The Watkins vote in 1994 bears scant resemblance to the Dole vote. Watkins runs stronger where Dole was weak and runs substantially weaker in the exurban counties in the northern part of Little Dixie. The 1996 Watkins vote for U.S. representative is strongly associated with the Dole vote. Watkins gained substantial support in the exurban counties in the corridor between Oklahoma City and Tulsa (called the "Hook" by Oklahoma mapmakers), but his support falls off precipitously in the traditional Little Dixie counties along the Texas and Arkansas borders.

Was Watkins's success a matter of traditional party voting, Christian realignment, or the appeal of the former incumbent? There is evidence to support each hypothesis. If we regress the county-level Watkins vote in 1996 onto the GOP share of registration, a significant, positive relationship is observed (b = .40, R^2 = .59). Watkins's election was a function of drawing on the core Republican constituency. When we add an additional control for the proportion of the county population that is evangelical (Bullock and Grant 1995), we observe no improvement in the model fit; GOP registration is still a significant predictor, but the evangelical presence in

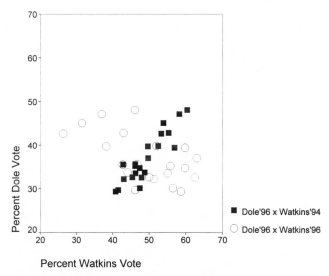

Fig. 11.4. Watson and Dole Votes in the Third District

the county has no significant impact on the Watkins vote. The last explanation—that Watkins's personal constituency transcended his party label—can be tested by the addition of one more variable: the share of the non-Republican vote won by Watkins in the 1994 gubernatorial race (percent for Watkins in 1994, divided by the percent for Watkins plus the percent for Jack Mildren, the Democratic nominee). When this variable for "Democratic defection" is introduced to the equation, a positive, statistically significant relationship is observed ($b = .16$ for Democratic defection [$p < .01$]; $b = .39$ for GOP registration [$p < .01$]; $b = -.09$ for evangelicals, [n.s.], $R^2 = .69$) that substantially improves on the initial prediction using the partisan base. Watkins's victory combined the base GOP vote with a portion of his old personal constituency to create a majority coalition. Whether the inroads made by Wes Watkins, Republican, can be traversed by other Republicans remains to be seen.

A Closer Look at Evangelical Voting and Party Switching

The county-level analysis indicated that the partisan change in the Third District was personality based and not the product of the Christian realignment (Bednar and Hertzke 1995). This is surprising given the role of the Christian Right in other GOP gains in the 1990s (Rozell and Wilcox, 1995). To get a better look at the behavior of the electorate, we draw on data gathered through 1996 exit polls conducted in the Third and Fourth Congressional Districts (Hertzke and Gaddie 1996). Of 474 voters in the Third District, 33.8 percent considered themselves to be born-again Christians, a slightly higher number than the estimated evangelical population of the state (Morgan, England, and Humphreys 1990). (See table 11.3.) The choices of these voters were decidedly partisan. Less than one in three cast ballots for Bill Clinton or for Democratic congressional nominee Darryl Roberts, even though 58 percent of born-again voters indicated that they were registered Democrats.

Republican success in inducing Democrats to switch over and vote Republican was dependent on the religious identification of the voter. Self-identified born-again Christians constituted 30 percent of all registered Democratic voters, and those Democrats split evenly between the Republican and Democratic candidates. Bill Clinton carried 65 percent of the vote among Democrats who did not consider themselves born-again but only 45 percent of the vote among born-again Democrats. Roberts fared little better, obtaining only 46 percent of the born-again Democratic vote. Born-again Democrats were far more likely to negatively evalu-

Table 11.3
Party and Religion in the Third District, 1996

	N	% Clinton	% Roberts	% Boren
All voters	458	42.4	43.8	44.8
Born-again*	144	27.8	29.0	27.1
Registered Democrats	300	59.0	58.6	60.5
Born-again*	84	45.2	46.3	42.3
Not born-again*	196	65.3	62.8	67.6
Registered Republicans	141	7.1	10.6	10.6

Source: The Carl Albert Center Poll: 1996 General Election.
*Respondents only
Margin of error = +/-4.6; confidence level = 95%

ate the Roberts campaign and generally distrusted Bill Clinton. Their defection on grounds of character reinforces the notion of responsible behavior advanced by Key (1966). It should be noted that Democratic defectors could also be projecting a negative evaluation to justify their defection.

Almost identical evidence of the born again–secular split in the Democratic Party is found in the poll results for the Fourth District, where incumbent J. C. Watts sought reelection against a well-funded but volatile Democratic state legislator, Ed Crocker. Watts won the race handily, and one reason was his ability to separate two groups of traditionally Democratic voters from their party. As indicated in table 11.4, about 29 percent of all voters were born again, more than half of those were

Table 11.4
Party, Race, and Religion in the Fourth District, 1996

	N	% Clinton	% Crocker	% Boren
All voters	459	42.0	37.7	41.4
Born-again*	131	30.5	26.7	29.8
Registered Democrats	263	62.9	55.8	59.1
Born-again*	70	48.6	41.7	48.6
Not born-again*	192	68.4	60.7	63.5
Registered Republicans	171	10.5	10.5	12.8
Black voter oversample	56	87.5	60.7	85.7

Source: The Carl Albert Center Poll: 1996 General Election.
*Respondents only
Margin of error = +/-4.6; confidence level = 95%

Democrats, and born-again Democrats constituted approximately 27 percent of all registered Democratic voters. Both Clinton and Crocker carried over 60 percent of the vote among secular Democrats but failed to gain even a majority of born-again Democrats. Overall, born-again voters only cast about one in three ballots for Clinton and one in four for Crocker. These patterns are virtually identical to those observed in the Third District.

An analysis of statewide registration and voting indicates the existence of a religious-based shift toward the GOP. When changes in the county-level registration of Republicans are regressed on the percent evangelical in the county, no significant positive relationship exists before 1994. Between November 1994 and January 1996, the increase in GOP registrants is significantly and positively related to the presence of large evangelical populations. Although the relationship is not overwhelming (R^2 = .29, b = .02, p < .0001), when considered in the context of Christian Right activism in the state, it appears that GOP growth is related to evangelical activism. When we also control for the base level of partisanship (Republican base registration), the explained variance increases to .37, and the evangelical variable holds significance.

There is also evidence of an independent impact by evangelicals on the Dole vote. When we control for the base GOP registration at the county level and for the percent evangelicals in the county, both are significant predictors of the Dole vote. The regression equation explains three-quarters of the variance, and both variables are positively related to the Dole vote (b = .62 for GOP registration [p < .0001]; b = .14 for evangelicals [p < .01]; R^2 = .75). In terms of both partisan identification and voting, the Christian Right is marching with the GOP in Oklahoma.

Conclusion

Oklahoma is a state in the midst of a political evolution that lags somewhat behind the rest of the South. Partisan identifiers are still solidly Democratic. Democrats still remain overwhelmingly in control of the state legislature and most local governments. Republican success has been largely confined to high-profile statewide and congressional elections where money and mass media can best be used to move Democrats away from their party.

Alexander Heard opined that when and if conservative Democrats lost their avenue of expression through the Democratic Party, they would move to the GOP. In the Deep South, the movement of such voters has often occurred in the wake of the empowerment of racial minorities, fulfilling V. O. Key's (1949) prophecy of black threat and white backlash. Underlying the movement of conservative whites who responded to the black threat was a perception that government had become too big, that the cost to taxpayers of subsidizing the sloth of others (most notably, in the eye of the Deep South voter, the black), and that Republicans offered relief from the national Democratic Party (Black and Black 1992).

The absence of a substantial black population renders this hypothesis suspect in Oklahoma. The underlying assumption about the black-threat-based response of conservative whites to the national Democrats—that a homogenous population, socialized to the Protestant work ethic, is repulsed by social engineering and high taxes for social welfare—can explain the movement of Oklahoma voters to the GOP. At the local and state legislative levels, where over 70 percent of all officeholders are Democrats, the linkages of voters to Democratic politicians are still highly personalized. According to one prominent Democratic senate leader, voters still know these people on a personal level; a campaign that ties them to the national Democratic Party does not work in localized constituencies precisely because local Democrats are not tied to the national party, and at a local level Democrats are capable of successfully running away from the national Democratic Party. Campaigns conducted in larger constituencies are necessarily less personal and therefore more reliant on mass media and money to communicate candidate images. For Democrats in Oklahoma, this has meant being tied to the unpopularity of the Clinton administration and the social agenda of the national Democratic Party.

The successful application of Christian Right strategy to campaigns in Oklahoma appears to have separated about half of born-again Democrats from their party's nominees for federal offices in 1996. The most recent increase in GOP registrants is related to the presence of evangelicals in communities. Oklahoma is far from "realigned" to the GOP at all levels. When compared to her immediate southern neighbors, the partisan changes in Oklahoma are more advanced than in Louisiana and Arkansas but lag behind Texas below the federal level.

There are threats to the growing GOP hegemony. Like neighbor Arkansas, Oklahoma suffers from an underdeveloped economy and a dependency on agriculture and natural-resource extraction. If continued economic prosperity does not come, the GOP will be confronted by Democrats who are recovering from the partisan shock of 1994. The current factional divisions in the Oklahoma GOP are muted by the air of success.

References

Aistrup, Joseph. 1996. *The Southern Strategy Revisited.* Lexington: University Press of Kentucky.

Albert, Carl B. 1990. *Little Giant : The Life and Times of Speaker Carl Albert.* Norman: University of Oklahoma Press.

Barone, Michael, and Grant Ujifusa. 1989, 1991, 1993, 1995. *The Almanac of American Politics.* New York: Barone & Co.

Barone, Michael, Grant Ujifusa, and Donald Matthews. 1977. *The Almanac of American Politics.* New York: Macmillan.

Bednar, Nancy, and Allen D. Hertzke. 1995. "Oklahoma: The Christian Right and the Republican Realignment." Pp. 91–108 in *God at the Grass Roots: The Christian Right in the 1994 Elections,* edited by Mark J. Rozell and Clyde Wilcox. Lanham, Md.: Rowman & Littlefield.

Black, Earl, and Merle Black. 1992. *The Vital South: How Presidents Are Elected.* Cambridge: Harvard Univesity Press.

Bullock, Charles S., III., and John Christopher Grant. 1995. "Georgia: The Christian Right and Grass Roots Power." Pp. 47–66 in *God at the Grass Roots: The Christian Right in the 1994 Elections,* edited by Mark J. Rozell and Clyde Wilcox. Lanham, Md.: Rowman & Littlefield.

Carmines, Edward, and James Stimson. 1989. *Issue Evolution.* Princeton, N.J.: Princeton University Press.

Giles, Michael W., and Melanie Buckner. 1993. "David Duke and Black Threat: An Old Hypothesis Revisited." *Journal of Politics* 55: 702–13.

Giles, Michael W., and Kaenan Hertz. 1994. "Racial Threat and Partisan Identification." *American Political Science Review* 88: 317–26.

Hale, Jon F., and Stephen T. Kean. 1996. "Oklahoma." In *State and Party Profiles: A Fifty-State Guide to Development, Organization and Resources,* edited by Andrew M. Appleton and Daniel S. Ward. Washington, D.C.: Congressional Quarterly Press.

Heard, Alexander. 1952. *A Two-Party South?* Chapel Hill: University of North Carolina Press.

Hertzke, Allen D., and Ronald Keith Gaddie. 1996. *The Carl Albert Center Poll: 1996 General Election.* Norman: University of Oklahoma.

Key, V. O., Jr. 1949. *Southern Politics in State and Nation.* New York: Knopf.

Kirkpatrick, Samuel A., David R. Morgan, and Thomas Kielhorn. 1977. *The Oklahoma Voter.* Norman: University of Oklahoma Press.

Lamis, Alexander. 1988. *The Two-Party South.* New York: Oxford University Press.

Morgan, David R., Robert E. England, and George G. Humphreys. 1991. *Oklahoma Politics and Policies.* Lincoln: University of Nebraska Press.

Oklahoma Department of Libraries. 1995. *The Oklahoma Almanac, 1995–1996.* Oklahoma City: Oklahoma Department of Libraries.

Rozell, Mark J., and Clyde Wilcox, eds. 1995. *God at the Grass Roots: The Christian Right in the 1994 Elections.* Lanham, Md: Rowman & Littlefield.

12

Florida: Political Change, 1950–1996

Michael J. Scicchitano and Richard K. Scher

In the last half of the twentieth century, Florida has experienced profound changes in its population. These changes have largely been driven by a massive migration of retirees seeking a warmer climate and younger persons seeking employment opportunities. The population of Florida nearly tripled from 1960 to 1995. Moreover, this migration has substantially changed the demographic character of the state. The percentage of white residents, for example, has grown steadily since 1900, and the percentage of African Americans has consistently declined. While the rest of the country has gotten younger, Florida's population has aged, and the state now ranks first in the percentage of the population that is sixty-five and older. In addition, the percentage of the population that is of Hispanic origin has nearly doubled since 1970; the state now has more than two million Hispanics. The change in the demographic characteristics of Florida has not been politically neutral. The political character of the state has undergone equally profound changes. This chapter will document the demographic changes that Florida has experienced in this century, with a focus on the last forty years. This background will help us to understand better the nature of the changes to Florida's political system. The chapter will then provide a detailed description of the partisan changes that have occurred in Florida since 1980. Finally, this chapter will examine the impact of demographic changes and party registration on Florida elections for both state and national offices.

The Changing Population of Florida

If there is one distinguishing feature of the demographic characteristics of Florida, especially in the latter half of the twentieth century, it is growth.

In 1900 Florida was one of the least-populated states in the East, but by 1996 it had become the second most populous state east of the Mississippi and the fourth most populous nationally. In every decade since 1900, Florida's population has grown by about 30 percent. In two of those decades, the growth was more than 50 percent. From 1950 to 1960, the population grew by nearly 80 percent. The population growth, however, has not been uniformly distributed across the state. Before 1950, the state's population center was north Florida, and particularly the Jacksonville area. But between 1950 and 1970, population growth was strongest in southern Florida. The central Florida region, with the development of Disney World and other recreational attractions in the Orlando area, has had the highest growth rates since 1970.

The growth in population has largely been fueled by two forces. Like the rest of the nation, Florida has experienced an increase in population from the baby boom generation. The most important reason for the growth rate in Florida, however, has been migration into the state. In the five-year period from 1985 to 1990, for example, nearly 1.5 million people moved into Florida from other states or countries.

The tremendous growth that Florida has experienced in the twentieth century, and particularly since 1950, has not maintained the demographic characteristics of the state that existed in 1900. Instead, there have been fundamental changes in the demographic patterns in the state. The most significant changes have occurred among three groups. First, the population of Florida has gotten older. Second, the racial composition of the state has changed, and the percentage of African American residents has declined. Finally, the percentage of Florida residents who are Hispanic has increased. The changes in the age, race, and ethnicity of residents have produced a state that is demographically—and politically—different than it was in 1950.

Changes in Age Patterns

A large number of those migrating to Florida since 1950 have been older people seeking a better climate for their retirement years. The changes in the age of Florida's residents are part of a complex national pattern of aging. Better medical care and nutritional and lifestyle behaviors have permitted people to live longer, while the baby boom produced a surge of younger people that has driven the average age of the population down. Florida did not escape the effects of the baby boom. Still, the state provides an extremely attractive climate for retirees who want to avoid harsh winters in the Northeast and Midwest. Retirees with fixed incomes also find

Florida's low taxes and lack of an income tax attractive. As a result of the in-migration of retirees, the age of Florida's population has increased more rapidly than that of other states, and now Florida ranks first in the nation in the number of residents who are sixty-five and older (Smith 1995).

Changes in Race Patterns

At the beginning of the twentieth century, Florida had a large African American population. In 1900, 44 percent of the state was African American and 56 percent was white. The number of African Americans in the state has increased since 1900. This growth, however, has not equaled the growth of whites. Migrants to Florida have mostly been older whites. As a result of the migration patterns, the relative percentage of African Americans in Florida declined consistently between 1900 and 1980. Since 1980, however, the racial composition of the state has stabilized at approximately 84 to 85 percent white and 14 percent African American.

Changes in the Hispanic Population

The last major change in the demographic character of Florida is the large increase in the number of Hispanic residents. From 1970 to 1990 the percentage of Hispanic residents has nearly doubled, to about 12 percent of the population. Many Hispanic residents, particularly of south Florida, are of Cuban origin. South Florida continues to attract residents from other locations in Latin America as well. The percentage of Hispanics in Florida should continue to grow in the next century; indeed, the increase in the Hispanic population between 1990 and 1995 was 28 percent (Allen 1997).

Partisan Changes in Florida

In the years following World War II, the political character of Florida changed from solidly Democratic to one in which the Republican Party, in many regions, has become competitive. The transition to this more competitive political environment was fueled by three forces (Scher 1997, 143–51). The first of these forces was the tremendous in-migration of more conservative, white, middle-class individuals from the North. A second force, related to the first, was the in-migration of large numbers of elderly persons who were also conservative and were more likely to vote for Republican candidates. These new arrivals had a profound effect on Florida politics, especially in the 1980s and 1990s, when the numbers of new conservative voters became sufficiently large to produce a competitive two-party state. Finally, many traditional Democrats began to question their loyalty to their party, which had become more liberal and "seemed no longer to represent southern interests and concerns" (Scher 1997, 145).

To understand Florida politics, it is important first to examine the changes in party registration in the state in the last two decades. Table 12.1 shows the percentage of the population registered as Democrats, Republicans, and as having no party identification (independents). This table indicates that, while the Democrats were clearly the dominant party in 1980, the political landscape is fundamentally different in 1996. In 1980, nearly two-thirds of registered voters were identified as Democrats. By 1996, less than one-half of registered voters were Democrats. During the 1980s and continuing into the 1990s, increasing numbers of voters registered as Republicans and independents. The number of Republicans has increased more than one-third, from less than 30 percent of registered voters to more than 40 percent. There are far fewer independents, but their percentage of registered voters has more than doubled, from 5.4 percent to nearly 12. By 1994 the combined percentage of Republican and independent voters was greater than the total percent of Democrats.

The rates of change in partisanship in Florida largely mirror the growth of the state's population. The right-hand columns of table 12.1 summarize the changes in the percentages of registered voters for the Democrats, Republicans, and independents over two-year periods between 1980 and 1996. The middle 1980s were a period of tremendous growth in the state.

Table 12.1
Partisan Identification in Florida, 1980–1996

	Dem.	Rep.	Ind.	% Change in Identification		
				Dem.	Rep.	Ind.
1980	65.8	28.8	5.4			
1982	63.0	30.8	6.2	-2.8	+2.0	+0.8
1984	61.0	32.8	6.2	-2.0	+2.0	0
1986	57.1	36.2	6.7	-3.9	+3.4	+0.5
1988	54.0	39.0	7.0	-3.1	+2.8	+0.3
1990	52.2	40.6	7.2	-1.8	+1.6	+0.2
1992	50.1	40.9	9.0	-2.1	+0.3	+1.8
1994	49.5	41.8	8.7	-0.6	+0.9	-0.3
1996	46.8	41.5	11.7	-2.7	-0.3	+0.3

Source: Florida Statistical Abstract

The decline in the percentage of Democrats was most dramatic during that period. From 1980 to 1992, Democrats experienced an average loss of 2 percentage points per biennium, with the greatest change in 1986 and 1988, when the combined decrease was 7 percent. The growth in the number of Republicans was greatest in these two years. By the middle 1990s, it appears that the decline in Democratic strength had slowed; in 1994, the decrease was only about one-half of a percentage point. In 1996, however, there was another large decline in the relative number of Democrats— nearly 3 percent. The Republicans did not, however, benefit from this decline, since the Republican registration also dropped slightly, but independents gained by 3 percent. Research indicates that the "motor voter" law contributed significantly to these changes (Mortham 1995). It is evident that partisan registration in Florida is still changing, and it is unclear when it will stabilize.

These data on changes in the registration pattern should not be interpreted as indicating that changes in party registration are uniform across Florida. There still are areas where Democratic or Republican registration is relatively stable. The patterns of these concentrations of party strength in Florida are complex. Democrats are still very strong in some rural areas and in some inner-city areas where there are concentrations of African American and low-income residents. This pattern of Democratic strength, however, is not found in some of the urban concentrations in the metropolitan Dade County area, home of large numbers of Hispanics who have traditionally voted for Republicans. In general, however, Republicans tend to be concentrated, as in other states, in the more suburban sections of metropolitan areas where voters are largely white and higher-income, although some heavily white rural areas are also becoming Republican.

The changes in party registration are not, of themselves, important. What is important is the impact of party registration changes on state and national elections in Florida. The following sections provide a detailed analysis of the change in election patterns for both national and state executive and legislative offices.

Presidential and Congressional Elections

The Presidency

The presidential elections in Florida were the first to demonstrate the emerging strength of the Republican Party. Figure 12.1 provides a summary of the results of presidential contests in Florida. From 1920 to 1948,

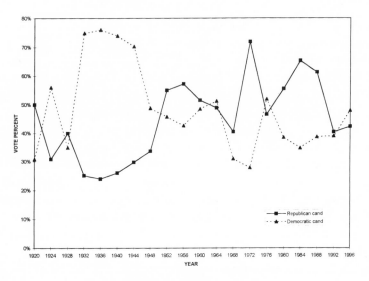

Fig. 12.1. Presidential Elections in Florida, 1920–1996

Floridians generally voted for Democratic presidential candidates. The only exception was the 1928 election, in which the state supported Hoover by a substantial margin over Al Smith, a Catholic from New York. In 1932, however, Floridians abandoned Hoover and voted for Roosevelt by a three-to-one margin. Starting with the Eisenhower election in 1952, a majority of Floridians were, for most elections, voting for Republican candidates. Since 1952, Democrats have carried Florida only three times, each time with a southern candidate. In 1964 Lyndon Johnson, in the course of a tremendous national victory, received a majority of only 2.3 percent of the Florida vote. Jimmy Carter, from adjacent Georgia, also won a narrow victory over the incumbent Gerald Ford. Voters abandoned Carter in 1980 and gave a substantial majority to Republican candidate Ronald Reagan.

In 1992 Democrat Bill Clinton ran a close second to the incumbent George Bush, but many potential Bush votes were siphoned off to the independent candidacy of Ross Perot. Clinton was able, in 1996, to best Dole in Florida. In this case, however, Clinton managed to position himself skillfully on several issues of importance to Floridians. Clinton was able to frighten elderly Florida voters with the warning that Dole, as a result of the large budget cut he promised, might be a threat to the health services and other benefits they receive from the federal government. Another important issue for Clinton in Florida was immigration. Dole's tough stands against illegal immigration and in favor of cutting benefits for illegal immigrants cost him substantial votes among Hispanics, especially Cuban Americans. Instead of strongly supporting the Republican candidate as they had done in 1992, Hispanics in Florida split their vote almost evenly between Dole and Clinton (Schneider 1996).

U.S. Senate Elections

While presidential elections in Florida have resulted in a rapid transition in favor of Republican candidates, the U.S. Senate contests are a more accurate indicator of the gradually changing nature of partisanship in the state. Figure 12.2 provides a summary of the U.S. Senate elections from 1920 to the latest election in 1994. The Democratic Party clearly dominated U.S. Senate elections to at least the late 1950s. From 1920 until 1962, only one Democratic candidate received less than 40 percent of the vote. That was Park Trammel, an incumbent who faced a strong challenge in 1928, a year in which Republican presidential candidate Herbert Hoover won Florida. Trammel returned in 1934, however, to win an uncontested election. Changes in the nature of U.S. Senate elections began to appear by the late 1950s and early 1960s. During this period, Florida's U.S. Senate seats were held by two strong incumbents, George Smathers and Spessard L. Holland. Holland, a former governor, eventually served four terms, while Smathers served three. Smathers retired in 1968 but would have been reelected had he run for a fourth term. Both Holland's and Smathers's

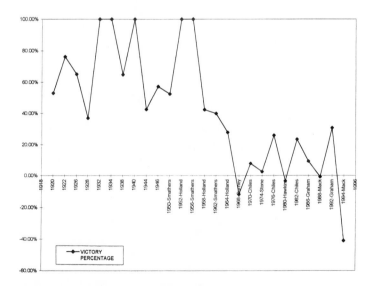

Sources: Congressional Quarterly Guide to U.S. Elections; Florida Department of State general election returns

Fig. 12.2. U.S. Senate Democratic Victory Percentage

reelection margins for their third terms in 1958 and 1962 were about 40 percent. While these are solid election victories, they are by less than the typical margin for the previous four decades. Holland won by less than 30 percent in his last reelection campaign in 1964. The dividing line in Florida U.S. Senate elections is between the 1964 and 1968 contests. The first Republican senator in at least half a century was elected in 1968, in an election for the seat Smathers had vacated. From 1968 until 1994, Republicans were elected four times. Moreover, both Democrats and Republicans had tight first-election tries. Dick Stone, a Democrat, and Paula Hawkins, a Republican, won by about 3 percent of the vote in their first (and only) victories. Connie Mack, a Republican, won by less than 1 percent in his first Senate victory in 1988. Once elected, some candidates were able to build support and win more substantial victories. Lawton Chiles's second and third victory margins were each about 25 percent, and Bob Graham, a popular former governor, achieved his second victory by more than 30 percent. None of these reelections, however, was as strong as the Democratic victories in the three decades from 1920 to 1950. Connie Mack, a Republican incumbent, won his second reelection by more than 40 percent in 1994. However, in a strong Republican year, Mack faced a weak opponent in the relatively inexperienced Hugh Rodham, who had the advantage (or liability) of being the brother of First Lady Hillary Rodham Clinton. It is clear that the Democratic Party will no longer dominate U.S. Senate elections in Florida as it did from 1920 until 1950. Instead, both Democratic and Republican candidates will face tough initial election campaigns. Only as incumbents will they be able to build more substantial election margins.

U.S. House Elections

The U.S. House elections in Florida largely mirror the results that are evident in the Senate elections. Table 12.2 summarizes the results of the U.S. House elections in Florida from 1950 to 1996. The table presents the year, the number of Democratic and Republican victors, and the average victory margin for Democratic and Republican senators. The last column in the table lists the percentage of House seats held by Republicans.

Democratic candidates dominated Florida House elections from 1920 to 1950. The first Republican was elected only in 1954, when William Cramer won the First Congressional District by a very tight 1.5 percent margin against a one-term incumbent who had narrowly been elected in 1952. Cramer was the only Republican congressman from Florida from 1954 until 1962 and was able to expand his victory margin to about 17 percent.

Table 12.2
U.S. House of Representative Elections in Florida, 1920–1996

	Dem. Seats	Avg. Dem. Margin (%)	Rep. Seats	Avg. Rep. Margin (%)	Rep. Seats (%)
1950	6	84.5			
1952	8	58.4			
1954	7	87.3	1	1.5	12.5
1956	7	48.2	1	12.7	12.5
1958	7	82.4	1	17.6	12.5
1960	7	64.6	1	16.8	12.5
1962	10	49.4	2	16.4	16.6
1964	10	73.7	2	21.1	16.6
1966	9	76.4	3	54.5	25
1968	9	38.5	3	74.5	25
1970	9	56.8	3	31.4	25
1972	11	39.1	4	50.4	26.6
1974	10	72.9	5	32.5	33
1976	10	67.2	5	29.0	33
1978	12	55.6	3	53	20
1980	11	39.1	4	44.6	26.6
1982	13	48.4	6	28.3	31.6
1984	12	53.5	7	67.6	36.8
1986	12	65.4	7	76.2	36.8
1988	10	64.9	9	52.7	47.4
1990	9	36.1	10	58.7	52.6
1992	11	63.3	12	62.8	52.2
1994	8	69.4	15	85.0	65.2
1996	8	70.7	15	70.1	65.2

Sources: Congressional Quarterly Guide to U.S. Elections; Florida Department of State general
election returns.

While the election of this single Republican candidate hardly represented an overwhelming change in Florida congressional elections, it was certainly an indication of more substantial changes to come. In the years that followed, the number of Republicans elected to Congress from Florida continued to grow. The size of the Florida congressional delegation has increased to reflect the increase in population, but the percentage of Republican-held seats does not merely parallel the increase in the number of congressional seats. By the 1980s, Republicans held one-third of the seats, and by the 1990s, they had surged to control more than 60 percent of the Florida delegation. Moreover, the size of the victory margin of Republican candidates has increased to rival that of Democratic candidates.

The number and percentage of total seats, moreover, does not accurately reflect the growing strength of the Republican Party in Florida. Congressional districts, of course, were drawn by the Democratic officials that still held a majority of the legislature (the districts in 1992 were drawn by a three-judge federal panel after legislators could not agree on a plan). Table 12.2 shows that, interestingly, the number of Republican congressional seats increased after redistricting allocated more seats to rapidly growing areas. Republicans held only one seat in the 1950s, two to three seats in the 1960s, three to five seats in the 1970s, six to nine seats in the 1980s, and twelve to fifteen in the 1990s.

Gubernatorial and State Legislative Elections

The Gubernatorial Elections

The elections for governor of Florida largely mirror the results for U.S. Senate and House elections. Table 12.3 lists the party of the victorious candidate as well as the percentage of the victory margin for gubernatorial elections in Florida from 1920 to 1994.

Again, we see that Democratic candidates for governor have dominated the elections from 1920 until the mid-1950s. The first Republican governor

Table 12.3
Gubernatorial Races in Florida, 1920–1994

Year	Victor's Party	Victory %	Year	Victor's Party	Victory %
1920	D	60	1960	D	19.7
1924	D	65.6	1964	D	14.8
1928	D	22.0	1966	R	10.2
1932	D	33.2	1970	D	13.8
1936	D	61.8	1974	D	22.4
1940	D	100	1978	D	11.2
1944	D	57.8	1982	D	29.4
1948	D	66.8	1986	R	9.2
1952	D	49.6	1990	D	13.0
1956	D	47.4	1994	D	1.6

Source: Congressional Quarterly Guide to U.S. Elections

was Claude Kirk, who was elected in 1966. The next Republican, Bob Martinez, was elected in 1986. Both were one-term governors. By 1960, however, the victory margins of Democratic governors were less than 20 percent, substantially smaller than the 56 percent average for the preceding forty years. The margin of victory for subsequent Democratic victors was only 15 percent. The gubernatorial elections from 1970 to 1994 were won by three relatively popular Democratic candidates who each served two terms—Rubin Askew, Bob Graham, and former three-term senator Lawton Chiles. Martinez, the sole Republican elected governor after the 1966 Kirk victory, won an open-seat election against a relatively unknown opponent, Steve Pajic, who received the nomination after a divisive Democratic runoff. Pajic was viewed by voters as a liberal, which made defeating Martinez difficult (see Black and Black 1987). Martinez was not able to win reelection against the popular and well-known Chiles. Chiles, after a first term in which he was not viewed as very successful, won an extremely narrow victory against Jeb Bush, son of the former president. Bush was well financed and was able to benefit from running in a year in which the Republican Party was generally successful across the nation.

While the Democrats largely dominated gubernatorial elections in Florida from 1970 to 1994, this dominance is substantially different from that evident in the 1920–1960 period. The victories from the late 1970s to the present were generally narrow Democratic victories won by capable and popular candidates. It is by no means certain that Democrats will continue to control the governor's office, and it is likely that in the next several elections the office will alternate between parties.

An interesting feature of Florida government is the election of cabinet officers. In most systems of government, the executive appoints, typically with the approval of the legislature, officials to run most cabinet offices. In Florida, the cabinet positions of secretary of state, attorney general, comptroller, treasurer, and commissioners of education and agriculture are elected.

While many states have multiple elected officials in the executive branch, Florida is unique both in the number and the range of such officials' duties, which are constitutionally and statutorily assigned. As a result, the cabinet serves as a collegial governing board for the executive branch (Scher 1994). It is easy to imagine the difficulty of governing in a system in which the chief executive officers of major departments are not controlled by the governor. It is even more difficult to govern when these individuals are from the opposite party. In 1986, Republican governor Bob Martinez's cabinet offices were all held by Democrats. In 1990, concurrently with the election of Democrat Chiles, two Republicans held cabinet slots, and in 1994 three of the cabinet positions were filled by Republicans.

Florida House and Senate Elections

The changing nature of partisanship and elections in Florida is also evident in the races for the state legislature. To understand the changes in Florida state legislative elections, it is important first to examine the partisan registration in house and senate districts. Table 12.4 presents the mean number of Democratic, Republican, and independent party registrations in the Florida House and Senate districts. Data are available only for 1988–1996, but even this short time span clearly demonstrates the changes in partisanship in Florida.

In 1988, the number of registered Republicans was substantially smaller than the number of Democrats. By 1996, however, the number of registered Republicans had increased to approach the number of Democrats. Moreover, by 1996, independents and Republicans outnumbered the registered Democrats. The rate of change for each party differs significantly. While the rate of change from 1988 to 1996 is a moderate 14 percent for Democrats, it is a much more substantial 40 percent for the Republicans. The increase in the number of independents, though starting from a relatively small number, is a surprising 120 percent. While many districts still have a strong Democratic majority, the trend since 1988 is for rapidly increasing numbers of Republican and especially independent registrations.

Another perspective on the changing nature of partisanship is provided by table 12.5, on state senate and house districts. This table lists the

Table 12.4
Average Party Registration in State House and Senate Districts, 1988–1996

	House Districts			Senate Districts		
	Dem.	Rep.	Ind.	Dem.	Rep.	Ind.
1988	27,200	19,595	3,511	81,602	59,010	10,534
1990	26,062	20,395	3,582	78,743	61,212	10,748
1992	27,654	22,274	4,550	82,964	66,824	13,651
1994	27,054	22,892	4,376	81,137	68,676	13,192
1996	31,064	27,575	7,734	93,212	82,727	23,212
% inc. '88–96	14.2	40.7	120	14.2	40.2	120.4

Source: Florida Department of State, general election returns

Table 12.5
Florida Legislative Districts with Majority Democratic
Registration (in percent)

	House (120 Districts)	Senate (40 Districts)
1988	71.6	72.5
1990	65.8	67.5
1992	64.2	67.5
1994	60.8	57.5
1996	55.0	52.5

Source: Florida Department of State official general election
returns

number of Florida House and Senate districts in which the Democrats
have a majority of the party registrations. In 1988 the Democrats had a
majority of those choosing a party in 86 of 120 house districts (71.7 percent) and 29 of 40 senate districts (72.5 percent). By 1996, only eight years
(and one redistricting) later, the Democrats and Republicans each held a
majority in about half of the house and senate districts. The registration
numbers clearly indicate that races for state legislative seats were more
competitive in the 1990s.

In addition to examining the party registration in each district, it is
important to examine the party composition of the Florida House and
Senate. The percentage of Democratic and Republican membership in the
legislature is presented in table 12.6.

This table demonstrates that there has been a significant change in the
party composition of the Florida legislature. In 1976, both the house and the
senate were about 75 percent Democratic. Since 1976, there has been a consistent decline in the number of Democratic legislators and a correspond-
ing increase in the number of Republicans. The percentages of the Democratic and Republican members of the house and senate are now about
equal. In 1996, for the first time since Reconstruction, Republicans took control of the Florida House. It is, however, unclear at this time if the trend
toward a greater Republican percentage of the legislature will continue.

Race and Politics in Florida

Florida provides an interesting opportunity to examine the impact of federal legislation and court decisions that made it possible for minorities to

Table 12.6
Partisan Makeup of Florida State Legislature, 1976–1996 (in percent)

	House (120 seats)		Senate (40 seats)	
	Democrats	Republicans	Democrats	Republicans
1976	76.6	23.3	72.5	25.0
1978	74.2	25.8	72.5	27.5
1980	67.5	32.5	67.5	32.5
1982	70.0	30.0	80.0	20.0
1984	64.2	35.8	80.0	20.0
1986	62.5	37.5	62.5	37.5
1988	73.3	26.7	57.5	42.5
1990	61.7	38.3	57.5	42.5
1992	54.2	40.8	50.0	50.0
1994	59.2	40.8	47.5	52.5
1996	49.2	50.8	42.5	57.5

Source: Florida Department of State general election returns

participate fully in the electoral process. The Voting Rights Act of 1962, extended in 1970, 1975, and 1982, effectively eliminated the roadblocks that states and local governments had erected to minority participation in elections. The 1986 *Thornburg v. Gingles* decision gave a clear indication that states should create minority legislative districts whenever possible. The Florida situation is unique from several perspectives. First, legislative districts for African Americans must be created in a state in which the percentage of blacks has declined throughout the century, apparently stabilizing at about 14 percent. Clearly, crafting legislative districts for African Americans in a declining population is no easy task. The second issue relates to the rapid increase, especially in south Florida, in the size of the Hispanic population. Both African Americans and Hispanics want to maximize their number of districts. Moreover, Hispanics in Florida, in contrast to many other states, are conservative and tend to vote Republican. The creation of Hispanic districts, therefore, further increases the number of Republicans in the legislature. The third issue relates in a somewhat different fashion to the population changes that Florida is experiencing. With the declining number of Democratic voters, the creation of districts for African Americans means that many traditional Democratic (African Americans) voters will be concentrated in these districts. This will further reduce the number of Democrats and increase Republican strength in adjacent districts.

Finally, it is important to understand that Florida's concentration of three distinct groups—white, African American, and Hispanic—has produced fierce electoral competition. The groups strive to promote candidates who share their race or ethnicity. This competition is particularly keen in the Dade County area, where all three groups exist in strength. The partisan conflict usually is evident at two levels. The competition between African Americans and whites to promote their Democratic candidates can be evident at the primary level. Hispanics, traditionally Republicans, enter the fray during the general election, when their candidate will oppose the primary winner. In recent years, however, Republicans have also been involved in significant internecine ethnic conflict in local primaries.

One example of racial conflict is the commission races in the city of Miami. M. Athalie Range became the first African American city commissioner in 1965. She was followed by a succession of African Americans who occupied her seat. In 1996, however, the seat was won by a Hispanic man. In fact, the commission seats in Miami now are occupied by four Hispanics and one white. There is a keen sense of frustration among blacks, who feel that the rise of Hispanic political power symbolizes the "unfulfilled promise" of a better life for African Americans in the Miami metropolitan area (Navarro 1997).

This pattern of race- and ethnic-based electoral conflict may, however, be changing. In the 1996 Miami mayoral (nonpartisan) election, white and Hispanic voters formed a coalition to promote a single candidate. With the increase in the number of younger Hispanic voters who are less conservative, these coalitions may become increasingly common. It is worth noting that Bill Clinton did extremely well among younger Cubans in 1996 (Fiedler 1996).

To aid in understanding the increase in African American representation in the Florida legislature, table 12.7 presents the percentage of African American house and senate members from 1976 through 1996. It is clear from the table that the number of African American legislators has increased substantially since 1976. In 1976, there were only a handful of African American members of the house and none in the senate. By 1996, the percentage of African American members in both chambers approached the percentage (approximately 14 percent) of African Americans in the state population. It is also interesting that the changes in the number of African American legislators is largely related to redistricting. African American members of the house jumped from 3.3 percent to 9.2 percent following redistricting in the 1980s.. The percentage of African Americans in the senate jumped from zero to 5 percent. The change

Table 12.7
African American Membership in the Florida Legislature (in percent)

Year	House (120 Seats)	Senate (40 Seats)	Year	House (120 Seats)	Senate (40 Seats)
1976	2.5	0	1988	10.0	5.0
1978	3.3	0	1990	11.6	5.0
1980	3.3	0	1992	11.6	12.5
1982	9.2	5.0	1994	10.0	12.5
1984	9.2	5.0	1996	11.6	12.5
1986	9.2	5.0			

Source: Joint Center for Political and Economic Studies; Florida Department of State general
election returns

following the 1992 redistricting primarily affected the Florida Senate,
where African American membership jumped from 5 to 12.5 percent.

The 1996 Elections

In 1996, there were no races for either governor or U. S. senator in
Florida. Attention was focused on the presidential election and the races
for the Florida legislature. For only the third time since 1952, a Democratic presidential candidate won Florida. Clinton's victory resulted from a
careful strategy that skillfully targeted certain groups as well as specific
geographic areas of the state. Clinton did particularly well among
women voters, receiving 52 percent of their vote to Dole's 41 percent.
Clinton, as expected, won a large majority of the African American vote.
He also did well among Hispanics. While Dole did win more Hispanic
votes than Clinton (48 percent to 44 percent), the president improved his
1992 performance by 13 percent. This improvement may be a signal that
Hispanic voters are becoming less conservative. Younger Hispanics in
particular are less concerned about foreign affairs and respond to appeals
based on other issues, such as the environment (Fiedler 1996). Even more
interesting was the president's performance among senior voters in
Florida. Clinton received 50 percent of the votes of those sixty years of
age and older, compared to Dole's 43 percent. Clinton spent millions of
dollars to inform seniors that Dole had opposed Medicare and that his
proposed budget cuts threatened to slow the increase in benefits. While
Dole gathered votes from those most concerned with character, Clinton

appealed to voters on the issues of education, the environment, and Medicare (Forman 1996).

In addition to targeting certain groups in the state, Clinton focused his efforts on winning the counties with the largest numbers of voters. Clinton won Dade, Broward, and Palm Beach Counties (Miami area). He also ran ahead of Dole in the Tampa–St. Petersburg area. Clinton did lose in Duval (Jacksonville) and Orange (Orlando) Counties, by 14,000 and 500 votes, respectively. These losses, however, are largely insignificant when compared to Clinton's plurality of more than 150,000 votes in Broward County.

The story in the Florida legislature, at least for the Democrats, was much different. Governor Chiles, to no avail, devoted considerable time and energy to attempting to return the legislature to Democratic control. The Florida Senate first became Republican in 1994. In 1996, the Republicans were able to hold, and slightly increase, their majority in the senate. Republicans also won a majority of seats in the Florida House. For the first time since Reconstruction, the Republicans held both chambers in a southern legislature.

The Republican victory in the house was crafted by a careful targeting of contested seats (nearly half of the house seats were not contested). In particular, twelve of the contested elections were open seats and another twelve were held by vulnerable Democrats. The Republicans were able to win enough of these seats to take control of the house. These victories were the result of the declining Democratic strength. They proved that well-funded Republicans who run effective campaigns can defeat Democrats.

Conclusion

The political situation in Florida has been one of the most dynamic of any southern state. The trend toward increasing numbers of Republican and independent voters means that Democratic candidates are no longer assured of victory. Elections will be increasingly competitive and will be won by the candidates who have the most resources and make the most effective appeals to voters. It is unclear at this time if current trends will continue and Republicans will come to dominate Florida politics. Another scenario is that there will be a partisan balance and elective offices will alternate between parties. It is also likely that the increasing independent vote will have a decisive influence on the outcome of state and even local elections.

References

Allen, Diane Lacey. 1997. "Hispanics in Florida." *Gainesville Sun*, 2 November, 1D.

Black, Earl, and Merle Black. 1987. *Politics and Society in the South.* Cambridge: Harvard University Press.

Fiedler, Tom. 1996. "Rewriting the Book on Florida." *Miami Herald*, 6 November, 16A.

Mortham, Sandra. 1995. "The Impact of the National Voter Registration Act of 1993 on the State of Florida." Tallahassee: Florida Secretary of State, November 15. This report can be found on the Internet at http://election.dos.state.fl.us/reforms/nvra.htm.

Navarro, Mireya. 1997. "As the Population Shifts, Many Florida Blacks Say They Feel 'Left Out.'" *New York Times*, 17 February, 16A, national edition.

Scher, Richard K. 1994."The Governor and the Cabinet: Executive Policy Making and Policy Management." Chap. 4 in *The Florida Public Policy Management System*, edited by Richard Chackerian. Tallahassee: Askew School of Public Administration and Policy and Florida Center for Public Management.

———. 1997. *Politics in the New South.* 2d ed. Armonk, N.Y.: M. E. Sharpe.

Schneider, William. 1996. "Immigration Issues Reward Democrats." *National Journal*, 30 November, 2622.

Smith, Stanley K. 1995. "Population Growth and Demographic Change." In *The Economy of Florida,* edited by J. F. Scoggins and Ann Pierec. Gainesville, Fla.: Bureau of Economic and Business Research.

13

Texas: Lone Star(Wars) State

James W. Lamare, J. L. Polinard, and Robert D. Wrinkle

Once upon a time, a long time ago, in a galaxy far, far away, there was a place called Texas. The Force was with a group called Democrats. It was rumored that in some states a dark side called Republicans was in power, but most Texans had never seen a Republican, so it was difficult to know whether or not they actually existed. The Force also was with White People. There were, of course, African Americans (they were called Colored or Negro then, at least in polite company) and Mexican Americans (they were called Latin Americans then), but they had none of the Force. At election time, if an African American or Mexican American attempted to vote as an individual, it was an act of courage rather than citizenship. It was, however, common "to vote" the minority groups, as in "don't forget to vote your Mexicans next week." Indeed, in South Texas so many trucks brought Latino farmworkers to the polls that the growers would tie different colored ribbons to the truckbeds so that after the workers had marked the correct ballot, they would return to the correct vehicle.

And the Force was only with Men. Although the colorful Miriam "Ma" Ferguson was elected in 1924, she was widely viewed as a stand-in for her ethically challenged husband, who had been booted out of the governor's office in 1917. Women played little role in the politics of this Texas of another era. But that was in a galaxy far away, and long, oh so very long, ago.

We are almost a half-century removed from the Texas that native son V. O. Key examined for his classic study of southern states (Key 1949). No single factor, such as race or oil and gas or conservatism or Key's "modified class politics," can describe the politics in Texas today. If there is a dominant theme to Texas politics today, it is change. Still, although Texas today bears little resemblance to the Texas of five decades ago, its contemporary politics are inextricably linked to its colorful past, particularly to the roots of its history as a frontier state and to its history of racial politics.

Texas history is, arguably, if not the most colorful history in the nation, the best known. Ask any high school student in Texas to identify a major event in the history of, say, Alabama or Iowa or South Dakota, and you're likely to receive only a blank stare. Ask any student, however, in virtually any state to identify the Alamo, and you'll get an answer that's at least in the ballpark. The history of Texas, of having served under six flags, of having been an independent republic, continues to influence the political ethic of the state, which retains, even now, a sense of a frontier state, with a fierce, if at times misguided, sense of independence.

Part of the legacy of the Texas frontier ethic has been the state's basic conservatism. Until the last two decades, electoral competition as well as legislative conflict broke along ideological rather than partisan lines; with few notable exceptions, the only elections that really counted were between conservative and liberal Democrats in the spring primaries. For the most part, conservatives won these battles. The usual scenario was success for liberals in the primary, only to be followed by defeat in primary runoffs. The process, as noted by historian George Norris Green, went as follows:

> Several conservative candidates split the conservative vote in the first Democratic primary, allowing the lone liberal to get into the runoff with the leading conservative. The conservative vote and money and newspapers then coalesce behind the conservative candidate in the second [runoff] primary, defeating the liberal, who invariably runs out of money and who never had any press support. (Green 1979, 197)

Public policy fights in the state legislature similarly were between conservative and liberal legislators, rather than Democrats and Republicans. This, of course, was due largely to the absence of the Republican Party in state and local politics, an absence that dated back to Reconstruction. In the immediate aftermath of the Civil War, Republicans controlled the state. Republican rule, however, was characterized by an unpleasant blend of corruption, tyranny, ineffectiveness, and violence. With the end of Reconstruction, the imposition of state laws (poll taxes and literacy tests, for example) barring nonwhites from meaningful political participation in Texas denied the Republican Party a natural constituency among black Texans to build a lasting power base in the state.

Over the next several decades, loyalty to the Democratic Party became deeply embedded in Texas's political culture. Identification with the Democrats was transmitted from generation to generation, resulting in such one-party dominance that Texans were described as "yellow-dog Democrats"—people who would rather vote for a yellow dog than any Republican.

Following Reconstruction, no Republican was elected to statewide office until John Tower broke through in 1961 to replace Lyndon B. Johnson in the U.S. Senate. Almost twenty years would pass before another Republican, this time Bill Clements in the 1978 gubernatorial race, would duplicate Tower's feat of winning a statewide election. During this period, Republicans fared little better in the state legislative races and enjoyed even less success as one went down the ballot. GOP primary elections reflected the Republican plight. In 1972, for example, only 114,000 voters cast ballots in the Republican primary, compared with 2.2 million people voting in the Democratic primary that year. However, after Clements's 1978 win (he would be defeated for reelection in 1982 and returned to office in 1986), Texas's elections steadily became more competitive.

Still, during the 1980s and 1990s, ideology remained more important than party affiliation. As Republicans began to contest and win state legislative seats, the conservative Democratic leadership in the state house and senate often would appoint GOP conservatives to committee chairs rather than reward the few Democratic liberals.

Texas also is a former state of the Confederacy, and race always has played a role in the state's politics. Historically, blacks in North and East Texas, and Mexican Americans in South and West Texas, have found themselves on the outside looking in when it comes to political power. The highest office won to date by an African American is the court of criminal appeals (Texas's highest court for criminal cases; the state supreme court addresses only civil cases); Morris Overstreet was elected in 1990. Mexican Americans have fared somewhat better, but this is a relative term and more a reflection of the absence of black success than Mexican American success. Raul Gonzales was elected to the Texas Supreme Court in 1986 and Dan Morales was elected attorney general in 1990; they remain the only two Mexican Americans elected to statewide offices. In 1996, Victor Morales won the Democratic primary, enabling him to challenge (unsuccessfully) Phil Gramm for the U.S. Senate; this is the highest office to which any member of a racial or ethnic group has been nominated in Texas.

Just as the partisan face of Texas is changing, however, so is the racial and ethnic distribution of political power in a state of flux. We turn now to an examination of the changing politics of party competitiveness and the politics of race.

Party Politics

It is difficult, if not impossible, to separate the politics of partisanship in Texas from the politics of race. Shortly after Lyndon B. Johnson signed the 1964 Civil Rights Act into law, he predicted to a friend that he had just ensured the end of the Democratic Party's electoral lock on the South. Certainly race has been a major factor in the Republican upsurge in Texas. As the national Democratic Party became identified as the party representing the interests of African Americans and other racial and ethnic minorities, white Texans increasingly considered the Republican Party a viable alternative. The passage of the 1965 Voting Rights Act (VRA) further contributed to the Democratic Party's image as the party of minorities, and the 1975 inclusion of Texas as one of the jurisdictions covered by the act cemented this image and accelerated white flight from the ranks of the Democrats.

Ideology also contributed to the emergence of the Republican Party in Texas. The nomination of liberal George McGovern as the Democratic Party's presidential candidate in 1972 increased the perception that the party was controlled by the liberal wing of American politics, and this, too, hastened the exodus of conservative white Texans to the GOP. As a consequence, party identification has changed markedly in recent years, but the basic conservatism of Texans has not (Dyer, Leighley, and Vedlitz 1997).

Along the partisan front, as detailed in figure 13.1, there has been steady growth of identification with the Republican Party, paralleled by a

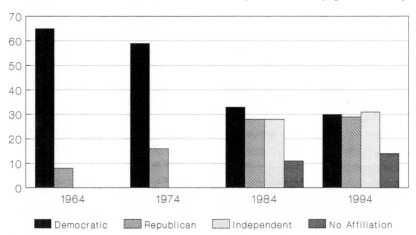

Source: Stanley and Windell, "Gender Politics in Texas Elections," paper presented at the 1995 meeting of the American Political Science Association; and Texas Poll Archives.

Fig. 13.1. Texas Partisanship, 1964–1994 (in percent)

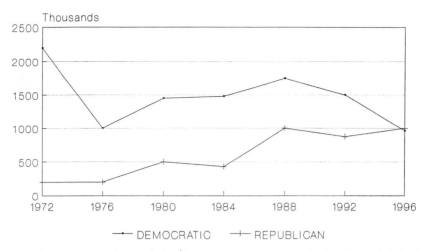

Source: Texas Secretary of State (http://www.sos.state.tx.us/function/elec1/results/70–92 html/.

Fig. 13.2. Primary Election Turnout

significant loss of support for the Democrats. In 1964, Democratic identification stood at 65 percent, eight times greater than Republican affiliation
(8 percent). By 1974, the gap had narrowed some, but Democratic identifiers still trumped Republicans by about four to one. The divide between
the parties had closed dramatically by 1984, with one-third of Texans
identifying as Democrats and 28 percent calling themselves Republicans.
Since that time, parity in party affiliation has been the norm.

Voting in Texas's open primary system has reflected this change in
party interest (see figure 13.2). The gap between voter turnout in the
Democratic and Republican primaries was enormous in 1972, narrowed
in the 1980s, and finally closed in the mid-1990s.

Demographic patterns also have spurred Republican growth in Texas.
Texas is a Sun Belt state with a steady influx of immigrants from other
states. Many of these new Texans come from traditionally Republican
states; scholarly research suggests that nearly one-fourth of Texas's
Republicans are not native to the state (Dyer, Vedlitz, and Hill 1988, 164).
Republican strength lies mainly among younger, higher-socioeconomic-
status, white non-Hispanic Texans, who reside in the more upscale suburbs and satellite communities that encircle the state's largest metropolitan areas. The Democrats draw their support predominantly from older,
native, lower-socioeconomic-status, rural Texans and the state's largest
minority groups, a point to be discussed more fully shortly (Dye, Gibson,
and Robison 1997, 767).

Table 13.1
Ideology in Texas (in percent)

	1968	1988	1994
Conservative	34	35	38
Liberal	15	19	17
Moderate/middle of road	40	40	38
Don't know	11	6	7

Sources: Chandler Davidson, *Race and Class in Texas Politics* (Princeton, N.J.: Princeton University Press, 1990); and Harte Hanks, *The Texas Poll,* Spring 1988 and Spring 1994.

In ideological terms, the more things change, the more they stay the same—at least in Texas. Table 13.1 indicates that, since 1968, the aggregate number of Texans calling themselves liberal, conservative, and moderate has been constant. The ratio of conservatives to liberals also has stayed at around two to one over this period. A 1982 survey found that 70 percent of Texans considered themselves at least somewhat conservative. Almost all Republicans and nearly two-thirds of the Democrats fell into this ideological camp (Office of the Secretary of State, 1982, table 3). As a result, electoral "victory is gained by trying to convince the electorate that a candidate is more conservative than his opponent" (Champagne and Collis 1984, 142). The difference in 1996, of course, is the party with which these conservatives now identify.

As mentioned above, part of the growth of the Republican Party can be directly attributed to the defection of conservative Democrats (Dyer and Haynes 1987), motivated to change affiliation because of the Democratic Party's overtures to minority groups (Burka 1986). Within the Republican Party there are variant conservative ideological perspectives (such as between the economic conservatives and the social conservatives) and varying degrees of commitment to conservatism. At a minimum, "the Republican party can be best described as having a conservative wing and a more conservative wing" (Champagne and Collis, 142).

Voting patterns have corresponded to these party and ideological trends. As indicated above, John Tower's election to the Senate in 1961 was the first Republican statewide victory in Texas since Reconstruction. Ironically, there is evidence that Tower was elected with the help of liberal Democrats who refused to support Tower's more conservative opponent, William Blakely (Gibson and Robison 1995, 195). Although Texas Republicans would win very few other elections at any level in Texas over the next twenty years, Tower's 1961 election is cited as the beginning of the two-party system in the state (Davidson 1990, 21).

Still, the Democratic Party continued to dominate most levels of Texas politics during the 1960s and 1970s. There were some Republican gains, most noticeably Clements's 1978 victory in the governor's race. By the end of the 1970s, however, although the GOP had established a greater presence than previously, Republicans still were relatively scarce in the legislative halls. At the beginning of the 1981 legislative session, Republicans held 25 percent of the legislative seats (at the beginning of the 1970s, they had held 7 percent).

Nonetheless, the GOP was now positioned to compete seriously for elective office. From 1960 to the mid-1980s the percentage of Texans who identified themselves as Republicans had been steadily, if gradually, increasing (from 8 percent in the early 1960s to 28 percent by the mid-1980s), while the Democrats were on a down elevator, with the Democratic percentage of the population dropping below 38 percent by 1984. In 1980 a Republican occupied the governor's office, a Republican was the state's senior U.S. senator, and Ronald Reagan, beloved by the conservatives in Texas, had just been elected president. The future was now for the GOP.

Well, not quite. Democrats surprised the Republicans in 1982 by recapturing the governor's mansion, sweeping the statewide offices, and maintaining strong majorities in both houses of the state legislature. The 1982 Democratic win can be attributed in part to a ticket that included both liberals and conservatives in the top spots, thereby holding both constituencies in the party, and by the united opposition to the dour Clements. In retrospect, this may have been the last hurrah for the Democrats in this century. In the 1984 elections Ronald Reagan easily carried Texas, Phil Gramm became the second Republican from Texas elected to the U.S. Senate, and, perhaps more important, Republicans gained seats in both the state senate and the state house. Republicans also made significant inroads in county elections, winning twice as many seats as they had held prior to the election.

Helped in part by the presence at the top of the ticket of Ronald Reagan in 1984 and favorite son George Bush in 1988, the GOP upsurge continued throughout the 1980s. Changing party loyalties continued to manifest themselves, both in the sense that some Democrats became Republicans (realignment) and in the sense that some Democrats moved away from the Democratic Party (dealignment) without aligning with the GOP. The net result: by the 1990s, party identification was virtually identical between the two parties.

The trend established in the 1980s continued into the 1990s. The Republicans suffered some difficult losses, the most visible being the defeat in 1990 of GOP gubernatorial candidate Clayton Williams at the hands of Democrat Ann Richards (or, more accurately, at the mouth of Williams, whose verbal gaffes in the last weeks of the campaign helped snatch defeat from the jaws of victory). But they continued to gain seats in almost every other venue. At the federal level, for example, Texas has supported the Republican candidate for president in every election since 1976. With the election of Kay Bailey Hutchison in 1993, both U.S. senators from Texas are now Republicans. Of the thirty members of the U.S. House of Representatives elected from Texas in 1996, fourteen are Republicans, including the highly influential majority leader of the House, Dick Armey, and the combative majority whip, Tom DeLay.

At the state level, George W. Bush, son of the former president, defeated incumbent Ann Richards in 1994 to become the second Republican governor of Texas since Reconstruction. The 1994 election also ushered in a Republican sweep of the three seats on the Texas Railroad Commission, which, because of its jurisdiction over the oil industry, is perhaps the most important elected administrative agency in the United States. The GOP also gained a majority on the 15-person state board of education. The state's elected commissioner of agriculture is a Republican, while other elected executives—for example, the attorney general, comptroller of public accounts, treasurer, and commissioner of the General Land Office—are Democrats. Although the leader of the Texas Senate, Lieutenant Governor Bob Bullock, is a Democrat, the voters in 1996 elected a Republican majority to the Texas upper house, something that had not happened in 125 years. The GOP also made a strong showing in races for the Texas House of Representatives, winning 68 of 151 seats in 1996.

Moreover, after the 1996 election, six of the nine members of the state's Court of Criminal Appeals are Republicans, and the GOP has a seven-to-two edge on the Texas Supreme Court. By 1991, 159 of the seats on the state's 380 district courts were occupied by Republicans, and since that time the number of GOP partisans holding these judicial positions has increased (Kingston, Attlesey, and Crawford 1992).

As these election results indicate, the issue no longer is whether Texas is a two-party state; rather it is whether Texas is becoming a one-party state with the Republican Party wearing the crown. If there is a cloud on the GOP horizon, it belongs less to the Democrats than to the religious right. The religious right is increasingly influential within the Republican Party in Texas; in 1996, this wing of the GOP held a virtual veto over the selection of Republican delegates to the national convention in San Diego. Governor Bush, often mentioned as a player in GOP presidential politics for 2000, is not part of the social-agenda wing of the party. Rather, he, like his father, identifies more closely with the moderate, economic wing. It may be ironic, but accurate, to say that Governor Bush's presidential aspirations are more popular among Republicans who are not Texans than among the movers and shakers in the contemporary Texas Republican Party.

The Politics of Race

In his classic study, Key suggested that race played a smaller role in Texas politics than in many other southern states. Instead, Key saw Texas politics as dividing along class lines that closely tracked political ideology (Key 1949, 261). No one familiar with Texas politics, however, would suggest that race and ethnicity are neutral factors in the state's political chemistry.

As with the emergence of the Republican Party in Texas, increased African American and Mexican American political influence is largely a development of the past twenty-five years. This increased influence in large part is a function of two factors: population patterns and the impact of the Voting Rights Act.

Although the percentage of African Americans in the overall Texas population has been decreasing in the past two decades, the concentration of this population in urban centers enhances its political influence. Over eight out of ten African Americans in Texas live in metropolitan areas; blacks make up at least 25 percent of the population in several of Texas's larger cities, a figure that translates into political power at election time.

The Mexican American population has been growing steadily, and the percentage of the overall Texas population that is Latino (almost all of Mexican origin) likewise has increased steadily. Mexican Americans currently constitute 28 percent of the state's population and are by far the largest minority group in Texas.

The increasing urbanization of the black population and the increasing numbers of Mexican Americans have coincided with the use of the Voting Rights Act to increase the political power, and representation, of these minority groups. The VRA was first extended to Texas in 1975; it is no coincidence that the growth of African American and Mexican American elected officials has occurred largely in the twenty years since that time. First, the VRA served to register thousands of eligible minority citizens. Then, beginning in the mid 1970s and accelerating into the 1980s, the act was used in successful challenges of the at-large voting structures of hundreds of city councils and school boards and the boundaries of state legislative districts and congressional districts. These legal challenges resulted in the creation of hundreds of electoral districts designed to enhance minority voting power. A quick glance at the data shows how successful these efforts were. In 1970 there were 29 African Americans serving in elective office in Texas; by 1993 this figure had increased to 472. In 1974 there were 540 Latino elected officials in Texas; twenty years later, there were 2,215.

The electoral success of the racial- and ethnic-minority candidates has been primarily at the local levels. This is significant, first, because these offices have a direct impact on the population and second, because they are the training grounds for movement to higher offices. In a very real sense, the VRA has produced an invisible revolution at the municipal and school board levels that almost certainly will begin to be manifested in higher state offices as Texas moves into the twenty-first century.

As alluded to earlier, partisan commitment in Texas takes a racial and ethnic cast (see figure 13.3). Anglos in Texas have steadily become more Republican over the last decade. Currently, 37 percent of this group identify with the GOP, an 11 percent increase since 1984. Correspondingly, there has been a 9 percent erosion of support among Anglos for the Democratic Party.

Interestingly, Democratic affiliation among African Americans and Hispanics has also slipped. Whereas 72 percent of blacks identified as Democrats in 1984, a decade later this number had dropped to 59 percent. This loss was not a gain for the Republicans, however. Indeed, only 2 percent of African Americans identified with the GOP in 1994, a fall of 5 per-

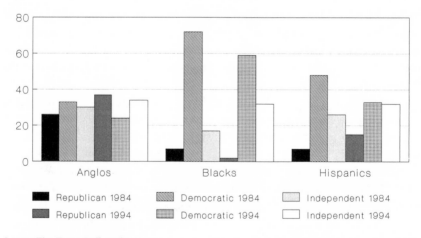

Source: The Texas Poll Archives

Fig. 13.3. Political Party Affiliation by Race/Ethnicity (in percent)

Table 13.2
Voting Participation and Ethnicity (in percent)

	Total Population	Eligible to Vote	Registered	Voting
Anglo	58	66	74	76
Hispanic	28	20	15	12
African American	12	11	9	10

Sources: Southwest Voter Research Institute; *Dallas Morning News,* 26 April 1993, A13; and Thomas Dye, L. Tucker Gibson Jr., and Clay Robison, *Politics in America: Texas Edition* (Upper Saddle River, N.J.: Prentice-Hall, 1997), 774–75.

cent from ten years earlier. Rather blacks in Texas are more inclined now to call themselves independents than they were in 1984. Similarly, Hispanic commitment to the Democrats has decreased from 48 percent to 33 percent during this time. Republican identification among Hispanics has doubled from 7 percent to 15 percent, and the number of Latino independents has expanded somewhat, from 26 percent to 32 percent.

To be sure, voting patterns in Texas suggest that on polling day African Americans and Latinos cast ballots for Democrats far more often than for Republican candidates (Dye and Gibson 1977, 774). However, there is a catch, for, as indicated in table 13.2, vote turnout among minorities, especially Mexican Americans, lags behind Anglo participation. As noted earlier, Hispanics make up 28 percent of Texas's total population, but because this is a very young population and because of the presence of noncitizens (estimated to be one in seven), only 20 percent of the state's eligible voters are Hispanic. Further winnowing the numbers, just 15 percent of the state's registered voters and 12 percent of its actual voters are Latinos. Hence, despite concerted efforts to register and mobilize the Hispanic vote in Texas, turnout remains problematic.

Anglos, on the other hand, are declining as a percent of Texas's total population but are overrepresented among the eligible (66 percent), the registered (74 percent), and the voters (76 percent) in Texas. Considering the shift among Anglos toward the Republicans, the future, at least over the short haul, remains bright for the GOP in the Lone Star State.

Conversely, the racialization of partisan politics might not bode as well for the state. Demographers estimate that sometime between 2009 and 2026, half of Texas's population will be comprised of "minorities." Most of this change will be the result of the growth of the Latino population, which will constitute 38 percent of the state's population by 2026. Indeed, by the end of the first quarter of the new century, 47 percent of school-age children will be Hispanic, creating "the potential for ethnic conflict because the white, aging 'baby boomers' will be faced with having to support schools that have mostly [Hispanic or black] kids."[1]

Overall, data indicate there has been much improvement in interracial feelings in Texas. In 1968, for example, 26 percent of the white population were willing to have a black as a roommate for their child at college, 36 percent were willing to invite a black to attend a social gathering at their home, 37 percent were willing to share a swimming pool with blacks, 43 percent to live next door to a black, 63 percent to let a black teach their children in schools, and 69 percent were willing to send their children to a racially integrated school.

Some twenty years later, attitudes had softened, especially among younger, higher-socioeconomic-status, non-Baptist Texas whites. A 1986 poll found much greater acceptance among all whites of African Americans as roommates at college (68 percent), in social gatherings at home (77 percent), in public swimming areas (78 percent), and as immediate neighbors (80 percent), teachers (84 percent), and students in integrated schools (81 percent). Moreover, there was very little resistance to working alongside African Americans, although 46 percent of whites rejected the notion of becoming related to blacks through marriage. Nearly 70 percent of white Texans said they would accept an African American president.

Similarly, the 1986 study found Anglos accepting of Latinos in diverse social, economic, and political settings. The number of Anglos rejecting these encounters rarely rose above 10 percent. African Americans and Hispanics expressed almost total acceptance of Anglos in all social, economic, and political situations examined.[2]

These findings suggest that this "era of better feelings" may inhibit translating majority-minority racial and ethnic differences into distinct, immutable partisan conflict in Texas. Intragroup splits between African Americans and Hispanics further complicate racial politics in Texas. Indeed, "blacks and Mexican Americans are more accepting of Anglos than they are of each other" (Dyer, Vedlitz, and Worschel 1989, 611). Thus, social distance might very well hinder coalition attempts, say, through the Democratic Party, among members of Texas's principal minority groups.

Conclusion

As Texas moves toward the twenty-first century, two parallel political tracks are visible. One is the partisan track, where the Republican Party continues to lay claim to the state. The GOP capture of the state senate in 1996 may be a preview of coming attractions with respect to the state house and the congressional delegation. Texas arguably has been a one-party GOP state in presidential elections for a generation, and Republicans have won three of the last five gubernatorial elections and already are heavily favored to win again in 1998. Forget Dixie: as far as Texas partisan politics is concerned, old times there may soon be forgotten.

The second track marks the increasing influence of the minority population in the state, particularly the Mexican American population. The demographics are clear; it is only a matter of time until the sociological minority population is a numerical majority, and these numbers, combined with increased educational and occupational gains, eventually will translate into political power.

Given the proclivity of both Mexican Americans and African Americans to vote Democratic, these two tracks may not be parallel for long. A clash seems inevitable, and this conflict may inform Texas politics for the next generation.

Notes

Title: with apologies to George Lucas.

1. Michael Wegner, assistant manager for research in the Office of the State Comptroller, quoted in Eskenazi 1994.
2. The results of the 1968 and 1986 surveys are discussed in the *Texas Poll*, Fall 1986.

References

Burka, Paul. 1986. "Primary Lesson." *Texas Monthly*, July.

Champagne, Anthony, and Rick Collis. 1984. "Texas." In *The Political Life of the American States*, edited by Alan Rosenthal and Maureen Moakley. New York: Praeger, 1984.

Davidson, Chandler. 1990. *Race and Class in Texas Politics*. Princeton, N.J.: Princeton University Press.

Dye, Thomas, L. Tucker Gibson Jr., and Clay Robison. 1997. *Politics in America: Texas Edition*. Upper Saddle River, N.J.: Prentice-Hall.

Dyer, James, and Don Haynes. 1987. *Social, Economic, and Political Change according to the Texas Poll*. Austin: College of Communication, University of Texas at Austin.

Dyer, James A., Jan E. Leighley, and Arnold Vedlitz. 1997. "Party Identification and Public Opinion in Texas, 1984–1994." In *Texas Politics: A Reader,* edited by Anthony Champagne and Edward J. Harpham. New York: W. W. Norton.

Dyer, James A., Arnold Vedlitz, and David B. Hill. 1988. "New Voters, Switchers, and Political Party Realignment in Texas." *Western Political Quarterly* 41 (March): 164.

Dyer, James A., Arnold Vedlitz, and Stephen Worschel. 1989. "Social Distance among Racial and Ethnic Groups in Texas." *Social Science Quarterly* 70 (September).

Eskenazi, Stuart. 1994. "Minority Groups Are Growing Share of Texas Population." *Austin American-Statesman,* 1 January, A1.

Gibson, L. Tucker, Jr. and Clay Robison. 1995. *Government and Politics in Texas.* Englewood Cliffs, N.J.: Prentice-Hall.

Green, George Norris. 1979. *The Establishment in Texas Politics: The Primitive Years.* Norman: University of Oklahoma Press.

Key, V. O., Jr. 1949. *Southern Politics in State and Nation.* New York: Knopf.

Kingston, Mike, Sam Attlesey, and Mary G. Crawford. 1992. *The Texas Almanac's Political History of Texas.* Austin: Eakin Press.

Office of the Secretary of State. 1982. *May Primary Election Analysis.* Austin: Office of the Secretary of State, 1982, table 3.

Part IV

The Soul of the South

14

The Soul of the South:
Religion and the New Electoral Order

John C. Green, Lyman A. Kellstedt,
Corwin E. Smidt, and James L. Guth

In the latest generation, southern politics has undergone a major transformation, moving from a one-party bastion to a crucible of two-party
competition. Many factors have contributed to this change: the effects of
race, the consequences of economic development and migration, and the
impact of religion. The last of these has received considerable attention
recently because of activities of the Christian Right. However, the impact
of religion extends beyond the "religious right" and is closely related to
the other changes in the region. Indeed, the sea change in the relationship
of southern religion and politics is critical to the new electoral order. Simply put, the soul of the South is being reincorporated into the politics of
the nation.

Here we review the political behavior of southern religious groups
using survey data, tracing continuity and change from the 1960s to the
1990s. We find that traditional religion is still an important feature of
southern elections but that it operates in a new context. The white Protestant alliance that undergirded the Democratic Party in the days of the
"solid South" is being reassembled in the Republican Party, while
increased religious diversity has helped extend into the South the coalition
of minorities long fostered by northern Democrats. This new electoral
order has had important national consequences: it allowed Newt Gingrich
to become Speaker of the House and Bill Clinton to win the White House.

Electoral Order and Southern Religion

Byron Shafer's (1991, 43–45) concept of an "electoral order" is a useful
way to discuss the role of religion in southern politics. An electoral order
is a stable political relationship between the social base, intermediary

organizations, and government institutions. The social base is made up of politically relevant demographic differences among voters, such as race and class; intermediary organizations include the formal mobilizers and representatives of such voters, principally political parties; and government institutions include officials elected by such means, such as the president and members of Congress. So, at any point in time, the electoral order is defined by the support of key social groups for the major parties and their candidates. And changes in social group support can ultimately produce a new order.

According to Shafer (1991, 43), religion is one of the fundamental social bases for electoral order in the United States, and one that is especially important in the South. Indeed, religion was, and still is, central to the region's distinctive culture and politics (Hill 1983). Scholars have noted that the "religious solid South preceded the political solid South" (Weaver 1968, 98) and that "the first will apparently outlast the latter" (Reed 1972, 57). It is thus surprising that students of southern politics have largely neglected religion. For example, Black and Black's two-volume treatise on southern politics (1987, 1992) barely mentions the topic, and John Petrocik's (1987) study of party coalitions in the South ignores it altogether. Of course, V. O. Key's masterly work (1949) was hardly better, and its neglect of religion has been replicated in the genre it inspired (e.g., Havard 1972; Lamis 1984). While there are some important exceptions (Baker, Steed, and Moreland 1983; Kellstedt 1990; Smidt 1983, 1989; Rozell and Wilcox 1996), religion has yet to become a standard feature of analysis of southern politics.

The reasons for this neglect are not hard to find. Much of the best work on southern politics has been informed by economic questions (Black and Black 1987) and the critical issue of race (Carmines and Stimson 1989). Just as important, southern religion can be difficult to understand, being both unusually homogeneous and remarkably diverse. On the first count, the South has been dominated by Protestant churches, and the concentration of pious Baptists and Methodists presents a sharp contrast to the religious diversity of the rest of the country (Hill 1966, 31–39). Thus many scholars assumed that southern religion did not vary. But on the second count, southern Protestants are hardly monolithic, exhibiting numerous differences in belief and practice (Harrell 1981): Baptists differ from Methodists, white from black Protestants, and believers from backsliders. This complexity has led many scholars to ignore southern religion on practical grounds.

Recent research on religion offers some conceptual tools with which to simplify this complexity. The first and most basic concept is "religious tradition," a grouping of religious communities that share a distinctive worldview. Religious tradition is best measured by combining affiliation with similar denominations (cf. Kellstedt et al. 1996a), and scholars typically recognize as the five largest traditions in the United States evangelical, mainline, and black Protestants; Roman Catholics; and the nonreligious or secular population. The first three are particularly important in the South.

The distinction between historically white evangelical and mainline Protestants is important but often subtle. Evangelicals are more orthodox in belief and practice, stressing "otherworldly" concerns, while mainliners are more modernist in belief and practice, putting greater emphasis on "thisworldly" matters (Kellstedt et al. 1996b). White Baptists in the South are evangelicals, and most white southern Methodists are mainliners. Indeed, the two largest Protestant denominations, the Southern Baptist Convention and the United Methodist Church, dominate the evangelical and mainline traditions, respectively, and their adherents are especially numerous in the South. Another critical distinction is between white and black Protestants. Given the effects of slavery and segregation, historically black Protestant churches constitute a separate religious tradition (cf. Sernett 1991). Although black Baptists and Methodists share beliefs and practices with their white counterparts, their worldview is quite different. A similar distinction occurs between the various Protestant traditions and non-Protestants, such as Catholics and seculars.

Another concept useful in reducing this complexity is "religious commitment," the extent of an individual's attachment to his or her religion. Religious commitment can be measured in many ways, ranging from church attendance to private devotionalism, but all help differentiate individuals who take their faith seriously from those whose attachments are merely nominal (Kellstedt et al. 1996a). Simply put, individuals with higher levels of commitment are the most likely to partake of the distinctive worldview of their religious tradition. Southerners are known for high religious commitment (Reed 1972), but the level of commitment is hardly uniform (Stark and Bainbridge 1985).

Taken together, these concepts allow us to identify seven religious groups that account for almost all southern adults: high- and low-commitment white evangelical Protestants, high- and low-commitment white mainline Protestants, black Protestants, Catholics, and seculars (see table 14.1). Given their small numbers in survey data, southern black Protestants and Catholics cannot be reliably divided by religious commitment, but we will comment on its apparent effects; not surprisingly, religious commitment is low among seculars.[1] Although a discussion of the effects of other demographic factors, such as income and gender, is beyond the

Table 14.1
Relative Size of Southern Religious Groups, 1960s–1990s (in percent)

	1960s	1970s	1980s	1990s
Protestants				
Evangelical				
High commitment	18	18	18	20
Low commitment	27	26	24	17
Mainline				
High commitment	13	7	7	7
Low commitment	15	15	10	9
Black	15	18	18	19
Catholic	6	11	13	13
Secular	5	6	7	12
Others	2	3	3	3

Sources: National Elections Studies; National Surveys of Religion and Politics

scope of this essay, we can report that statistical controls do not substantially change the relationship between religion and politics reported below (Kellstedt et al. 1996a).

These religious groups are related to southern distinctiveness in various ways. First, high-commitment evangelicals represent the core of traditional southern religion, with the other three white Protestant groups representing modest departures from it in both belief and practice. Second, the three remaining groups were excluded from traditional southern religion: blacks because of the "color line," and Catholics and seculars because of what might be called the "papal line" and the "theistic line," respectively.

These religious groups were also connected to the electoral order in the era of the solid South. All four groups of white Protestants were allied in support of the Democratic Party. The strength of this alliance produced a powerful faction in the coalition of minorities that the Democratic Party assembled at the national level, and which helped elect Democratic presidents and majorities in Congress, from Grover Cleveland to Jimmy Carter. High-commitment evangelicals were the core of this white Protestant alliance, apparently remaining loyal even in the face of regional rebellions, such as the states' rights agitation in 1948. Certainly it was low-commitment white Protestants who were the most likely to defect to third-party candidates in recent times (Gilbert, Johnson, and Peterson 1995). Mainline Protestants were also less firmly anchored to "southern Democracy," being the most likely to defect to the Republicans, the party of their coreligionists outside the region (as in 1956). Black Protestant, Catholic, and secular voters were largely excluded from this alliance; in response, they sometimes allied themselves with northern Democrats in intraparty battles and sometimes defected to the GOP in general elections. The task before us is to assess how these patterns have continued or changed in the last generation and to examine their impact on the new electoral order.

The Religious Composition of the South

A good place to begin such an assessment is with the relative size of our seven religious groups from the 1960s to the 1990s (table 14.1). After all, the size of a social group sets the upper bounds on its contribution to the electoral order. One source of continuity is high-commitment evangelicals, who made up roughly one-fifth of the adult population over the period. In fact, this group of white Protestants was the only one that maintained its relative size between 1960 and the 1990s. In contrast, low-commitment evangelicals declined from over one-quarter to about one-sixth of the population. An even sharper decline occurred among mainline Protestants, especially the high-commitment group, whose experience parallels that of low-commitment evangelicals. By the 1990s, white Protestants had contracted from almost three-quarters of the southern citizenry to just over one-half. Thus, the core of the white Protestant alliance remained intact in relative terms, while its periphery was reduced.

The other side of this pattern is a steady increase in religious diversity. Black Protestants grew by more than one-quarter over the period, so that by its end they matched the number of high-commitment evangelicals. Catholics and seculars grew even faster, more than doubling by the 1990s. Indeed, these last two groups together eventually outnumbered high-commitment evangelicals on the one hand and all mainline Protestants on the other. No doubt these changes reflect the effects of southern economic development and migration, trends that eroded the position of Protestantism, and especially the mainline, outside of the South. So, religious groups once excluded from traditional southern religion expanded as the white Protestant alliance contracted. As we will see below, these changes in the religious composition of the southern electorate are associated with transformations in the electoral order.

Religion and Political Behavior

What about political changes among these religious groups? Table 14.2 examines three common measures of political behavior over time: vote

Table 14.2
Southern Religion and Political Behavior, 1960s–1990s

	1960s		1970s		1980s		1990s	
	Dem.	Rep.	Dem.	Rep.	Dem.	Rep.	Dem.	Rep.
Presidential Vote (%)								
Protestants								
Evangelical								
High commitment	42	58	33	67	31	70	31	69
Low commitment	65	35	36	64	39	61	43	57
Mainline								
High commitment	45	55	27	73	33	67	35	65
Low commitment	41	54	35	65	35	65	44	54
Black	91	9	88	12	89	8	86	14
Catholic	57	30	40	59	45	55	60	40
Secular	58	42	43	57	32	68	45	55
House Vote (%)								
Protestants								
Evangelical								
High commitment	74	26	70	30	62	38	36	64
Low commitment	81	19	71	29	64	36	40	60
Mainline								
High commitment	61	39	61	39	58	42	42	58
Low commitment	60	40	61	39	56	44	37	63
Black	92	8	93	7	92	8	86	14
Catholic	75	26	78	22	64	36	54	46
Secular	80	20	65	35	60	40	54	46
Party Identification (%)								
Protestants								
Evangelical								
High commitment	71	20	58	30	53	36	32	52
Low commitment	71	18	55	26	52	33	40	45
Mainline								
High commitment	57	32	48	43	40	51	36	49
Low commitment	52	38	49	36	45	44	39	46
Black	83	10	80	9	83	10	80	12
Catholic	66	20	67	19	54	31	49	39
Secular	62	23	55	26	50	35	35	40

Sources: National Elections Studies; National Surveys of Religion and Politics

choice in presidential and House elections and party identification. To make temporal comparisons easier, the first two measures are restricted to the major-party vote. This decision matters little in House elections, but it can make a big difference for the presidency—a matter we will take up below. For party identification, partisan leaners are combined with the other partisans and pure independents are not shown. Each of these measures shows basically the same pattern, with the presidential vote being the most volatile and party identification the least.

By the 1960s, high-commitment evangelicals were already beginning to move away from southern Democracy. Partly in reaction to John Kennedy's Catholicism, but also because of the Goldwater and Nixon campaigns, almost three-fifths of this group cast GOP presidential ballots during this decade. Republican support expanded to more than two-thirds in the 1970s and maintained its high level in the 1980s and 1990s; meanwhile, Democratic support fell to less than one-third of the two-party vote. A slower but no less dramatic shift occurred in House vote and party identification. Up through the 1980s, high-commitment evangelicals voted overwhelmingly for Democratic congressional candidates and on balance identified with the Democratic Party. But in the 1990s, this key group shifted sharply toward the GOP in both regards.

The other white Protestant groups show similar patterns. Low-commitment evangelicals voted solidly Democratic at the presidential level in the 1960s and then switched to the Republicans in the succeeding decades, but at a lower rate than their high-commitment coreligionists (and with some backtracking in the 1990s). House vote and partisanship also followed the high-commitment group but at a lower level. Mainline Protestants displayed a variation on this theme. The high- and low-commitment groups started the period voting for Republican presidential candidates, a trend that expanded in the subsequent decades. On House vote and partisanship, these groups also moved more quickly in the Republican direction. Here the high-commitment group was generally more Republican, but not as consistently as among evangelicals. Both white Protestant traditions reached a rough parity in Republican presidential vote in the 1980s, and in House vote and partisanship in the 1990s.

Black Protestants were dramatically and consistently different. Over the entire period, they were solidly Democratic at the ballot box and in partisanship. Southern Catholics and seculars showed more variation. Both groups were squarely in the Democratic camp in the 1960s but voted for GOP presidential candidates in the 1970s and 1980s. Catholics returned to the Democratic column in the 1990s, and they were also consistently Democratic in House vote and partisanship, albeit at a declining rate. In partial contrast, southern seculars remained in the Republican presidential column in the 1990s and showed a modest tilt toward the GOP in partisanship. In House vote, however, seculars resembled Catholics. Although the small number of cases makes it difficult to assess the impact of religious commitment on southern black Protestants and Catholics, it appears that members of the high-commitment group intensified their Democratic leanings over the period.[2]

Religious commitment had an independent effect on turnout (Kellstedt et al. 1996a). In each time period and for all religious traditions, high commitment was associated with higher levels of voting, and although turnout declined across the board from the 1960s to the 1990s, the downturn was smallest among the high-commitment groups (including high-commitment black Protestants and Catholics). Not surprisingly, seculars had relatively low levels of participation. Because of the effects of socioeconomic status, mainline Protestants had the highest turnout and black Protestants the lowest, with evangelicals and Catholics in between (data not shown).

Thus, the transformation of the electoral order in the South had twin religious engines: political change among white Protestants and growing religious diversity. On the first count, high-commitment evangelicals conducted a steady march into the very center of the Republican camp, and other white Protestants arrived in the same neighborhood by more circuitous paths. Meanwhile, black Protestants remained solidly in the Democratic fold, Catholics remained on balance Democratic, and seculars showed mixed behavior.

Religion and Changes in the Electoral Order

We can illustrate the combined impact of these factors on the electoral order by looking at major-party vote totals at the beginning and end of the period. Table 14.3 reports the relative contribution of each religious group to the Democratic and Republican presidential coalitions in the 1960s and the 1990s, and changes between them. Very similar results obtain for House vote coalitions and party identification (data not shown). These patterns starkly reveal the emerging electoral order, with each party's coalition developing a different core constituency.

Not surprisingly, the new core of the Republican coalition is high-commitment evangelicals. This group rose from one-quarter of the Republican vote in the 1960s to one-third in the 1990s, a gain of 8 percentage points. Because of this group's stable size, most of the difference must be attributable to political change and turnout differential. All the

Table 14.3
Religion and the Electoral Order: Presidential Vote (in percent)

	1960s		1990s		Change	
	Dem.	Rep.	Dem.	Rep.	Dem.	Rep.
Protestants						
Evangelical						
High commitment	16	25	14	33	-2	+8
Low commitment	24	22	12	17	-12	-5
Mainline						
High commitment	14	18	7	14	-7	-4
Low commitment	11	20	8	11	-3	-9
Black	19	4	33	6	+14	+2
Catholic	8	5	13	9	+5	+4
Secular	6	5	7	9	+2	+4
Others	2	1	6	1	+4	0
TOTAL	100	100	100	100		

Source: National Elections Studies; National Surveys of Religion and Politics

other Protestant groups declined as a proportion of the GOP vote, especially low-commitment mainliners. So, overall, white Protestants fell from better than four-fifths to three-quarters of the Republican coalition. Given the increasing GOP bent of these three groups, much of this change results from declines in size and from turnout differential. The GOP also made modest gains among black Protestants, Catholics, and seculars, but taken together, such increases exceed the gains of high-commitment evangelicals, so that these groups grew from less than one-sixth of the GOP presidential vote to one-quarter. These figures are attributable to both population growth and political change.

The new core of the Democratic coalition is black Protestants—an ironic version of southern distinctiveness. In the 1960s, this group accounted for about one-fifth of the Democratic vote, and by the 1990s, one-third, representing a 14 percentage point gain, the largest of any religious group. This change reflects not only population increase among African Americans but also their enfranchisement since the 1960s. No doubt their impact is reduced by low turnout. These dramatic gains helped the Democrats make up for equally dramatic losses among white Protestants, especially among low-commitment evangelicals. Indeed, the losses among both evangelical groups equals the gains among black Protestants. Overall, white Protestants fell from almost two-thirds to about two-fifths of the Democratic vote over the period. These differences result from both population and political change, and probably turnout differentials as well. Democrats also made modest gains among Catholics and seculars (as well as other religious groups), so that these groups rose from one-sixth to one-quarter of the vote.[3]

Religion and the New Electoral Order

Thus, by the 1990s the southern electoral order had two new centers of gravity: high-commitment evangelicals for the GOP and black Protestants for the Democrats. The major parties divided the other religious groups about evenly, contributing to two-party competition and reinforcing other changes in southern politics (Kellstedt et al. 1996a). On the one hand, the remaining southern distinctiveness increasingly helped the GOP, and on the other hand, the South has become less distinctive, to the benefit of the Democrats. These patterns appear to have progressed throughout the decade, with 1996 showing them most fully.

Table 14.4 takes a closer look at the voting behavior of our religious groups in the 1990s and illustrates these trends in more detail (see Green et al. 1996, chaps. 14, 15). The table displays the two-party congressional and presidential vote in chronological order from 1990 to 1996. First, note the steady Republican gains among high-commitment evangelicals, shifting from majority support for Democratic House candidates in 1990 to overwhelming backing of Republicans in 1994 and 1996. Similarly high levels of support appear for the GOP presidential tickets, continuing a pattern established in the 1980s. These bearers of traditional southern religion were crucial to recent Republican gains in Congress, including the election and reelection of Newt Gingrich as Speaker of the House, and they also provided a "fire wall" in the Republican presidential defeats in 1992 and 1996. Social issues were of particular interest to this theologically conservative group (Kellstedt et al. 1996a), and no doubt the church-based mobilization of the Christian Right is partially responsible for its solidification as a strong Republican constituency (Green et al. 1997).

The other white Protestant groups show patterns similar to the high-commitment evangelicals, but their support for Republicans was often less strong and their path through the 1990s less even. For instance, low-commitment evangelicals often voted less Republican than the high-commitment group, especially in the 1996 presidential election, where their 55 percent for Dole was hardly bigger than their 53 percent for Republican congressional candidates in 1990. This pattern resembles the mainline groups, although in this decade low-commitment mainliners were fre-

Table 14.4
Religion and Southern Political Behavior: Republican Vote in the 1990s
(in percent)

	1990	1992		1994	1996	
	Cong.	Cong.	Pres.	Cong.	Cong.	Pres.
Protestants						
Evangelical						
High commitment	46	53	62	69	76	76
Low commitment	53	52	58	57	69	55
Mainline						
High commitment	54	56	68	56	60	62
Low commitment	60	60	54	61	66	58
Black	6	7	10	10	9	10
Catholic	44	50	43	43	43	38
Secular	49	54	55	37	37	55

Source: National Surveys of Religion and Politics

quently more supportive of GOP congressional candidates.

Mainline Protestants are less likely to have been influenced by the Christian Right and are attracted to the Republican standard largely for economic reasons—a position consistent, by the way, with the Protestant ethic of personal achievement and free enterprise (Kellstedt et al. 1996a). Of course, this kind of individualism often conflicts with the moralism of the old-time religion. Such a division occurred among northern Protestants in the 1920s and has finally appeared in the South. In any event, Republicans have benefited from both groups of southern Protestants, and the challenge to the party is to maintain, strengthen, and refine this new version of the white Protestant alliance.

The strong Republican support of white Protestants is hardly monolithic, however, particularly when compared to black Protestants' steadfast presence in the Democratic camp throughout the 1990s. Indeed, without this strong support, the Democrats would not have remained competitive in the South. Of course, the original source of this support—the struggle for civil rights—was crucial to the erosion of the Democratic allegiance of white Protestants. Certainly the construction of a biracial Democratic coalition was made easier by the exit of many traditionalist whites to the GOP. This expanded black constituency also depends heavily on church-based mobilization, much like high-commitment evangelicals among Republicans (Lincoln and Mamiya 1990). Indeed, southern Democracy is now unthinkable without black churches and parachurch groups—an irony of historic proportions.

The growing Catholic and secular populations in the South have also helped the Democrats, but their support is less strong and has developed less evenly. Southern Catholics were flirting with the Republicans in 1992 but reverted to their Democratic proclivities as the decade wore on, especially in 1996. Southern seculars were even less predictable, backing Bush in 1992 and Dole in 1996, but not the Gingrich-led Republican congressional candidates in 1994 and 1996. However, when these groups are combined with large minorities of white Protestants, some of whom are theologically liberal, and the solid support of black Protestants, the Democrats can compete in the South, as Bill Clinton and Al Gore showed in 1992 and 1996. Such a coalition of minorities is, of course, the stuff of Democratic politics at the national level. Here, too, northern politics has invaded the once solid South.

Are these trends likely to continue? We are confident they will, and table 14.5 offers a small but potent piece of evidence in support of this expectation. The table looks at the political behavior of high- and low-commitment evangelicals in 1992 controlling for age.[4] We choose evangelicals for this illustration because of their consistent and dramatic pattern of political change; other groups show more complex age patterns.

First, note the now familiar differences between the high- and low-commitment groups, with the former generally more Republican. But the most interesting pattern is by age within both commitment groups: with only a few exceptions, the younger cohorts are markedly more Republi-

Table 14.5
Political Behavior of White Southern Evangelicals, Controlling for Religious Commitment and Age, 1992 (in percent)

	Presidential		Congressional		Partisanship	
	Dem.	Rep.	Dem.	Rep.	Dem.	Rep.
High commitment						
All	24	76	32	68	26	45
18–29 years	33	67	31	69	15	60
30–44 years	14	86	25	75	17	57
45–59 years	19	81	37	63	30	32
≥ 60 years	36	64	42	58	51	24
Low commitment						
All	40	60	47	53	36	46
18–29 years	35	65	43	57	31	59
30–44 years	34	66	30	70	24	45
45–59 years	44	56	54	46	34	46
≥ 60 years	50	50	77	23	72	28

Source: 1992 VRS Exit Polls

Table 14.6
Religion and Southern Political Behavior: Support for Perot (in percent)

	1992	1996	Both
Protestants			
Evangelical			
High commitment	15	7	11
Low commitment	18	12	16
Mainline			
High commitment	12	4	9
Low commitment	22	5	13
Black	2	2	2
Catholic	19	6	13
Secular	23	42	30

Source: National Surveys of Religion and Politics

can than the older ones. Indeed, in most cases, there is a steady increase in Republican support as we move from the last generation of the solid South (60 years or over) to the "buster" generation (18 to 29 years). Interestingly, it is the "boomer" generation that causes most of these discrepancies. If these patterns for evangelicals represent the underlying dynamic in southern politics, and we think they do, then this new electoral order will continue to emerge well into the next century.

Thus far we have purposely avoided a crucial element of politics in the 1990s, namely, Ross Perot. Table 14.6 reports on the support for Perot in 1992, 1996, and both years combined. Clearly, Perot's support was strongest among the low-commitment groups (including black Protestants and Catholics as well). The epitome of low religious commitment is the seculars, who showed the strongest support for Perot in both elections—and were the only group to increase their support in 1996. These findings comport well with the work of Gilbert et al. (1995) who find that support for third-party candidates is associated with low levels of religious commitment. In the South, as elsewhere, Perot appealed to people disconnected from social bonds and in transition politically (Green 1997). Thus, the Perot campaign performed the traditional role of third-party candidates: serving as a halfway house during changes in the electoral order.

The Soul of the South

If nothing else, the preceding analysis confirms the importance of religion as one of the fundamental social bases in the electoral order in the South and, by implication, in the nation. As we have seen, the impact of southern religion on politics is characterized by strong continuities and dramatic changes. The bearers of traditional southern religion, high-commitment evangelicals, are good examples of both: they have maintained their relative size and distinctive outlook in the face of major social changes and in response shifted their attachments from the Democrats to the Republicans. Other Protestant groups have declined in number but also shifted their political support, so that the white Protestant alliance is being recreated in the Republican Party. Like high-commitment evangelicals, black Protestants have displayed both continuity and change: fierce loyalty to the Democrats, combined with increased size and levels of participation. Catholics and seculars have grown in numbers, helping to bring the Democratic coalition of minorities to the South.

Thus, at the end of the twentieth century, the soul of the South is being reincorporated into the politics of the nation, with religious groups peculiar to the southern experience anchoring both major-party coalitions in the South. These changes in the social base of the electoral order have had important repercussions for intermediary political organizations and government institutions.

First, these shifts have given both the Republicans and the Democrats strong incentives to build sophisticated organizations in a region once bereft of electoral competition. These shifts have also provided incentives for religious-based social movements, from the civil rights movement to the Christian Right, dedicated in large measure to getting religious communities to the polls.

Second, the result of those votes can be seen in elected officials: an increase in Republican officeholders in Congress and state and local offices, and a parallel rise in the number of African Americans and non-Protestants. And for the greatest prize of all, the presidency, both parties are competitive if they choose their candidates and platforms with care. Changes of this magnitude, if they persist, are bound to produce significant alterations in public policy.

Notes

1. The following analysis is based on the National Elections Studies (NES) Cumulative File (1960 to 1988) and the National Surveys of Religion and Politics conducted at the University of Akron in 1992 and 1996 (see Kellstedt et al. 1996a for details). The sample size varies by decade for the NES data (1,890 in the 1960s; 3,648 in the 1970s; 2,994 in the 1980s); the Akron data sets had sample sizes of 4,001 and 4,037 respectively. The NES data are made available by the Inter-University

Consortium for Political and Social Research; the National Surveys of Religion and Politics were supported by grants from the Pew Charitable Trusts. The authors are solely responsible for the interpretations presented here. Denominational affiliation was coded into religious traditions according to Kellstedt et al. (1996a). Religious commitment was measured by church attendance (high commitment was coded as attending more often than "a few times a year," low commitment as attending "a few times a year" or less). Contact the authors for additional details in the coding of religious variables in these data sets.

2. Trends among southern Protestants and Catholics resembled those among their coreligionists outside of the South, but southern seculars were quite different. See Kellstedt et al. (1996a).

3. Traditional distinctions between the Deep and the Rim South appear in these data. High-commitment evangelicals and black Protestants appear to be more important to their respective party coalitions in the Deep South, while these groups are less important in the Rim South.

4. We use the 1992 VRS exit poll for this purpose because of its greater sample size. These data were made available through the Roper Center. The authors are solely responsible for the interpretations presented here.

References

Black, Earl, and Merle Black. 1987. *Politics and Society in the South.* Cambridge: Harvard University Press.

———. 1992. *The Vital South.* Cambridge: Harvard University Press.

Baker, Tod A., Robert P. Steed, and Laurence W. Moreland, eds. 1983. *Religion and Politics in the South.* New York: Praeger.

Carmines, Edward G., and James A. Stimson. 1989. *Issue Evolution: Race and the Transformation of American Politics.* Princeton, N.J.: Princeton University Press.

Gilbert, Christopher P., Timothy R. Johnson, and David A. M. Peterson. 1995. "The Religious Roots of Third Party Voting: A Comparison of Anderson, Perot, and Wallace Voters." *Journal for the Scientific Study of Religion* 34: 470–84.

Green, John C. 1997. "The Third Party South." In *The 1996 Presidential Election in the South,* edited by Laurence W. Moreland and Robert P. Steed. New York: Praeger.

Green, John C., James L. Guth, Corwin E. Smidt, and Lyman A. Kellstedt. 1996. *Religion and the Culture Wars.* Lanham, Md.: Rowman & Littlefield.

Green, John C., Corwin E. Smidt, Lyman A. Kellstedt, and James L. Guth. 1997. "Bringing in the Sheaves." In *Sojourners in the Wilderness: The Christian Right in Comparative Perspective,* edited by Corwin E. Smidt and James M. Penning. Lanham, Md.: Rowman & Littlefield.

Harrell, David Edwin, ed. 1981. *Varieties of Southern Evangelicalism.* Macon, Ga.: Mercer University Press.

Havard, William C., ed. 1972. *The Changing Politics of the South.* Baton Rouge: Louisiana State University Press.

Hill, Samuel S. 1966. *Southern Churches in Crisis.* New York: Holt, Rinehart, & Winston.

———. 1983. Introduction to *Religion and Politics in the South,* edited by Tod A. Baker, Robert P. Steed, and Laurence W. Moreland. New York: Praeger.

Kellstedt, Lyman A. 1990. "Evangelical Religion and Support for the Falwell Policy Positions: An Examination of Regional Variation." In *The Disappearing South,* edited by Robert P. Steed, Laurence W. Moreland, and Tod A. Baker. Tuscaloosa: University of Alabama Press.

Kellstedt, Lyman A., John C. Green, James L. Guth, and Corwin E. Smidt. 1996a. "Grasping the Essentials: The Social Embodiment of Religion and Political Behavior." In *Religion and the Culture Wars,* by John C. Green, James L. Guth, Corwin E. Smidt, and Lyman A. Kellstedt. Lanham, Md.: Rowman & Littlefield.

———. 1996b. "The Puzzle of Evangelical Protestantism." In *Religion and the Culture Wars,* by John C. Green, James L. Guth, Corwin E. Smidt, and Lyman A. Kellstedt. Lanham, Md.: Rowman & Littlefield.

Key. V. O., Jr. 1949. *Southern Politics in State and Nation.* New York: Knopf.

Lamis, Alexander P. 1984. *The Two-Party South.* New York: Oxford University Press.

Lincoln, Eric C., and Lawrence H. Mamiya. 1990. *The Black Church in the African-American Experience.* Durham, N.C.: Duke University Press.

Petrocik, John R. 1987. "Realignment: New Party Coalitions and the Nationalization of the South." *Journal of Politics* 49: 347–75.

Reed, John Shelton. 1972. *The Enduring South.* Lexington, Mass.: D. C. Heath.

Rozell, Mark J., and Clyde Wilcox. 1996. *Second Coming: The New Christian Right in Virginia Politics.* Baltimore: Johns Hopkins University Press.

Sernett, Milton G. 1991. "Black Religion and the Question of Evangelical Identity." In *The Variety of American Evangelicalism,* edited by Donald W. Dayton and Robert K. Johnston. Knoxville: University of Tennessee Press.

Shafer, Byron E. 1991. "The Notion of an Electoral Order: The Structure of Electoral Politics at the Accession of George Bush." In *The End of Realignment?* edited by Byron E. Shafer. Madison: University of Wisconsin Press.

Smidt, Corwin E. 1989. "Change and Stability in the Partisanship of Southern Evangelicals: An Analysis of the 1980 and 1984 Presidential Elections." In *Religion in American Politics,* edited by Charles Dunn. Washington, D.C.: Congressional Quarterly Press.

———. 1983. "'Born Again' Politics: The Political Attitudes and Behavior of Evangelical Christians in the South and Non-South." In *Religion and Politics in the South,* edited by Tod A. Baker, Robert P. Steed, and Laurence W. Moreland. New York: Praeger.

Stark, Rodney, and William Bainbridge. 1985. *The Future of Religion.* Berkeley and Los Angeles: University of California Press.

Weaver, Richard. 1968. *The Southern Tradition at Bay.* New Rochelle, N.Y.: Arlington House.

Index

About the Contributors

DAVID A. BREAUX is an associate professor of political science at Mississippi State University. He has published journal articles and book chapters on southern politics and state legislative elections.

DAVID M. BRODSKY is professor of political science at the University of Tennessee–Chattanooga.

SCOTT E. BUCHANAN is a doctoral candidate in political science at the University of Oklahoma. He is the author of journal essays and book chapters on southern politics.

CHARLES S. BULLOCK III is Richard B. Russell Professor of Political Science at the University of Georgia. He is a widely published writer on the politics of the South and the coauthor of *Runoff Elections in the United States.*

DAYE DEARING is a research analyst at the John C. Stennis Institute of Government at Mississippi State University. Her research interests include southern politics, legislative redistricting, and devolution.

RONALD KEITH GADDIE is assistant professor of political science at the University of Oklahoma. He is coauthor of *David Duke and the Politics of Race in the South* and *The Almanac of Oklahoma Politics, 1997–1998.*

JOHN C. GREEN is director of the Ray C. Bliss Institute of Applied Politics at the University of Akron and the author of numerous studies on the Christian Right in American politics. He is coeditor of *The State of the Parties* (2d ed.).

JAMES L. GUTH is professor of political science at Furman University and the author of numerous studies on the Christian Right in American politics.

THOMAS A. KAZEE is professor of political science at Davidson College. He is the editor of *Who Runs for Congress?*

LYMAN A. KELLSTEDT is professor of political science at Wheaton College and the author of numerous studies on the Christian Right in American politics.

JOHN C. KUZENSKI is assistant professor of political science at the Citadel. He is codirector of the Citadel Symposium on Southern Politics and the author of journal essays and book chapters on southern politics.

JAMES W. LAMARE is dean of social and behavioral sciences at the University of Texas–Pan American. He is the author of *Texas Politics: Economics, Power, and Policy* (6th ed.).

WAYNE PARENT is associate professor of political science at Louisiana State University and the coeditor (with Huey Perry) of a book on African American politics.

HUEY PERRY is Chancellor's Fellow and professor of political science at Southern University in Baton Rouge, Louisiana.

J. L. POLINARD is professor and chair of the Department of Political Science at the University of Texas–Pan American. He is the coauthor of *Electoral Structure and Urban Politics* and *State and Local Politics*.

MARK J. ROZELL is associate professor of political science at American University and the coauthor of *Second Coming: The New Christian Right in Virginia Politics*.

RICHARD K. SCHER is professor of political science at the University of Florida and the author of *Politics in the New South*.

MICHAEL J. SCICCHITANO is professor of political science at the University of Florida.

DON E. SLABACH is a research analyst with the John C. Stennis Institute of Government at Mississippi State University. He has published research on southern politics and state policy development.

CORWIN E. SMIDT is professor of political science at Calvin College and the author of numerous studies on the Christian Right in American politics.

HAROLD W. STANLEY is associate professor and chairman of the Department of Political Science at the University of Rochester. He is the author of articles on voting, political parties, and elections and *Voter Mobilization and the Politics of Race; Senate vs. Governor, Alabama 1971;* and *Vital Statistics in American Politics.*

GARY D. WEKKIN is professor of political science at the University of Central Arkansas and a widely published writer on Arkansas politics.

ROBERT D. WRINKLE is a professor in the Department of Political Science at the University of Texas–Pan American. He is the coauthor of *Electoral Structure and Urban Politics* and *State and Local Politics.* His current research interests include public policy, electoral structure, and minority politics.

89280